14 DAY BOOK
**This book is due on or before
the latest date stamped below**

CALIFORNIA STATE UNIVERSITY, NORTHRIDGE LIBRARY

The Matriarchs of England's Cooperative Movement

The Matriarchs of England's Cooperative ═══ Movement ═══

A Study in Gender Politics and Female Leadership, 1883–1921

BARBARA J. BLASZAK

Contributions in Labor Studies, Number 56

GREENWOOD PRESS
Westport, Connecticut • London

Library of Congress Cataloging-in-Publication Data

Blaszak, Barbara J.
    The matriarchs of England's cooperative movement : A study in gender politics
and female leadership, 1883–1921 / by Barbara J. Blaszak.
      p. cm.—(Contributions in labor studies, ISSN 0886–8239 ;
no. 56)
    Includes bibliographical references and index.
    ISBN 0–313–30995–7 (alk. paper)
    1. Women in cooperative societies—Great Britain—History.
2. Cooperation—Great Britain—History. 3. Women—Employment—Great
Britain—History. 4. Women's Co-operative Guild—History.
    I. Title. II. Series.
    HD3424.G7B55 2000
    334′.082′0941—dc21   99–43403

British Library Cataloguing in Publication Data is available.

Copyright © 2000 by Barbara J. Blaszak

Library of Congress Catalog Card Number: 99–43403
ISBN: 0–313–30995–7
ISSN: 0886–8239

First published in 2000

Greenwood Press, 88 Post Road West, Westport, CT 06881
An imprint of Greenwood Publishing Group, Inc.
www.greenwood.com

Printed in the United States of America

The paper used in this book complies with the
Permanent Paper Standard issued by the National
Information Standards Organization (Z39.48–1984).

10 9 8 7 6 5 4 3 2 1

Copyright Acknowledgments

The author and publisher gratefully acknowledge permission for the use of the following material:

Material from the Women's Cooperative Guild Papers (Margaret Llewelyn Davies and Lilian Harris
Papers) is reprinted courtesy of the British Library of Political & Economic Science, London
School of Economics and Political Science.

Material from the Women's Cooperative Guild Manuscript Collection is reprinted courtesy of The
University of Hull Brynmor Jones Library.

Material from the Co-operative Union Archive is reprinted courtesy of the Co-operative Union.

To my husband, who discovered it's more pleasant to teach a Luddite wordprocessing than to stand in the pouring rain holding smelly sweatclothes.

Contents

Acknowledgments

This book has a history almost as interesting as the one it tells. I began work on it in 1981, but laid the materials aside when my career went in the direction of academic administration. During the time I spent in England in 1981, the late Roy Garrett at the Cooperative Union Library in Manchester was most helpful to me, as was the staff at the British Library of Political and Economic Science at the London School of Economics, and Norman Higson, then the documents collection librarian at the Brynmor Jones Library at the University of Hull. Mr. Higson and his wife were especially kind, taking me for picnics on the Yorkshire moors and having me to their house for dinner. The hospitality of Peter and the late Rewa Robertson, the former owners of the Hollies Hotel, also helped make Hull feel like home to me. It would have pleased Rewa to know that my research efforts finally materialized into a book.

I would like to thank Le Moyne College for the sabbatical that finally enabled me to find the time to return to the materials I had collected, which had been gathering dust for more than fifteen years. The generosity of the college's Faculty Research and Development Committee was of great assistance in my efforts to resuscitate my project. The committee partially funded my trip to England in 1998, when I spent long hours at the British Newspaper Library in Colindale reading the *Co-operative News*. The staff there was most patient with my incessant requests for photocopying. I also visited Manchester during that trip, and Gillian Lonergan at the Cooperative Union Library made the materials I needed available to me. Subsequently, she put me in touch with Sue Bell of the Cooperative Women's Guild, who arranged for permission for me to use the photographs that appear at the head of each chapter. I would like to thank the women on the National Executive Committee for that permission and also the staff at CWS Photographic for the beautiful reprints they sent me of the original photographs.

The staff at Le Moyne College's interlibrary loan department was most helpful, obtaining for me books and journal articles which we did not have in our collection. Mary Lee Shanahan was of special assistance in getting materials when they were urgently needed. Susan Behuniak of Le Moyne's political science department and Julie Gibert of the history department at Canisius College read the first draft of the manuscript and made many helpful suggestions for which I am in their debt. My colleague Doug Egerton made possible the manuscript's final completion by agreeing to chair the history department for me during the summer of 1999. Finally, Ellen Giraud was most accommodating during the preparation of the camera-ready manuscript for Greenwood Press.

This book has benefitted from the years it spent in hibernation. During that time many scholars have contributed to the fields of labor and women's history; I have been able to take advantage of their work. Had I completed this book in the 1980s, it would have told a less illuminating story. My personal experiences as an academic administrator have also informed this book. As a woman who has occupied leadership positions, I have been made very aware that gender suffuses politics in academe and determines their course.

Summer, 1999
Le Moyne College
Syracuse, New York

Introduction: Women in the English Cooperative Movement

English cooperators, whose consumers' movement traced its origins to the enterprise founded by the Rochdale Pioneers in the 1840s, began increasingly to talk about the Cooperative Commonwealth to come in the years after the First World War.[1] At the 1925 Cooperative Congress the delegates approved a change in the rules governing the Cooperative Union to include among the objects of that national organization "the ultimate establishment of a Co-operative Commonwealth."[2] Cooperators were unable to say when the Commonwealth would arrive, but they could describe how. It would evolve gradually from the mundane business of selling groceries to working-class housewives. As these women began to realize the possibilities that the "co-ops" provided for accumulating savings and learned that cooperation gave their class an opportunity for ownership and a voice in its business enterprises, it was supposed that they would be increasingly motivated to buy their provisions from their cooperative stores and nowhere else. All over the world, not just in England, little cooperative stores would then grow in size and establish wholesale outlets from which to buy the goods they sold. This had already happened in England, and Scotland too, back in the 1860s. These wholesale outlets would then enter into the production of some items and start depots abroad to obtain imported commodities, transporting them home aboard cooperative ships, as the English and Scottish Wholesale Societies had already begun to do by the start of the twentieth century. The entire enterprise would be owned by the members of cooperative societies, the ordinary people who had taken out shares in their local stores and received returns on their investments according to the number of shares they owned and the amounts they spent on provisions. These shareholders would direct their stores, and indeed, the entire Cooperative movement democratically, by voting at the stores' members' meetings and by electing representatives to national cooperative bodies and gatherings.

Cooperators considered cooperation the antithesis of capitalism, so their

Turn-of-the-century membership card of the Women's Cooperative Guild. Reproduced courtesy of the Co-operative Women's Guild.

Cooperative Commonwealth would not be organized around such capitalistic principles as competition and the profit motive. Cooperators reasoned the advent of the Commonwealth would coincide with a more equitable—fair but not necessarily equal—distribution of wealth. This more equitable distribution of goods would be the inevitable result of cooperation having replaced capitalism as the basis of the economic system. Without competition for individual profit, it was reasoned that people would work for the welfare of the community, not permitting anyone to have too little, and no one would be driven to monopolize too much. Labor would not be brutally exploited in the Commonwealth and consumers would not be cheated by being offered adulterated or shoddy goods; nor would they be duped by false advertising. All this implied a miraculous character transformation for the human race. The Commonwealth would make it unnecessary for each person to guard his or her own self-interest because the environment in which he or she lived, shopped, and worked would no longer be based on competition and profit for individual gain. The welfare of others, of the community, would be uppermost in everybody's mind. All would cooperate with one another because all would realize that the welfare of each and the welfare of the many were inseparable.[3]

Cooperators believed that capitalism contributed to the debasement of moral values, and cooperation to their enhancement. Thus the Commonwealth would bring about a New Moral World, a phrase coined by the British utopian socialist, Robert Owen. Owen was considered by cooperators to be one of the ideological founders of their movement. But they rejected any suggestion that their Commonwealth was utopian. To them, a utopia was a planned community imposed upon the masses by some idealist who believed that he knew what was in the best interests of the oppressed, just as the altruistic Owen had believed. In such a community there was unlikely to be freedom, even when an equitable distribution of wealth had been achieved. Cooperators argued that this had been proved by the failure of the communities Owen and his followers had tried to found in the early decades of the nineteenth century. Their rejection of Owenite community building, however, was not an abandonment of ideals, as Sidney Pollard suggested in his study of the Cooperative movement.[4] It was merely, as other historians of the movement have claimed, an adjustment to the practical realities of working-class life, which cooperators believed the Owenite community builders had neglected to take into consideration.[5] Cooperators acknowledged their debt to Owen. They owed their critique of capitalism and theories about character formation to him. But they considered that he had gotten several things wrong. They argued that the working class had to initiate its own schemes for personal and collective amelioration. Workers could neither depend upon the paternalism of wealthy individuals like Owen, nor upon the state. Moreover, they believed the direction in which those schemes should evolve could not be determined *a priori* as Owen had attempted, since a democratic vote of the participants in them needed to be taken at every critical juncture. Consequently, cooperators believed the Rochdale Pioneers, not Owen, were the actual fathers of their movement. In their opinion, the Pioneers had grafted Owenite ideals onto the practical stock of working-class self-help.[6]

Although the twenty-eight men who constituted the Rochdale Pioneers were neither impoverished nor all from the working class,[7] they began their business venture as a result of the witness they bore to the effects of economic depression in their community and the country at large. It was the decade of the "hungry '40s." Britain was then suffering through a downward phase in the cyclical economic patterns that industrialization had established, and this particular recession was especially severe. Unemployment in the industrial districts of England and Scotland, along with famine in Ireland, produced the conditions that gave the decade its sobriquet. They also bred political unrest. The Chartists demanded the franchise for working-class men; the Anti-Corn Law League wanted the repeal of the tariffs that kept the cost of bread high; and a variety of radicals agitated for everything from sanitary legislation, in order to clean up the growing cities, to a reduction in the working day to ten hours. The objective of all these reformers was the improvement of the situation for the working class, and thus a solution to the "condition of England question"—the division of the country into what Benjamin Disraeli characterized as two nations, rich and poor.

In Rochdale, the advent of the power loom had rendered redundant the handloom weavers of the town's flannel industry. Industrialization in Rochdale's county of Lancashire introduced cotton factories with their susceptibility to the trade downturns of the early industrial period, and caused the disruption of the more autonomous patterns of work and life typical of the era of domestic manufacture. Economic change and recession prompted Rochdale's working men to organize into trade unions and to strike. They and sympathizers with them joined the Chartists and the Owenite socialist groups that had sprung up in the town. In 1844, twenty-eight of these Chartists and Owenites pooled their resources and opened a store in Toad Lane to sell such staples as butter, sugar, flour, and candles to anyone who cared to join them in their venture into shopkeeping. All that was required of a prospective member was that he or she be willing to accumulate shares in the store by installment payments. Any profits the store made from its sales would generate returns for the shareholders at a rate of interest of 3½% a year, with the remaining profits payable to shareholders according to the amount of money they spent at the store. Eventually, this enabled shareholders to eat their ways to nest eggs, as George Jacob Holyoake, one of the nineteenth-century propagandists and historians of the Cooperative movement, pointed out.[8]

The Pioneers originally had as their ultimate objective the accumulation of sufficient capital to enable them to found a community on the Owenite model. That had been the aim of the participants in the so-called Pre-Rochdale Cooperative movement, which had flourished in the 1820s and early 1830s. The Pioneers had initially modeled their venture on those of cooperators who had preceded them. However, the success of their endeavor, its imitation by people in other communities, and the prosperity the 1850s brought to what has become known as the "labour aristocracy" that patronized the stores served to alter their goals. Cooperators came to realize that their efforts could raise their standards of living without a retreat to an Owenite community. They also began to believe that eventually their system of communally owned enterprises where fair prices, accurate weights, and well-made goods prevailed would replace retail trading. Moreover, they reasoned that the replacement of the entire capitalist system of exchange and production would be possible if the stores clubbed together to establish their own wholesale buyers and manufacturers of the goods they sold. Cooperators considered such a direction of their efforts consonant with their original Owenite ideals because it would lead to the replacement of competition, and individual self-interest in the pursuit of private profits, by the social ownership of the means of exchange and production, in the interest of mutual aid. But the Pioneers failed to retain all of their Owenite ideals. Indeed, when it came to Owenite ideals about gender, the Pioneers had never had them in the first place. As Barbara Taylor has demonstrated in *Eve and the New Jerusalem*, Owenism postulated a New Moral World wherein gender relationships were revolutionized to end the oppression of women.[9] The Pioneers imagined no such transformation. Their imaginations were prisoners of traditional Western thinking in regard to gender relationships. In the nineteenth century, this thinking had particular implications for the meaning of exchange and production. As Joan Scott has observed, the Western intellectual tradition is built on binary oppositions wherein "leading terms are accorded primacy," even though those primary terms would have no meaning were it not for their opposition to their partners, and even when what is portrayed as dichotomous is actually interdependent.[10] She has argued that in the confines of a patriarchy, sexual difference is used "to encode or establish meanings."[11] This tendency was especially marked in a patriarchy such as the one that prevailed in England before the first wave of feminism. The result was that "meanings of gender bec[a]me tied to many kinds of cultural representations, and these in turn establish[ed] terms by which relations between women and men [were] organized and understood."[12]

J. M. Ludlow, Christian Socialist and advocate of cooperation, exemplified this gendered encoding of meaning at work within the minds of cooperative men when he said: "Consumption [is] the animal element, production the divine."[13] Ludlow was a lawyer by profession and liberally educated. Like all nineteenth-century men, he was acquainted with the West's classical heritage. Middle-class men like Ludlow were introduced to this heritage through formal education, whereas the autodidacts of the working class found it on their own. His remark exhibits his Aristotelian gender prejudices and contextualizes in terms of Pythagorean polarities nineteenth-century thinking with respect to consumption and production. It consequently reveals the gendered prejudices that prevailed about those roles among cooperators. According to the Pythagorean Table of Opposites, the human experience could be divided in two—male and female. Male was right, female left; male was light, female dark; male was civilization, female the natural world; male was good, female evil.[14] The male element was superior to the female, or, as Ludlow put it, "divine" as opposed to "animal." Interestingly, as the nineteenth century progressed and respectable women began increasingly to be confined to the private and men to the public spheres, the Victorians unwittingly created a culture in which the ancient Greeks would have been comfortable. Within that culture, consumption was encoded as female and therefore inferior to the male activity of production. Men were associated with the task of producing the goods women bought. Whether as the workers who actually manufactured the commodities or as the owners and investors in the enterprises that made them, men were the producers. Consumption was thought to require neither strength—valued by working-class male culture[15]—nor intelligence—valued by middle-class male culture. For men to engage in a movement of organized consumers was therefore problematic to the point of being potentially emasculating.

There is a folktale among cooperators about that cold, dark December evening in 1844 when the Pioneers first opened their store. Supposedly, the men became apprehensive about the venture upon which they were about to embark and were reluctant to take down the shutters and commence business. It was then that a woman who happened to be present stepped forward to remove the shutters and declare the store open. Perhaps she knew from talking with other women in the neighborhood that all the housewives were eager to see what the store offered and would be waiting expectantly outside, anxious to try doing business with this new type of establishment. It has been calculated that over 60% of a nineteenth-century working-class household's budget was spent on food.[16] Since women did the shopping, this made them very much aware of the difficulty of balancing the family's income and expenses against its dietary needs.[17] Any new venture that promised to help them in the arduous task of ensuring family survival would interest them. Although it has been claimed that Lancashire working-class activists in the early nineteenth century often organized around family issues,[18] the Pioneers were nevertheless unable to appreciate how eager working-class women were to try shopping at their store, simply because men did not do the shopping. Nor would it have been likely that they would have attended to what they might have disparagingly characterized as "gossip" among the neighborhood's women, even if it were about their store. They would therefore have had good reason to be reticent about embarking on the business of shopkeeping. They neither did the household shopping, nor valued the opinions of women, nor had a background in retail trade. Their wives certainly knew much more about groceries and probably more about shopkeeping than they did. What may have increased their reticence even more was their awareness that their whole venture was dependent for success upon the loyalty of women shoppers. To give women the power over the fate of a movement men had created was unprecedented. Indeed, the research of Peter Gurney suggests that cooperative men engaged in what amounts to self-deception as a consequence of their worries about the "basket power" of cooperative women. However, because Gurney does not read the evidence as a feminist, he fails to see the thinking of male cooperators in those terms.

Gurney observes that male cooperators considered participants in their movement "active" consumers, as opposed to the "passive" ones of the capitalist economy.[19] Gurney also says that they characterized shopping at the cooperative stores as a rational choice and associated it with self-control because it demonstrated a person's ability to defer gratification in an effort to save.[20] The application of a feminist analysis to Gurney's observations leads to a revealing conclusion. Reason and self-control have traditionally been attributed to men within the Western tradition, while women are characterized as emotional and disorderly. Living within this tradition accordingly compelled male cooperators to think of cooperative consumption as an active, masculine activity as opposed to a passive, feminine one. Male cooperators were extremely uncomfortable about engaging in a business having to do with consumption, and they consequently built an elaborate intellectual defense of their activity in order to protect their masculinity.

While Gurney may not have deconstructed the self-deception maintained by male cooperators, he does argue that the cooperative culture the movement generated had a female orientation because of the "distinctive universe of values" it created.[21] These values came to be embodied in the concept of the Cooperative Commonwealth, with its noncompetitive, caring, and unselfish economy that was deemed more moral than capitalism's. Associative values are more often attributed to women than to men, and, in the nineteenth century especially, women were considered these values' natural guardians.[22] Women, sheltered in the home, protected those values from the ravages of the vice-ridden public world that it was men's misfortune to inhabit. Thus, just as women were held to be morally superior to men, cooperation was considered morally superior to capitalism. Within the binary intellectual tradition of the West, cooperative culture was therefore a woman's culture. But there is evidence to indicate that some women who participated in the movement considered the whole phenomenon of cooperation theirs.

In *The Women's Co-operative Guild*, written in 1904, Margaret Llewelyn Davies refers to cooperation as a woman's movement because of its orientation around consumption, and she speaks of the "basket power" that female shoppers wield as what will make possible its eventual world-wide triumph.[23] She gloried in women's power as consumers and realized that women could use it as leverage to effect change. She also recognized that consumption involved hard work and that women should demand some recognition of this fact. Whether it was the working-class woman able to afford only the barest necessities for her family or the middle-class one with money to spend on luxuries to adorn her home, women were the keys to the maintenance of both the cooperative and capitalist economies. Women consumers shopping in either the cooperative or capitalist economies could not be characterized as passive. The accuracy of Llewelyn Davies's estimations have been confirmed by the research of historians. The work of Ellen Ross on working-class women in London shows how such women struggled to sustain their households, and Lori Loeb's study of middle-class women's consumption reveals that the choices they made drove the economy.[24] Chris Waters notes that the language of consumer rights first appeared in the late nineteenth century.[25] It is no accident that this development coincides with first wave feminism, even though, as Waters observes, male socialists were also interested in such rights.[26] Nevertheless, male cooperators worried that consumption involved passivity and were consequently driven to devise the theories Gurney discusses to defend their movement as "manly." It was difficult for them to square their masculinities with the consumer orientation that cooperation involved.

For cooperative men to have imagined that any type of consumption was passive shows their lack of appreciation for the effort women spent on homemaking, especially in working-class households where the very survival of the family depended on the housewife's efforts. Of course, a housewife's work involves more than consumption. Women everywhere and in all eras have been and are engaged in the business of production because of the household tasks they perform and the children they bear.[27] But in the nineteenth century, as industrialization replaced the domestic economy, it dissociated work done in the home from the earning of wages. Work that continued to be performed in the home was therefore no longer considered productive work. Of course, many poor or unmarried women continued to work for wages in their homes.[28] Depending on their socioeconomic class, they might be engaged in anything from providing services, like piano lessons, to producing goods by piecework.[29] Indeed, as industrialization progressed, it paradoxically could create situations which contributed to the temporary increase in the numbers of people employed in production in the home and in the sweated trades.[30] Moreover, Ellen Ross has proved that even after marriage, many working-class women in particular had to work for wages. She has calculated that as much as 80% of the male manual workers in England earned too little, too irregularly to support a non-wage-earning wife.[31] However, these women wage earners were invisible because of the gender ideology that came to prevail at mid-century and that insisted that woman's place was in the home.[32] There she was presumed to engage in tasks that did not earn wages and were therefore unproductive.

The ideal woman in the home was, of course, the married woman—not the spinster sister or widowed mother—because it was assumed that marriage is the natural state in which all adult women should live. Once married, it was presumed that a woman's husband would support her. After the advent of economic prosperity in the 1850s, the luxury of having a non-wage-earning wife became attainable for certain portions of the working class. This luxury did not "trickle down" to the working class from the middle class, as has sometimes been maintained; nor was it indicative of some attempt at the imitation of middle-class values on the part of the working class.[33] Rather, as Sonya O. Rose and Anna Clark in particular have argued, working-class culture generated its own gendered ideas about what was respectable behavior for men and women.[34] Rose contends that male workers came to define their masculinity according to the conditions of their employment. A working-class male was a "man" if his job required physically demanding or difficult tasks and if it paid enough for him to support a family.[35] Historians who have researched the development of the family wage concept among the working class have seconded the latter of these two conditions in particular as tending toward the working-class definition of masculinity.[36] With respect to working-class women, Rose has shown that those who aspired to raise their families' status came to associate domesticity with respectability.[37] This led some to conceal from census takers the "shameful" fact that they might occasionally have to supplement their husbands' wages by earning some of their own.[38] In fact, the investigations of Elizabeth Roberts and Diana Gittens reveal that working-class wives generally did not even consider it "working" if their labor was casual.[39] Working for wages meant to them full-time labor done outside the home.[40] In sum, from mid-century it became expected among the upper echelons of the working class for women to work for wages as girls, but to give up their jobs either upon marriage or the arrival of the first child.

Interestingly, in Rochdale's county of Lancashire, exceptions to this pattern

were typical. Women employed in Lancashire's cotton mills sometimes continued in their jobs despite either marriage or motherhood.[41] The Rochdale Pioneers undoubtedly knew of such women; some were probably even married to
them. A number of the Pioneers were weavers, and weavers did not earn a family wage; their wives and children had to work.[42] In *The Struggle for the
Breeches*, Anna Clark notes that Lancashire working-men's culture prior to
1850, at least, tended to be much more inclusionary of women than the working-men's culture which prevailed among the predominantly skilled trades of
London.[43] It is reasonable to suppose that married women's habits of working
outside the home in cotton-manufacturing districts contributed to this openness.
Historians like Jane Lewis, Jill Liddington, and Jill Norris have even gone so far
as to claim that the practice of married women continuing in employment in
Lancashire created more egalitarian gender relations, with men offering to help
with the housework and working-class women freely organizing at the end of
the century to demand the vote.[44] Perhaps this explains why folklore has it that
there was a woman present to remove the shutters at the opening of the Toad
Lane store. However, Anna Clark rejects the conclusions about Lancashire gender relations that Lewis, Liddington, and Norris draw. Clark maintains that
"textile culture" remained patriarchal even though it may have been more inclusive and less misogynistic than the "artisanal culture" that prevailed elsewhere
among skilled working men.[45] More egalitarian gender relations never developed. Mike Savage's research on gender relations in the cotton mills of Preston
offers further proof of Clark's thesis. Savage's work reveals that a male network
of fathers, husbands, and overseers determined the circumstances of female employment.[46] Moreover, he attributes patriarchal control in the workplace to the
persistence of "patriarchal modes of domination within the family and neighbourhood."[47] In other words, men who helped with the housework did not relinquish their patriarchal prerogatives.

It is important to investigate what place the Pioneers envisioned for women
in their Toad Lane venture, because some of them were Owenites. Barbara
Taylor in *Eve and the New Jerusalem* discusses the feminist perspectives which
motivated many of the men and women attracted to Owenism.[48] Accordingly, it
must be asked: if women were going to be the customers at the Pioneers' store,
could they be anything else?

A year after opening their store, the Pioneers passed by democratic vote of
the shareholding members a series of amendments to the laws they had written
in 1844 for governing their enterprise. The alteration they then made to their
first law clarified who could become a member through the addition of inclusive
language: "Each person on *his or her* admission to membership shall take out
four shares in the capital [italics added]."[49] Obviously, the Pioneers intended
women to be shareholding members of their establishment with voting power
and any other rights and privileges owing to such investors. However, the
change they made to their thirteenth law guaranteed that few women would
venture to take advantage of this opportunity.

Rule thirteen had not been female-friendly to begin with. It read:

Any person desirous of becoming a member of this society shall be proposed and seconded by two members at a meeting of the officers and directors, and if approved by the majority of those present shall be eligible for election at the next weekly meeting.[50]

It is difficult to imagine a woman putting herself in such a public position despite the inclusionary nature of Lancashire working-men's culture and the feminist pretensions of Owenism.[51] It is also difficult to imagine a room full of married men, in a country which gave married women no right to own property, and where couverture prevailed, voting to permit membership for either their wives or the wives of others.

In 1845, the Pioneers amended this rule by adding: "Each person on the night of *his* admission, shall appear personally in the meeting room and state *his* willingness to take out four shares of one pound each [italics added]."[52] The requirement of a personal appearance and public speaking before a room full of men, the absence of gender-inclusive language, and the necessity of committing what a working-class housewife would consider a substantial amount of money makes clear that the Pioneers intended to put shareholding beyond the possibility of the married working-class women who shopped at their store. In the first step that the Rochdale Pioneers took toward the creation of the Cooperative Commonwealth about which their grandchildren spoke, women's work was envisioned as different from men's. They were to be the customers, buying to equip the private sphere of the home. Men, on the other hand, were to be active in the public sphere of the cooperative enterprise, directing it as voting shareholders. The Pioneers were emphatic about maintaining gender role boundaries because cooperation, unlike trade unionism, Chartism, or even Owenism, organized people as consumers, not as producers. It therefore had the potential of emasculating the men involved in it.

The Pioneers were as successful as they were emphatic about maintaining gender role boundaries. As the Cooperative movement they started spread, it became typical for families to take out their memberships in cooperative societies in the husband's name. The husband therefore became the only person in the family eligible to vote at the society's meetings or to stand for election to its offices or committees. In fact, some societies even prohibited anyone but the male members from attending their meetings. Others went so far as to forbid nonmembers from using their reading rooms and libraries. The wife might shop at the store. Her loyalty might contribute to its financial success. Her purchases accumulated the dividend her family received. But she was not a member and was entitled to none of the rights and privileges of a member. To be fair, store managers considered the dividend that a wife's purchases accumulated to be the woman's property, even though they were under no legal obligation to do so. Also, there were cooperative societies whose rules encouraged female membership and participation. Some of these permitted as many adults in a household as desired to become members. However, such societies were rare until the twentieth century, especially in Lancashire, and rules that tended to the exclusion of women were not formally dropped by the societies belonging to the Cooperative Union until after World War I, which helps to explain the increases in membership the movement experienced in the 1920s[53]: all women shoppers then became eligible to take out their own memberships. However, even after the Second World War, cooperators continued in their rigid thinking about gender roles.

In 1961, Arnold Bonner, a tutor at the Cooperative College, wrote the book *British Co-operation* to replace the dated text in use at the College. In the final chapter of the book there is a section entitled "Builders of the Commonwealth." In this section he reiterates the Pioneers' position on gender roles within the Cooperative movement. He says, "Every time the housewife decides to buy from the co-operative society she is advancing the Commonwealth, every time she decides to buy elsewhere she is maintaining capitalism."[54] Women contribute to the creation of the Cooperative Commonwealth by buying, men contribute to it by investing. Bonner says:

Other vital decisions are made by *people* with money to invest. Co-operative enterprise cannot exist and develop without capital. . . . Yet there are many ardent socialists willing to lay down their lives on the barricades, who will more readily stake their money in the football pools in the hope of winning some of that of their fellows than invest in their own co-operative businesses and so benefit all [italics added].[55]

It is clear from his allusion to the "football pools" that the investing "*people*" to whom Bonner is referring are men. In sum, the Cooperative Commonwealth might dare to attempt the elimination of distinctions in wealth and power born of class, but intended to do nothing about those born of gender.

The Cooperative movement thus appears as infertile ground for the generation of a women's organization. Yet, in 1883, a body calling itself the Women's League for the Spread of Cooperation was formed. This body eventually became the Women's Cooperative Guild, which had a "relational" feminist agenda.[56] In other words, it argued for public roles and voices for women in order to help them perform their traditional duties as wives and mothers. The Guild was thus an anomaly in late nineteenth-century Britain where "equal rights" feminism had established itself. Equal rights feminists campaigned for women's rights to education, to entry to the professions, and to the vote on the grounds that women are no different from men and consequently should be treated no differently from them. Within the context of the history of feminism in England, the Guild was a harbinger of a phenomenon historians have variously designated as "new feminism," "welfare feminism," "maternalist feminism," or "separate spheres feminism." All these terms refer to the relational feminism that came to prevail in England after World War I and are meant to distinguish it the from earlier equal rights feminism, which sought to remove restrictions on women and create formal equality between the sexes. While a number of historians have argued it may misrepresent both the "old" and the "new" feminism to draw too hard a line between them,[57] the differences between their ideologies and agendas were significant enough to divide the women of the National Union of Women's Suffrage Societies, who felt they were forced to choose between the equal rights orientation of Millicent Fawcett and the relational perspective of Eleanor Rathbone in the years after World War I.[58]

Some historians have attributed the shift from equal rights to relational feminism among women's advocates to the effects of the war, arguing that equal rights feminism had created gender war. After witnessing the carnage of war between nations, feminists soured on continuing their confrontation with men and sought to apply the more conciliatory agendas and tactics of new feminism.[59] Other historians contend that the enfranchisement of women, which followed on the heels of the war, served to draw attention to gender differences rather than to their elimination, contributing to the appearance of a feminism based on gender differences.[60] For example, men and women were presumed to make voting decisions differently. Politicians accordingly scrambled to appeal to the new voters who were considered so fundamentally different from men. This encouraged women's leaders like Eleanor Rathbone to try to seize the opportunity to secure legislation that would benefit women in their traditional roles as wives and mothers.[61] Finally, some historians have suggested that the growing awareness of working-class women's concerns drove feminists to realize that "formal" equality between men and women would do little to ameliorate conditions for working-class women.[62] The circumstances of these women's lives, with their poverty and incessant childbearing, rendered them incapable of taking advantage of formal equality. Feminists therefore concluded that some sort of societal reorganization would be necessary in order to create the conditions of "real" equality for such women.[63] Many feminists believed that the state could assist in this reorganization by legislating the "endowment of motherhood," which would pay women for the work of reproduction in which they engaged in the home.[64] In this instance, the experience of World War I combined with concerns about the health of working-class women's offspring to buttress the feminist case, although not always in ways feminists would approve. Susan Pedersen has observed that the war provided feminists with a nationalist argument for the endowment of motherhood. They could contend that just as soldiers are paid for their service to the state, mothers should be paid for providing it with citizens.[65] And, as Deborah Dwork has shown, worries about the birthrate inclined conservatives favorably to some sort of state-sponsored scheme for helping mothers provide for their children.[66] However, nationalists, conservatives, and even socialists interested in constructing a comprehensive welfare state never intended that any maternal assistance program should liberate women from patriarchal control.[67] On the other hand, the new feminists hoped both to safeguard women's traditional sphere and break its association with "economic dependence and political marginality."[68] They wanted to make the home a base for liberation instead of bondage, thereby subverting patriarchy.[69]

The Guild operated from a new-feminist perspective and stressed the differences between men and women. Its leaders realized that formal equality could not free the working-class housewife from economic dependence. They hoped by combining cooperation and state-sponsored welfare legislation to create real equality for the working-class woman in her role as wife and mother. The relational perspective of the Guild was suited to the Cooperative movement. Given the rigid gender roles male cooperators sought to maintain, it is impossible to imagine equal rights feminism taking root there. Interestingly, cooperation's association with Owenism may also have contributed to the Guild's predisposition to new feminism because Owenism's analysis of gender differences was very similar to new feminism's. In *Eve and the New Jerusalem*, Barbara Taylor describes the feminist views of two leading Owenites, William Thompson and Anna Wheeler. Thompson and Wheeler argued that even if laws were changed to give women formal equality, the impact on women would be negligible if the societal and cultural conditions that kept women oppressed remained in place.[70] That was the position of new feminists and it was also the position of one of the Guild's most famous leaders, Margaret Llewelyn Davies, who believed formal equality for women would achieve little until the dawn of the Cooperative Commonwealth.[71] In the Commonwealth she imagined there would be no societal or cultural distinctions between the sexes. Her conception of the Commonwealth was thus different from that of male cooperators like the Pioneers and Arnold Bonner, and different even from that of many women cooperators. Male and many female cooperators had no visions with respect to the reconfiguration of gender relations and refused to imagine the eradication of gender-based social and cultural hierarchies.

Although the Guild was created and led by women cooperators with a relational feminist perspective, the notion of involvement beyond shopping for women in the movement actually originated with two men who believed women were naturally suited to be educators because of their experiences as mothers. Also operating in these men's minds was the Victorian stereotype of women as the custodians of ideals and virtue, a stereotype that proved attractive to women cooperators as well. There are no personal papers recording what transpired between the two men who sought to create expanded roles for women within the Cooperative movement; nor is what happened between them, their wives, and their friends recorded anywhere. But a series of coincidences in the 1880s makes possible the reconstruction of events that led to the founding of the Guild. This account of the Guild's origins will attribute its foundation much more to the agency of men than do previous histories of this organization.[72] In so doing, it is not intended to portray cooperative women as passive, voiceless victims of male whims—only to acknowledge that men set the boundaries in which the women had to operate.[73] Previous histories of the Guild have failed to recognized the importance of the limitations cooperative men set for women because they have neglected to consider that the organization's genesis was determined by official concerns within the Cooperative movement in the 1880s. In that decade many male leaders of the movement were worried about deficiencies in the cooperative education of the rank and file. This led to the inauguration of classes for cooperators, the writing of a textbook for them, the formation of a national committee to oversee cooperative education, and also the start of a woman's page in the weekly newspaper of the movement. The newspaper column triggered the formation of the Guild as a women's group dedicated to instructing the working-class housewives who shopped at the stores in the higher principles of cooperation. All of these developments involved the same two men, their wives, and the couples' circle of male and female friends.

In 1882, Ben Jones and his friend, Arthur H. D. Acland, began to organize classes for cooperators in London. Jones believed, "We [cooperators] need a careful and systematic teaching of the principles and practice of Cooperation."[74] Jones was the director of the London branch of the English Wholesale Society and Acland an Oxford don and Liberal member of Parliament who had become an advocate of cooperation. At that year's annual cooperative congress Jones expressed his concerns about deficiencies in cooperative education, quoting the words of a Cambridge don who shared his opinions and had spoken at the 1879 Congress:

If the mass of your members are not sufficiently instructed in economic science, in the facts of commerce, in the state of this and other countries, in the history of trade, in general knowledge, and in particular knowledge of what you aim at and how you seek it . . . there arises a real danger to the Co-operative Movement; your members become a hindrance and your possessions become a peril.[75]

As it turned out, Jones and Acland were as much worried about the ignorance of the women shopping at the stores as they were about that of the predominantly male shareholding members. They considered it especially important that women be given instruction in the "principles" and "practice" of cooperation because most of them were only in it for the "divi." Crane Brinton has observed in his study of utopian movements that their leaders tend to be eager to make sure the followers do not settle for too little.[76] Acland and Jones thought the "divi" was too little because they believed cooperation had the potential to transform the world. What may have also come into play as a motivating factor for Acland and Jones was a phenomenon Chris Waters noticed with respect to socialists. He observed that Independent Labour Party leaders worried that wives uncommitted to the ideals of socialism might undermine their husbands' fervor.[77] Acland and Jones may have felt similarly; therefore they were keen to instruct women in cooperative principles and concluded that the best way to teach women was by having other women do it. Their wives eagerly agreed to help with the task.

Jones's wife, Annie, was a working-class woman who had spent her youth in a Lancashire cotton mill. How she came by her erudition is unclear; very little is known about her. She eventually became president of the Women's Cooperative Guild and proved herself to be an articulate spokesperson in that role. Acland's wife, Alice, was a well-educated, middle-class lady who was as passionate about the cause of cooperation as her husband. Both women had four children, but Alice's middle-class status guaranteed her more help with them and the household tasks, freeing her for other pursuits. Of the two women, Alice was the one chosen for the venture her husband and his friend had in mind.

The men approached the editor of the *Co-operative News*, who was Acland's friend, and arranged for Alice to write a series of articles on "Women's Lives" for the paper in 1882. The next year Alice was appointed the editor of the paper's new women's column, the "Woman's Corner." In her first column she revealed the agenda her husband and his friend had set for her and the "Corner," which she enthusiastically supported. She asked the question, "Why are [women] held in such low esteem by men?"[78] She answered that it was women's own fault because "we fail to be all we might be."[79] Alice was not suggesting that women should be like men and do men's work. Rather, she was arguing that they needed training in order to make them more than "playthings" and "housekeepers," to make them the "helpmeets" of men.[80] It was the duty of "every true-hearted" woman to be helpful, and if she were a cooperator, to assist the cause of cooperation.[81] She then brought up the subject of cooperative education for women:

In this matter of co-operation, for instance, why should not we women do more than we do? Why should not we have our meetings, our readings, our discussions? Why should not *we* hold co-operative "mothers' meetings," when we may bring our work and sit together, one of us reading some co-operative book aloud, which may afterwards be discussed?[82]

Alice was suggesting what amounts to women's seminars on cooperation. With this column began the implementation of Jones and Acland's plan to use women who were knowledgeable about cooperation to instruct others in its "principles" and "practice."

In the "Corner's" second column, Melinda Greenwood, daughter of the founder of the English Wholesale Society, a man acquainted with Ben Jones at the London branch, wrote to the column to express the hope that women would begin to attend the national congresses, if only as spectators.[83] The following week, a certain S. Newman wrote to say she thought "there ought to be women on store committees."[84] She was apparently ignorant of cooperation's aim to eradicate competition, because she was ready to enter into a contest with the men to see which sex could do more for the movement. The third week, however, brought letters that were less ambitious than Newman's about women's roles in the movement. They suggested activities for women more in tune with those "every true-hearted" woman should pursue. One correspondent said she believed that "we women have a part to perform in our own quiet way. . . . In addition to whatever influence we may have over our husbands and brothers, we have the care and responsibility of educating and training the great army of future co-operators."[85] Another correspondent suggested ways women cooperators could convert other women to shopping at the stores: "My opinion is that women can push forward this grand cause of co-operation as much as anyone, if they try—not merely by asking their neighbours to join the stores—but by showing them proofs of the benefits they derive from the store."[86]

On February 3, Melinda Greenwood wrote to the column again, and her letter was in keeping with the tempered expectations for women's roles in the movement that had appeared the previous week. In fact, it summarized what Ben Jones and Arthur Acland had set out to achieve:

We come across many women who do not understand co-operation in its true meaning; they only know it in its "dividend" sense, and not in its higher sense of elevating themselves and their children and fellow-creatures. Some of them have never had the opportunity of learning what its true principles are. In the first place, they have been attracted by the dividend, and if they have children growing up, perhaps some of them may have attended the evening or science classes, and used the library. These have been links, but as to what co-operation means, and what are its aims, they know nothing at all. If something was written about it plain and simple *by a woman*, I think they would be more interested in it [italics added].[87]

Here women's mercenary focus on the dividend is condemned, as Jones and Acland would approve. Moreover, according to the men's plan, Greenwood urges women to undertake the task of educating their sisters. She went on to give more specifics: that knowledgeable women like the correspondents to the "Corner" should volunteer to write short letters every week on cooperation, keeping "it plain and simple, so that any woman who could read might understand it."[88] Thus male cooperators would be relieved of the task of composing elementary texts and could devote their energies to more sophisticated efforts at cooperative education. Ben Jones and Arthur Acland, for instance, were busy writing their textbook, *Working Men Co-operators*, which would appear in 1884, and could not take the time to instruct women. They had also become involved with the founding of the Cooperative Union's Central Education Committee, designed to act as an advisory board for the movement on the subject of cooperative education. This was the context of personal relationships, gender role presumptions, and movement-wide concerns in which was born the Women's League for the Spread of Cooperation, otherwise known as the Women's Cooperative Guild.

The week after Greenwood's second letter there appeared in the "Woman's Corner" the letter from Mary Lawrenson that is credited with instigating the formation of the Guild. Lawrenson was one of Greenwood's dearest friends. Her letter suggested Acland form a "Central Board" and draw up a plan for holding the mothers' meetings she had envisioned in her first column.[89] Lawrenson began her letter by quoting from a book she had just finished reading, *With Harp and Crown*. One of the characters in the book, a man, says, "I see a time when men shall acknowledge that the truest chance for the world is to cultivate and raise the women."[90] She then added that she hoped one of the objects of the organization of cooperative mothers that would emerge from Acland's efforts would be to devise ways to ensure that women became and stayed paragons of virtue. She said:

No woman who has given thought to these matters can see without regret young girls sauntering about the streets after work hours, as though the greatest happiness in life consisted in attracting the admiring notice of—well, we will call them young men—fellows whose smartest sayings are at the cost of the silly ones who gain for themselves ridicule in place of admiration.[91]

The founders of the first organized body of cooperative women had begun to stake out a territory for their activities, and it was a field of work for women that male cooperators like Ben Jones and Arthur Acland could approve. It fit their gendered assumptions about women's roles. The matriarchs of the Cooperative movement would look after the education and welfare of women and children. They would perform these tasks for the purpose of keeping alive cooperative ideals that were under siege from "divi-mindedness." They would safeguard the virtue of women, especially girls, assuming that "to cultivate and raise the women" was "the truest chance" for cooperation.

This study of women in the English Cooperative movement focuses on the period from 1883 to 1921. It opens with the founding of the "Woman's Corner" of the *Co-operative News* and closes with the retirement of Margaret Llewelyn Davies, the longest-serving general secretary of the Women's Cooperative Guild. These were critical years for feminism. As discussed earlier, new feminism replaced the equal rights variety in this period. These were also critical years for the Cooperative movement. As Peter Gurney illustrates in *Co-operative Culture and the Politics of Consumption in England*, cooperation throve in these years, but also began to manifest internal difficulties and confront external threats that would reduce both the movement's vitality and its prosperity in the years to come.[92] Earlier historians of the movement, like Sidney and Beatrice Webb, observe of the period that the stores attracted more customers and members, but fewer of them were "true" cooperators.[93] Most participants in the movement were in it for the dividends and cared nothing about the movement's history or its aspirations for the future. Few participated in the running of the cooperative societies to which they belonged. The movement's evolution of national organizations with federal structures created leaders who were distant from the rank and file, undermining further the average member's incentive to become involved. The effect of these developments subverted the movement's efforts to run itself democratically.

Cooperation's moral commitment to offer the consumer value for money meant the stores sold plain articles, which competed poorly for market share with the flashy goods that commercial capitalism began to offer as the nineteenth century gave way to the twentieth. What made matters worse for cooperation was its refusal to engage in the sorts of advertising that capitalists were developing to market their products. Cooperators believed the new vogue in advertising to be designed merely to deceive the consumer.[94] The result was that this movement desirous of eradicating competition could not compete in the marketplace and was itself in danger of extermination. Cooperative stores could provide value and variety when compared to the small retail traders that predominated before the late nineteenth century. But they offered no such advantages to the consumer when compared with the department and chain stores that began to take over the retail trade in the 1880s. Moreover, next to such stores, the "co-op" looked pretty drab.[95] The cooperative store had no attractive window displays, tastefully arranged counters, or overly solicitous sales clerks. It looked like a warehouse, and its clerks could be brusque.

Political changes as much as economic ones challenged cooperators between 1880 and 1920. The growth in popularity of a socialism that advocated the creation of welfare state coverage for everyone from "the cradle to the grave" to guarantee a minimum standard of living was interpreted by some cooperators as a threat to the principle of self-help on which they had built their movement. Although most nineteenth-century cooperators voted Liberal, their movement was committed to political neutrality. The emergence of the Labour Party, which relied on the trade unions to which so many cooperators belonged, prompted them to re-examine this commitment. The First World War caused them to abandon it. During the war, the government had been reluctant to consult cooperators about rationing policies and threatened to tax the "profits" of this movement that claimed that it did not make "profits," but merely accumulated "savings" from mutual trading.[96] The Cooperative Party was therefore formed to defend the movement, and it often ran candidates in conjunction with Labour.

Women cooperators wanted to help the men meet the challenges that confronted cooperation. However, the extent to which their help was welcomed became the issue with which they had to deal. It is proposed to examine in this book the gender politics of the Cooperative movement at the turn of the century and to consider what sorts of female leaders they produced. The first section of the book investigates what freedoms of speech and movement women were permitted as well as what resources they were given. The second section looks at the women leaders these conditions produced. The final section reveals the results of women's efforts to contribute to the creation of the Cooperative Commonwealth, by considering the conflicts cooperative women had with one another and with the men who controlled the movement. The book concludes that the accomplishments of the matriarchs of the movement were limited because of the patriarchy in which they operated. Other historians have investigated women's participation in the Cooperative movement. Some, like Alistair Thomson, have even recognized that the movement remained tightly controlled by men despite women's efforts to change that.[97] However, all previous work on women in cooperation has overestimated what the women managed to achieve because it has failed to explore the dynamics of the gender politics within the movement.[98] This even includes a quite recent book by Gillian Scott, which focuses on the post–World War I history of the Guild.[99] Scott concedes that the women who led the Guild in the interwar period were in thrall to male agendas but perversely maintains that this was contrary to the situation in which cooperative women operated before the First World War. Scott fails to see that men established the boundaries within which women were permitted to operate, and these limitations undermined women's efforts either to run their affairs democratically or according to their feminist *cum* cooperative values characterized as "caring and sharing" by two other scholars of the Women's Guild.[100]

The first chapter in the section titled "Women's Space/Women's Place" argues that men supervised and restricted women's freedom of speech within the Cooperative movement. It uses as evidence the women's column in the *Cooperative News* for the years between 1883 and 1919. It finds that many women were afraid to write to or for the column. Even when exchanging recipes they used initials or pseudonyms, which male cooperators rarely used when writing to the paper because of the brotherhood they considered as existing among themselves as participants in the movement. Women, however, apparently felt uncomfortable in the public space of the *News*.

The amount of space given women's concerns in the paper is also examined, including the size of the women's column and its position in the newspaper. It is noticed that the column's editor had little control over its contents. Male cooperators believed their newspaper represented their movement. They wanted nothing to appear in the *News* that might endanger the movement's welfare and it was up to the paper's general editor, a man, to determine what did. Thus under a sympathetic general editor the women's column was free to discuss such "sensitive" topics as the laws and mores governing marriage. But under an unsympathetic general editor any suggestion that marriage could be a patriarchal dictatorship was censored. Women were not permitted to complain in the column about husbands who gave them insufficient money for the household expenses while retaining for themselves enough spending money to enjoy leisure activities. Instead they had to gush about the joys of domesticity and companionate marriage, without even so much as suggesting that in such marriages the burden of being companionable is usually placed on the wife. Editors of the women's column complied with these restrictions in order to preserve what little freedom and space they were permitted.

The second chapter in the section uses the statistics the Women's Cooperative Guild kept to track both its growth in size and the activities of its members. These statistics illustrate the extent to which women were marginalized within the Cooperative movement. The Guild had initially been conceived as a separate space for women's work on behalf of cooperation. However, guildswomen began to make incursions on activities men had reserved for themselves, because it proved impossible to separate women's from men's work within a movement whose business it was to supply the household. Every decision men made on store management committees affected the housewives who shopped at the stores. Guildswomen consequently felt justified in arguing that they were entitled to representation on such committees so that they might perform their natural roles as wives and mothers more effectively. Men were caught off guard by such relational arguments for women's rights. Those arguments seemed at once to uphold traditional views of women's roles and to undermine male hegemony. Men responded by fiercely defending their territories. Only in areas where cooperation was weakly established were men willing to accept women's presence in offices and on committees that men were accustomed to monopolizing. Thus in Lancashire, the home and stronghold of cooperation, the Guild's statistics show women making few gains in their attempts to influence the movement.

The second chapter also discusses the impact that male prejudice had on the Guild as an organization. Because most of its members were married working-class women the Guild had very little money of its own. It depended for funding on the movement with which it was affiliated. However, that movement was controlled by men on both national and local levels. Male cooperators were parsimonious when it came to providing the Guild with the resources it needed. They withheld access to rooms that guildswomen wanted for their meetings; they denied them sufficient funding for their activities. Lack of funding meant that branches could not afford to send representatives to district, sectional, or national meetings of the Guild. This undermined the Guild's claim that its federal structure was democratically run by representatives from the branches. Insufficient funds also meant that many guildswomen who rose through the ranks of that organization to positions of leadership beyond the branch level were neither working class nor housewives, or were in their middle years and no longer burdened with the expenses and work of raising a family. However, the Guild's leaders considered that their organization was dedicated to addressing the concerns of married working-class housewives and mothers, even though its rank and file and its leadership often differed from each other in composition, and even though conflicting perspectives on issues developed within the organization as a result of the discrepancies in the material conditions of life that existed between ordinary members and their leaders. For example, the leadership was often more radical on socioeconomic, gender, and international issues than the rank and file would tolerate. This contributed to conflicts between the national leadership and the branches, and also caused the great majority of women who shopped at the cooperative stores never to bother to join the Guild.

The section titled "Angels in the Store" considers the careers of several of the Women's Cooperative Guild's national leaders. The first chapter looks at the early years of the Guild. It examines the perspectives on cooperation, gender, and class held by the women who led the organization between 1883 and 1889 and compares them to those held by ordinary members. Since neither these leaders nor the rank and file left private papers,[101] the only sources for this information are the minute books kept by the Central Committee of the Guild, the reports of Guild national congresses printed in the *Co-operative News*, and the articles and correspondence featured in the "Woman's Corner." These sources reveal the obstacles guildswomen encountered in their attempt to create a community of women within the Cooperative movement and in their efforts to help the men in the construction of the Cooperative Commonwealth to come. Both the leaders and the rank and file of the Guild held certain presumptions about class, for example, which they reinforced in one another and which were as antithetical to sisterhood among guildswomen as they were to cooperation's vision for the future. This reveals an ironic situation. When the leaders stayed in touch with the wishes of the ordinary members, they merely echoed the uninformed prejudices of those women, contributing nothing to the creation of the better world for which cooperators hoped. However, when they attempted to lead, they lost touch with the average member and, in turn, the average member lost interest in the Guild.

Personality also counted for much in the management of the Guild, in particular with respect to its relations with male cooperators. The men preferred certain personality types and expected certain behaviors. Consequently more could be accomplished by women who were deferential, demure, or diplomatic than women who were confrontational, which is not to say confrontational behaviors never prospered. Mary Lawrenson had a directness about her that many men interpreted negatively. Yet she became the first woman ever elected to a national office in the Cooperative movement when she won election to the Southern Section of the Cooperative Union's Central Board. However, she failed to remain in leadership positions either within the movement or the Guild, and that was the result of her personal style. Cooperative women preferred nonconfrontational female leaders as much as men did. They knew such leaders were less likely to drive men to defensive positions.

The second chapter of this section focuses exclusively on Margaret Llewelyn Davies, who was the Guild's general secretary for thirty-two years and who is usually considered to have had a positive influence on the organization.[102] This examination attempts to deliver a critical assessment of Llewelyn Davies and her career. It ignores neither the dissident voices of her opponents nor the impact of her private life on her public one. It uses as sources her private papers and her publications. The chapter finds that her class advantages, coupled with developments internal to the Guild, enabled her to attain and keep her position of leadership. It observes that her unmarried, childless situation limited her appreciation for the regard cooperative women had for private life, despite its hard work and sacrifices.[103] On the other hand, it argues that Llewelyn Davies's unmarried status also made her a critical observer of marriage and prompted her to use the Guild to agitate for reforms that would make women more independent of their husbands.

It was during Llewelyn Davies's tenure as general secretary that the Guild adopted the same federal structure that the Cooperative Union utilized. In her 1904 history of the Guild, she likened this structure to a tree. The trunk was the Guild's Central Committee over which she presided; the main limbs were the sections; and the lesser limbs attached to them were the districts. Finally, to the lesser limbs were attached the branches, representing the Guild's branches. She said, "The object aimed at in this organisation is healthy independence in local work, combined with response to the policy and suggestions coming from the centre."[104] However, under her direction there tended to be more "response to the policy and suggestions coming from the centre" than "healthy independence in local work." Though she claimed to be a democrat, she was proud of the centrist management configuration she directed. The analogy she made between it and a tree says much about the difference between matriarchal and patriarchal organizational structures. Patriarchal structures tend to be configured after "top-down" models, whereas matriarchal ones utilize organic imagery, which sends the message that the leaders nurture and sustain the followers. However, matriarchal structures can be just as hierarchical and oppressive of dissident voices as patriarchal ones. After all, if one cuts a branch from a tree, the branch will die. It is therefore not surprising to find Llewelyn Davies boasting about how much male cooperators admired the Guild's organization because it had better control over its rank and file than the men's organizational structures had over the wider movement. She noted that a male admirer once exclaimed, "Why touch it at any point, and it's known at the Central."[105] This was more than the men could say of the Cooperative Union after which the Guild was modeled. The Union often found itself incapable of imposing its will on the individual cooperative societies, which belonged to it, but which jealously guarded their independence.

The Guild's political culture as much as its organizational structure stifled grassroots activity. The Guild encouraged an atmosphere at its national meetings in particular that discouraged the participation of its less assertive members. Slavish devotion to the parliamentary procedures evolved by the man's world of politics produced this unwelcoming environment. The final section of the book is titled "The Dysfunctional Commonwealth." In its first chapter the failure of cooperative women organized into the Guild to create an alternative political culture to the one suggested to them by male models is held responsible for their inability to overcome the class, regional, and generational divisions that existed among them. The chapter finds that some guildswomen were anxious to maintain these divisions, while others presumed such barriers to sisterhood could be so easily crossed that few fundamental cultural changes would be necessary to do so. In both cases, these attitudes prevented guildswomen from grasping the extent to which differences among themselves obstructed their efforts to create a community of mutually supportive women within the Cooperative movement.

Special consideration is given to the manner in which the issues of women's suffrage and divorce law reform divided the women. In the absence of any surviving private papers, the "Woman's Corner" of the *Co-operative News* is an important source for the attitudes of many of the Guild's forgotten leaders and members on these issues. In particular, the use of the "Woman's Corner" led to the rediscovery of Mrs. Bury, from the Darwen branch of the Guild in the county of Lancashire. Mrs. Bury was an outspoken advocate for the opinions of rank-and-file guildswomen whose wishes were often ignored by Margaret Llewelyn Davies and other national leaders.

Mrs. Bury was articulate and confident in her convictions, but sensitive to her constituency. She was uncomfortable with the overly centralized federal structure the Guild had adopted, considering that it suppressed grassroots initiatives and minority opinions. To her, it seemed to encourage the notion that guildswomen should think alike simply because they all belonged to the same organization, thus ignoring important differences in opinions, born of class or region, which should be heard. It is interesting to note that although Mrs. Bury held a number of national offices during her association with the Guild, nowhere in the archives kept by the Cooperative movement is there a record of her Christian name. Perhaps that is appropriate. She had conservative views on marriage and preferred to conform to the social conventions of her era with respect to her own title.

As a result of World War I, the Cooperative movement faced the increasingly hostile policies of a national government looking for ways to fund the carnage on the Continent and ration food on the home front. This led many rank-and-file guildswomen to believe that agitation on behalf of women's issues, which tended to upset male cooperators, should be set aside in the interest of presenting a united front against the government's threats to cooperation. These same threats also made male cooperators more willing to negotiate with the Guild over what women's role in cooperation should be. In particular, after the movement decided to abandon its traditional policy of political neutrality and women won the vote, cooperation's men began to see women as voters with the potential to force the government into policies friendly to the movement. In addition to their traditional roles as shoppers at the stores and educators of women and children, women were now encouraged to shoulder the task of voting against cooperation's enemies. However, although male cooperators conceded that women had their uses, they continued to deny them access to national offices and managerial committees. Cooperative women were partly to blame for this. They had failed to argue for expanded roles from the standpoint of equal rights feminism. Their relational feminism had encouraged the men to see them as different from men and, regrettably, to categorize them as deficient because they were different.[106] But, the women had little alternative if they wanted any voice at all within cooperation, given the reticence of the men to admit the fluidity of the boundary between public and private, men's work and women's, in their consumers' movement.

The last chapter examines the tortuous course of these gender politics, focusing on the enmity between the Women's Cooperative Guild and the Cooperative Union. Between 1914 and 1918 the Guild and the Union were in conflict over a number of issues, including the Guild's right to agitate for divorce law reform, its right to select the topics of study for women in courses funded by the Union's Central Education Committee, and its right to set a policy independent of the larger movement. The men of the Union believed that they should have the final say over the Guild's direction because the Guild was dependent on them for funding. In sum, a dispute was underway in the public sphere between the Guild and the Union, a dispute very similar to one that might occur in a working-class household. When a husband provided his wife with money to spend on household expenses, he conceded to her jurisdiction over the money's disbursement. Still, he did not expect her to spend it in ways he would not approve, and reserved the right to veto her decisions. The research of Ellen Ross reveals the extent to which arguments between working-class couples over the budgeting of money had the potential to become so vocal even the neighbors would hear them, and so violent they sometimes required police intervention.[107] The compromise that the Guild and the Union achieved to settle their differences was also similar to one which a working-class couple might reach. They agreed to continue arguing, but not in front of the "neighbors." In other words, it was arranged for there to be regular meetings between representatives of the Guild and the Union to discuss any differences they might have. A united front could then be presented against the movement's enemies when they dared to threaten cooperation.

Finally, it is necessary to add that this book's perspective on the gender politics played between the sexes in the Cooperative movement is informed by the theories of feminist geographers with respect to space and marginalization. As Audrey Kobayashi has asserted, "'space' [can be] used to consolidate difference . . . subordination is rendered through separation and unequal access."[108] In their battles with the men in control of the Cooperative movement for meeting rooms, funding, and election to office, cooperative women certainly discovered the truth of Kobayashi's observation. Cooperative men controlled access to space, and that enabled them to marginalize women within the movement.

The work of feminist geographers is also applied to the book's analysis of the consequences of the differences that existed among cooperative women and their impact on the women's ability to make the space they were permitted one that was inclusive. It is argued that the Guild's leaders, for instance, played at identity politics, organizing women as women and presuming of them a solidarity that ignored class, regional, and generational differences. This, as Kobayashi says, led "to oppressions based on intragroup differences."[109] Cooperative patriarchy was not solely responsible for oppressing women in the movement; it was assisted by the women's failure "to negotiate [their own] complex and divided selves" in a way that could prevent them from turning their Guild into yet another hierarchy of power.[110]

Further limiting the accomplishments of cooperative women was their relational feminism. Its difference-based orientation tended to leave traditional gender divisions unchallenged, and therefore essentialized women as caregivers and educators of their families and children.[111] If male cooperators could not imagine women being interested in concerns beyond the home, it was because cooperative women never argued for a voice in public affairs for any reason other than that it would help them perform their traditional roles better. Many feminist scholars have commented on this limitation of relational feminism, pointing out that it uses the same intellectual framework as those anti-feminists who want to trap women in their traditional roles.[112] On the other hand, there are those who contend relational feminism has the capacity to challenge the boundaries between men and women because it forces into the public forum the concerns traditionally deemed to be the private affairs of the patriarchal family, such as motherhood and childcare.[113] However, after forcing these issues into the open, relational feminism has failed to prevent the creation of ghettos in the public sphere for women and their concerns. It has therefore been unable to break down traditional boundaries.

Cooperative women were unable to choose an equal rights feminist ideology because of male resistance, the Guild's focus on the needs of working-class women, and the legacy of Owenism. Male cooperators associated equal rights feminism with middle-class ladies who wanted to subvert the natural distinctions between the sexes.[114] Guildswomen agreed, since the formal equality those middle-class ladies sought would do little to benefit working-class women. The legacy of Owenism also predisposed cooperation's female leaders to concentrate on securing real rather than formal equality. It led them to believe it was possible to reconfigure societal relationships in order to achieve a cooperative utopia where even women who remained in traditional roles would no longer be rendered dependent and powerless. If the Cooperative movement never adequately addressed inequities resulting from gender, both male and female cooperators were responsible.

NOTES

1. Peter Gurney in *Co-operative Culture and the Politics of Consumption in England, 1870–1930* (Manchester: Manchester University Press, 1996), 45, dates the advent of this discussion a little earlier. He observes that it began in the 1890s and picked up pace after the turn of the century.

2. Quoted in Arnold Bonner, *British Co-operation* (Manchester: Cooperative Union Ltd., 1970), 477.

3. For additional information on the utopian ideology of Cooperation, see Stephen Yeo, "Introductory: Rival Clusters of Potential: Ways of Seeing Co-operation," in Stephen Yeo (ed.), *New Views of Co-operation* (New York: Routledge, 1988); and Gurney, *Co-operative Culture and the Politics of Consumption in England*, chapter 2.

4. Sidney Pollard, "Nineteenth Century Co-operation: From Community Building to Shopkeeping," in Asa Briggs and John Saville (eds.), *Essays in Labour History* (London: Macmillan & Company Ltd., 1960).

5. This is the argument of George Jacob Holyoake's history of the Rochdale Pioneers, *Self-Help by the People* (London: Holyoake & Company, 1858), 1–3; and Gurney also makes this claim in *Co-operative Culture and the Politics of Consumption in England*, 4.

6. Holyoake makes this boast in *Self-Help by the People*, 1–3.

7. There is some dispute among cooperators about how many the Rochdale Pioneers were in number. Some sources put their head count at thirty-four. Arnold Bonner in *British Co-operation* accepts only twenty-eight and also provides their occupations,

ages, and political afiliations—Chartist or Owenite (510–512). He describes them as being "well-paid skilled artisans, some in business on their own account" (45). This would prove the socioeconomic group most attracted to cooperation throughout the history of the movement.

8. George Jacob Holyoake, *The History of Co-operation in England*, vol. 2 (New York: AMS Press, 1971), 111–112.

9. Barbara Taylor, *Eve and the New Jerusalem* (New York: Pantheon Books, 1983).

10. Joan W. Scott, "Deconstructing Equality-versus-Difference: Or, the Uses of Poststructualist History for Feminism," *Feminist Studies* vol. 14, no. 1 (Spring 1988), 37.

11. Ibid.

12. Ibid.

13. Quoted in Bonner, *British Co-operation*, 134.

14. Marilyn A. Katz, "Daughters of Demeter: Women in Ancient Greece," in Renate Bridenthal, Susan Mosher Stuard, and Merry E. Weisner (eds.), *Becoming Visible* (Boston: Houghton Mifflin Company, 1998), 49.

15. Sonya O. Rose describes the components of working-class masculine identity in *Limited Livelihoods. Gender and Class in Nineteenth-century England* (Berkeley: University of California Press, 1992), 129–130.

16. Ellen Ross, *Love and Toil: Motherhood in Outcast London, 1870–1918* (New York: Oxford University Press, 1993), 41.

17. Ibid., 28.

18. Anna Clark, *The Struggle for the Breeches: Gender and the Making of the British Working Class* (Berkeley: University of California Press, 1995), 159.

19. Gurney, *Co-operative Culture and the Politics of Consumption in England*, 195.

20. Ibid., 158.

21. Ibid., 61.

22. Susan Kingsley Kent, *Sex and Suffrage in Britain, 1860–1914* (Princeton: Princeton University Press, 1987), 32.

23. Margaret Llewelyn Davies, *The Women's Co-operative Guild, 1883–1904* (Kirkby Lonsdale, Westmorland: Women's Cooperative Guild, 1904), 65.

24. Ross, *Love and Toil*, 28; and Lori Loeb, *Consuming Angels: Advertising and Victorian Women* (New York: Oxford University Press, 1994), 21.

25. Chris Waters, *British Socialism and the Politics of Popular Culture, 1884–1914* (Manchester: Manchester University Press, 1990), 25.

26. Ibid.

27. Wally Seccombe argues in "Patriarchy Stabilized: The Construction of the Male Breadwinner Wage Norm in Nineteenth-century Britain," *Social History* vol. 11, no. 1 (January 1986) that working-class wives in particular saw themselves as producers because they labored in the home to produce family survival (57).

28. For a discussion of wage labor outside the home by married women, see Elizabeth Roberts, "Working Wives and their Families," in Theo Barker and Michael Drake (eds.), *Population and Society in Britain, 1850–1980* (London: Batsford Academic and Educational Ltd., 1982). She claims (141–142) that it did not decline markedly over the course of the nineteenth century. On the other hand, Jane Lewis and Sonya O. Rose, "'Let England Blush': Protective Labor Legislation, 1820–1914," in Ulla Wikander, Alice Kessler-Harris and Jane Lewis (eds.), *Protecting Women: Labor Legislation in Europe, the United States and Australia, 1880–1920* (Urbana, IL: University of Illinois Press, 1995) argue the contrary (93).

29. Sally Alexander, Anna Davin, and Eve Hostettler, "Labouring Women: A Reply to Eric Hobsbawm," *History Workshop* vol. 8 (1979) investigates the variety of

women's work (177). So does Roberts in "Working Wives and Their Families," in Barker and Drake (eds.), *Population and Society in Britain*, 142–143.

30. Rose, *Limited Livelihoods*, 20.

31. Ross, *Love and Toil*, 77.

32. Both Clark, *The Struggle for the Breeches*, 238–243, and Taylor, *Eve and the New Jerusalem*, 78–79, see the mid-century as the time of this ideology's establishment in the consciousnesses of the working class.

33. All recent scholarship agrees that domesticity for working-class wives evolved out of the gender dynamics of the working class itself. See the following: Susan Pedersen, "The Failure of Feminism in the Making of the British Welfare State," *Radical History Review*, no. 43 (Winter 1989); Jane Lewis, "The Working-class Wife and Mother and State Intervention, 1870–1918," in Jane Lewis (ed.), *Labour and Love: Women's Experience of Home and Family, 1850–1940* (New York: Basil Blackwell, 1987); Elizabeth Roberts, *A Woman's Place: An Oral History of Working-class Women, 1890–1940* (New York: Basil Blackwell, 1984); Anna Clark, *The Struggle for the Breeches*.

34. Rose, *Limited Livelihoods*, 129–130 and Clark, *The Struggle for the Breeches*, 94. Other scholars agree with Rose and Clark. See Pedersen, "The Failure of Feminism," 98–99; Lewis, "The Working-class Wife and Mother and State Intervention, 1870–1918," in Lewis (ed.), *Labour and Love*, 103; Roberts, *A Woman's Place*, 137.

35. Rose, *Limited Livelihoods*, 129–130; and Pedersen, "The Failure of Feminism," 98.

36. Harold Benenson, "The 'Family Wage' and Working Women's Consciousness in Britain, 1880–1914," *Politics and Society* vol. 19, (1991); Sonya O. Rose, "Gender Antagonism and Class Conflict: Exclusionary Strategies of Male Trade Unionists in Nineteenth-century Britain," *Social History* vol. 13, (1988); Wally Seccombe, "Patriarchy Stabilized."

37. Ellen Ross supports this thesis in *Love and Toil* and in "'Not the Sort that Would Sit on the Doorstep': Respectability in Pre–World War I London Neighborhoods," *International Labor and Working Class History*, no. 27 (Spring 1985).

38. Rose, *Limited Livelihoods*, 79

39. Roberts, *A Woman's Place*, 136; and Diana Gittens, *Fair Sex: Family Size and Structure, 1900–39* (London: Hutchinson, 1982), 95.

40. Gittens, *Fair Sex*, 95.

41. This pattern is observed by Elizabeth Roberts in "Working Wives and their Families," in Barker and Drake (eds.), *Population and Society in Britain*, and in her "Women's Strategies, 1890–1940" in Lewis (ed.) *Labour and Love*; also by Jill Liddington and Jill Norris in *One Hand Tied Behind Us* (London: Virago Press Ltd., 1978).

42. Rose, *Limited Livelihoods*, 161.

43. This is the main thesis of Clark's *Struggle for the Breeches*.

44. Jane Lewis, *Women in England, 1870–1950: Sexual Divisions and Social Change* (Bloomington, IN: Indiana University Press, 1984), 28; Liddington and Norris, *One Hand Tied Behind Us*, chapter 7.

45. Clark, *The Struggle for the Breeches*, 31.

46. Mike Savage, "Capitalist and Patriarchal Relations at Work: Preston Cotton Weaving, 1890–1940," in Linda Murgatroyd et al. (eds.), *Localities, Class and Gender* (London: Pion Limited, 1985), 179–184.

47. Ibid., 193.

48. Taylor, *Eve and the New Jerusalem*, xiii–xv.

49. Quoted in Bonner, *British Co-operation*, 524.

50. Ibid.

51. Clark, *The Struggle for the Breeches*, agrees (132). She notes that among textile workers it would be incorrect to assume that their nominal inclusion of women should be interpreted as indicating sexual equality or the nonexistence of patriarchy.

52. Bonner, *British Co-operation*, 524.

53. Peter Gurney's *Co-operative Culture and the Politics of Consumption in England* provides useful statistics on the Cooperative movement taken from the work of G.D.H. Cole, one of cooperation's premier historians (241–242).

54. Bonner, *British Co-operation*, 487.

55. Ibid. What is worse, this quotation is from the revised 1971 edition of Bonner's work.

56. The term relational feminism is derived from Karen Offen, "Contextualizing the Theory and Practice of Feminism in Nineteenth-century Europe," in Bridenthal et al. (eds.), *Becoming Visible*.

57. Kent, *Sex and Suffrage in Britain*, 54–59, 86–89; Jane Lewis, "Dealing with Dependency: State Practices and Social Realities, 1870–1945," in Jane Lewis (ed.), *Women's Welfare/Women's Rights* (London: Croom Helm, 1983), 14; Scott, "Deconstructing Equality-versus-Difference," 39–48.

58. Brian Harrison, *Prudent Revolutionaries. Portraits of British Feminists between the Wars* (Oxford: Clarendon Press, 1987), chapters 1 and 4; Harold L. Smith, "British Feminism in the 1920s," and Hilary Land, "Eleanor Rathbone and the Economy of the Family," in Harold L. Smith (ed.), *British Feminism in the Twentieth Century* (Amherst, MA: University of Massachusetts Press, 1990).

59. Susan Kingsley Kent, "Gender Reconstruction after the First World War," in Smith (ed.), *British Feminism in the Twentieth Century*.

60. Joan W. Scott, *Only Paradoxes to Offer* (Cambridge, MA: Harvard University Press, 1996), 169.

61. Harrison, *Prudent Revolutionaries*, chapter 4; Land, "Eleanor Rathbone," in Smith (ed.), *British Feminism in the Twentieth Century*; and Pat Thane, "The British Labour Party and Feminism, 1906–1945," in Smith (ed.), *British Feminism in the Twentieth Century*; Susan Pederson, *Family, Dependence and the Origins of the Welfare State: Britain and France, 1914–1945* (Cambridge: Cambridge University Press, 1993), chapter 3; Lewis, "The Working-class Wife and Mother and State Intervention, 1870–1918," in Lewis (ed.), *Labour and Love*.

62. Philippa Levine, *Feminist Lives in Victorian England: Private Roles and Public Commitment* (London: Basil Blackwell, 1990), 174.

63. Sally Alexander, "The Fabian Women's Group, 1908–52," in Sally Alexander, *Becoming a Woman and Other Essays in 19th and 20th Century Feminist History* (New York: New York University Press, 1995), says this reorganization was the goal of the Fabian Women's Group (157).

64. Pedersen, "The Failure of Feminism," 88; Harrison, *Prudent Revolutionaries*, 79 and 104.

65. Pedersen, "The Failure of Feminism," 91. Also see her "Gender, Welfare, and Citizenship in Britain during the Great War," *American Historical Review* vol. 95, (October 1990).

66. Deborah Dwork, *War Is Good for Babies and Other Young Children: A History of the Infant and Child Welfare Movement in England, 1898–1918* (London: Tavistock Publications, 1987).

67. This is Pedersen's thesis in *Family, Dependence and the Origins of the Welfare State*.

68. Pedersen, "The Failure of Feminism," 91.

69. Pat Thane identifies this as one of the goals of the women in the Labour Party in "The Women of the British Labour Party and Feminism," in Smith (ed.), *British Feminism in the Twentieth Century*, 129.

70. Taylor, *Eve and the New Jerusalem*, 17.

71. Llewelyn Davies, *The Women's Co-operative Guild*, 161.

72. Llewelyn Davies, *The Women's Co-operative Guild*; Catherine Webb, *The Woman with the Basket* (Manchester: Cooperative Wholesale Society's Printing Works, 1927); Jean Gaffin and David Thoms, *Caring and Sharing: The Centenary History of the Women's Co-operative Guild* (Manchester: Cooperative Union Ltd., 1983); Gillian Scott, "'The Working-class Women's Most Active and Democratic Movement': The Women's Co-operative Guild, 1883–1950," D.Phil. thesis, University of Sussex, 1988 which has been recently published as *Feminism and the Politics of Working Women: The Women's Co-operative Guild, 1880s to the Second World War* (London: UCL Press Ltd., 1998).

73. Jane Lewis also recognizes this fact of life for women in *Women in England*, xi.

74. Quoted in Desmond Flanagan, *A Centenary Story of the Co-operative Union of Great Britain and Ireland* (Manchester: Cooperative Union Ltd., 1969), 28.

75. Quoted in Bonner, *British Co-operation*, 119.

76. Crane Brinton, "Utopia and Democracy," in Frank E. Manuel (ed.) *Utopias and Utopian Thought* (Cambridge, MA: Houghton Mifflin Company, 1966), 57.

77. Waters, *British Socialism and the Politics of Popular Culture*, 167–168.

78. "Woman's Corner," *Co-operative News*, January 6, 1883.

79. Ibid.

80. Ibid.

81. Ibid.

82. Ibid.

83. "Woman's Corner," *Co-operative News*, January 13, 1883.

84. "Woman's Corner," *Co-operative News*, January 20, 1883.

85. "Woman's Corner," *Co-operative News*, January 27, 1883.

86. Ibid.

87. "Woman's Corner," *Co-operative News*, February 3, 1883.

88. Ibid.

89. "Woman's Corner," *Co-operative News*, February 10, 1883.

90. Ibid.

91. Ibid.

92. Gurney, *Co-operative Culture and the Politics of Consumption in England*, chapters 8 and 9.

93. Sidney and Beatrice Webb, *The Consumers' Co-operative Movement* (London: Longmans, Green & Company, 1921), 48–49. Gurney disputes their assertion in *Co-operative Culture and the Politics of Consumption in England*, but unconvincingly (2–12, 24–25, 33–49).

94. Gurney, *Co-operative Culture and the Politics of Consumption in England*, 66.

95. Ibid., 234.

96. Ibid., 137.

97. Alistair Thomson, "'Domestic Drudgery Will Be a Thing of the Past': Co-operative Women and the Reform of Housework," in Yeo (ed.) *New Views of Co-operation*, 109.

98. Gaffin and Thoms, *Caring and Sharing*; Scott, "The Working-class Women's Most Active and Democratic Movement."

99. Scott, *Feminism and the Politics of Working Women*.

100. Gaffin and Thoms even chose these values for the title of their book on the Guild.

101. Mary Lawrenson has left private papers. They consist of some letters that are so few in number that they can be read in the space of a morning. The originals are in the Women's Cooperative Guild central office near London. The Cooperative Union Library in Manchester has photocopies.

102. Gaffin and Thoms, *Caring and Sharing*, chapter 2; Scott, *Feminism and the Politics of Working Women*, chapter 4.

103. Judy Giles, *Women, Identity and Private Life in Britain, 1900–50* (New York: St. Martin's Press, 1995), 44, notes that working-class women responded to poverty and injustice by aspiring to a better life which meant for them a separation of the spheres in which women's domesticity connoted respectability.

104. Llewelyn Davies, *The Women's Co-operative Guild*, 36.

105. Ibid., 37.

106. Feminist scholars have made similar observations with respect to the new feminism. See Kent, *Sex and Suffrage in Britain*, 226–227; Lewis, *Women in England*, 104–105; Martha Vicinus, *Independent Women: Work and Community for Single Women, 1850–1920* (Chicago: University of Chicago Press, 1985), 283.

107. Ross, *Love and Toil*, chapter 2.

108. Audrey Kobayashi, "The Paradox of Difference and Diversity," in John Paul Jones III et al. (eds.), *Thresholds in Feminist Geography* (Lanham, MD: Rowman & Littlefield Publishers, Inc., 1997), 6.

109. Ibid., 5.

110. Gill Valentine, "Making Space: Separatism and Difference," in Jones et al. (eds.), *Thresholds in Feminist Geography*, 75.

111. Jane Lewis makes this point with respect to family allowances, for which new feminists like Eleanor Rathbone agitated, "Models of Equality for Women: The Case of State Support for Children in Twentieth-century Britain," in Gisela Bock and Pat Thane (eds.), *Maternity and Gender Policies: Women and the Rise of European Welfare States, 1880s–1950s* (New York: Routledge, 1991), 74–75. However, Susan Pedersen argues that Rathbone never intended to essentialize women in that way; see her "Eleanor Rathbone 1872–1946," in Susan Pedersen and Peter Mandler (eds.), *After the Victorians: Private Conscience and Public Duty in Modern Britain* (London: Routledge, 1994), 118.

112. Kent, "Gender Reconstruction after the First World War," in Smith (ed.), *British Feminism in the Twentieth Century*, 66; Kent, *Sex and Suffrage in Britain*, 226–227; Scott, "Deconstructing Equality-versus-Difference," 39; Smith, "British Feminism in the 1920s," in Smith (ed.), *British Feminism in the Twentieth Century*, 61; Harrison, *Prudent Revolutionaries*, 112; Mary Poovey, *Uneven Developments: The Ideological Work of Gender in Mid-Victorian England* (Chicago: University of Chicago Press, 1988), 6; Anne Phillips, *Divided Loyalties: Dilemmas of Sex and Class* (London: Virago Press Ltd., 1987), 103; Wikander et al. (eds.), *Protecting Women*, 4; Lewis, "Models of Equality for Women," in Bock and Thane (eds.), *Maternity and Gender Policies*, 74–75; Lewis, *Women in England*, 104–105; Vicinus, *Independent Women*, 283.

113. Seth Koven and Sonya Michel, "Womanly Duties: Maternalist Politics and the Origins of Welfare States in France, Germany, Great Britain, and the United States, 1880–1920," *American Historical Review* vol. 95 (October 1990) make this argument (1079).

114. Harrison in *Prudent Revolutionaries* (148) notes the tension that existed between workers' organizations and feminists and suggests that new feminism was better at resolving it.

Lilian Harris, assistant general secretary of the Women's Cooperative Guild and confidante of Margaret Llewelyn Davies. Reproduced courtesy of the Co-operative Women's Guild.

Part I

Women's Space/Women's Place

AMY SHARP.
1886-1889.

ROSALIND NASH.
1889-1904.

ANNIE BAMFORD TOMLINSON.
Since 1904 ; Editor, " Woman's Outlook " since 1919.

Members of the Guild who edited the Women's Pages of the
" Co-operative News," which Lady Acland also edited for a time.

Chapter 1

The "Woman's Corner" of the *Co-operative News*

In September 1895, Catherine Webb, who would serve as interim editor of the "Woman's Corner" for a few months in 1904, wrote a series of articles for that column of the *Co-operative News*. They reported the proceedings of the year's annual congress of the Women's Cooperative Guild. At Guild congresses it was customary for papers to be read to educate those in attendance about issues of concern for cooperators. Resolutions would then be proposed and voted on by the delegates. In this instance, "a resolution in favour of profit-sharing among workmen was put, but before it was carried Mr. Tutt rose on behalf of the women to ask that the word workmen be altered to workers, to include women."[1]

Webb reported that both she and the delegates present, including Elizabeth Tournier, vice-president of the Guild, had noticed the exclusionary term "workmen," but "trusted to the [Cooperative] movement to include women workers, as it was always the practice to do in any [cooperative] society employing women."[2] The women were confident of their right to equal treatment within the Cooperative movement. The man made no such presumptions, and proposed an amendment which would mandate the enforcement of equality. Unfortunately, Richard Tutt's understanding of the situation for women in cooperation was the more accurate assessment of the reality of women's place in the movement.

Sometimes sympathetic men are more aware of efforts to keep women marginalized than are women themselves. Women can often be overly grateful for any concessions granted them, while their male allies are more inclined to recognize clearly those concessions as palliatives that would never satisfy men. In the secondary source literature that studies women's place in the late nineteenth- and early twentieth-century British working-class movement it is apparent that historians have divided similarly in their interpretations of the evidence of women's marginalization, although those divisions fail to correspond to the

historian's gender. This division is owing to the tendency of the sources to reflect both the optimistic female point of view as well as the more pessimistic
one of male sympathizers with feminism, forcing historians to make judgment
calls. For example, in her investigations of the Labour Party, Pat Thane argues
that women played significant roles in the construction of the welfare state[3] and
in local Independent Labour Party chapters.[4] Chris Waters, on the other hand,
observes that Independent Labour Party women were relegated to such activities
as the washing-up after meetings and entertainments.[5] Like Thane, Seth Koven
and Sonya Michel conclude that women helped shape the maternalist policies
adopted by many states at the previous turn of the century,[6] while Susan Pedersen is less sanguine about their accomplishments.[7] Sonya O. Rose, Jenny Morris, and Wally Seccombe have examined the exclusionary tactics of male trade
unionists which limited women's right to work, especially in the skilled trades.[8]
Such restrictions often involved trade union advocacy of legislation ostensibly
designed to "protect" women from unhealthy workshop conditions, and historians are divided on the merits of such legislation no less than were the men and
women who lived with it.[9] Finally, within one study it is even possible to find
two conflicting opinions about the extent of women's freedom and power. In
One Hand Tied Behind Us, Jill Liddington and Jill Norris argue that Lancashire
working men were accepting of female independence because so many women
in that county had factory jobs, while at the same time demonstrating that those
men opposed women's suffrage, preventing the Trades Union Congress from
supporting it despite the agitation of female trade unionists.[10]

Historians of the Women's Cooperative Guild may be counted among the
"optimists" with respect to women's place in the British working-class movement, since they have insisted that the guildwomen's confidence that they would
be treated equally was better founded than Richard Tutt's suspicions. The
aforementioned Catherine Webb was one such historian. In her *Woman with the
Basket*, she speaks of the Guild's triumph over male opposition and attributes it
to the egalitarian ideology that formed the basis of cooperation.[11] More recent
historians, such as Jean Gaffin and David Thoms, have seconded that opinion.[12]
So, too, have historians of the Cooperative movement like Beatrice Potter,
G.D.H. Cole, and Peter Gurney, all of whom suggest that the Guild had a salu-
tary affect upon the movement, especially when it promoted reforms on behalf
of labor and women, because such commitments helped keep the successful
business enterprise that cooperation became true to its utopian roots in
Owenism.[13] However, these historians make the mistake of presuming that cooperation's egalitarian and idealistic agenda extended beyond class to gender
and that the Guild was freer to make policy choices than it actually was. For
example, Gillian Scott has argued that the Guild had the freedom "to make policy decisions untrammelled by the priorities of those insensitive to the needs of
guildswomen."[14] And in their study of the radical suffragists in Lancashire, Liddington and Norris have asserted that the Guild could "form its own policy on
the basis of its members' opinions."[15] However, male opposition and, at best,
ambivalence to women's public activism actually determined Guild policies. An
examination of the use of language and space in the "Woman's Corner," which
was for all practical purposes the Guild's column in the official newspaper of

the Cooperative movement, reveals the extent to which the men in control of the movement and its publications established the parameters within which women functioned in print and, consequently, within the movement. As Joan Scott has argued, language provides "a point of entry for understanding how social relationships are conceived."[16] As feminist geographers maintain, space can be used to marginalize and subordinate.[17] A study of the use of language and space within the cooperative press can thus reveal much about the gender politics operating within the Cooperative movement.

The *Co-operative News* began publication in 1871 as the first newspaper conducted "by" cooperators rather than "for" them, as past newspapers advocating the cause of cooperation had been.[18] It was published by the Cooperative Newspaper Society, which was empowered to make such business decisions regarding the paper as its size and cost. Content was considered a business matter because the first issue of the *News* declared that a newspaper is "the flag of a party . . . the sign by which the world knows it," and asserted that the cause of cooperation would have a great future if cooperators show "good sense and a capacity for concert and progress."[19] In sum, opinions that were judged contrary to what the proprietors of the paper deemed in the best interests of the movement were unlikely to appear in its pages.

In 1875, Samuel Bamford was appointed editor of the *News*.[20] The paper was heavily in debt when he took it over, but his efforts to increase circulation turned the paper's fortunes around.[21] There are no surviving records detailing the course of the editorial discussions that led Bamford to grant space in the *News* to women cooperators in 1883, but the first editor of the "Woman's Corner," Alice Acland, hinted in her inaugural column that the "Corner" was a bid to increase circulation by making the paper more attractive to women:

The fact is that, for women, the *News* has been just a little bit dull! Reports of meetings, and of discussions at conferences and at congresses, are very interesting . . . to those who by reading them may gain instruction which will help them to act . . . and any man at any moment may find himself called upon to act . . . for *women* it is different. Woman's work in life varies so much from men's work, that she is not called upon to *act* in these matters.[22]

Ironically, Acland then went on to complain that all male cooperators expected of their women was to "come and *buy*" at the stores, and suggested that another reason the "Corner" had been created was that male cooperators had begun to feel "a little ashamed of themselves" for expecting so little of the women.[23] However, shame figured little in Bamford's calculations. He expected women to "come and *buy*" his paper in order to help discharge the debt on it. Bamford knew that in working-class households the wife was in charge of the housekeeping budget. Bamford was a Lancashireman; research done by Ellen Ross shows that in that county it was customary for the husband to turn over to his wife each week his entire wage packet for household expenses.[24] If the wife was a cooperator, she would take her husband's earnings to the cooperative store each week, spending carefully to make the money stretch. She would need some incentive to spend the penny needed to buy Bamford's weekly publication. Bamford hoped that a women's column would provide that incentive. By the late nineteenth century, other weeklies had begun to run women's columns, and he may also have wanted to keep his paper competitive with them.

Bamford was a skillful businessman of working-class origins. Born near Rochdale, he had worked his way up through the Cooperative movement and, in fact, owed his education to science and art classes offered by the Rochdale Equitable Pioneers' Society.[25] Before he permitted the *News* to offer a permanent column for women he tested the waters, offering Acland the opportunity to write three months of articles entitled "Women's Lives" for the paper in 1882. Acland was chosen to write these articles and ultimately to edit the "Woman's Corner" because Bamford and her husband, Arthur Acland, were friends. Arthur Acland and his friend Ben Jones had brought Bamford's attention to the need for a women's column to educate female cooperators, but Bamford first had to make sure it would pay. Many years after the "Corner's" foundation, Alice Acland recalled how difficult it had been to convince the Cooperative Newspaper Society to allow space for a women's column in the paper.[26] She also claimed that Bamford was a supporter of the column. One of the reasons this "supporter" came to censor women's speech in the "Corner" had to do with his concern about the opposition to the column's existence among those to whom he reported. Unfortunately, just as there are no records of the editorial discussions leading to the establishment of the "Woman's Corner," none remain of the decision-making process governing the column's content. But the column itself speaks eloquently as to what was expected in that regard, because of its location in the newspaper and the manner of its treatment of "sensitive" topics.

Prior to 1919 the *Co-operative News* tended to run from twenty to thirty-plus pages in length. The "Woman's Corner" usually appeared anywhere from page eighteen to page twenty-eight, depending on the size of the edition. It was placed after the national, cooperative, and international news; after book reviews, serialized fiction, editorials, and letters to the editor; and sometimes after advertisements, personals, obituaries, and various announcements of upcoming cooperative activities. The only cooperative constituencies more marginalized than women in the pages of the *News* were children and employees of cooperative stores and manufactories, who, incidentally, trade unionists and even some cooperators charged, endured poor working conditions.[27] When their columns first appeared in the late 1880s, the "Junior Co-operators' Page" followed the "Corner," with the "Employes' [*sic*] Column" coming after it.[28] As has been noted, feminist geographers have observed that space can be used "to consolidate difference" and render subordinate "through separation and unequal access" those categorized as different.[29] They claim as well that "restrictions" on space can be used as forms of social control.[30] So while it is tempting to think that placement at the back of the paper made the "Corner" more accessible to busy housewives who might read the *News* from a "distaff" direction, it is questionable that Bamford had that in mind when he positioned the column in his paper.[31] The "Corner" was literally in the corner and was thus aptly named.

Since there are no records of the "Corner's" founding, how it got its name is a mystery. However, it is reasonable to conclude that its first editor was consulted and approved it, perhaps even conceived it. Although Acland advocated a wider sphere for women, she could neither imagine nor approve of them in nontraditional roles.[32] To her a corner was an appropriate characterization for the separate sphere in which women could work for their own improvement as well as that of others. She once said that her goal was to leave her "corner of the world (however tiny) . . . a little better than [she] found it."[33] Her preferred method of activism was to move "in a quiet womanly way."[34] Thus she opposed public speaking by women.[35] Neither she nor Amy Sharp, who became her assistant in 1884 and successor in 1886, considered the "Corner" public space. Rather, they saw it as a safe haven where women inexperienced in sharing their opinions with one another would find support and encouragement.[36] Acland thought she could use it to build a community of women, according to a phenomenon Lori Loeb describes in her study of middle-class female consumers, where she detects self-disclosure contributing to the building of communities among women.[37]

Whether women actually regarded the "Corner" as a private space for expressing themselves and building a community may be measured by the number of them signing their full names when they wrote to it, as well as by the repeated and often unproductive pleas of its first editors for substantive discussion of the issues of the day by correspondents.[38] In the 1880s and 1890s, in particular, women writing to the "Corner" preferred pseudonyms, initials, or the names of their home towns, even when they wrote merely to request or contribute recipes. Men tended to use such aliases in their letters to the editor of the *News* only when expressing controversial opinions.[39] Contributors like Amy Wright, who wrote to say how much she enjoyed the "Corner" and felt "at home there," likening it to "the study of a home, where we may read and think for ourselves," were rare during the first two decades of the column's existence.[40]

The case of Mary Lawrenson is the "Corner's" most striking example of women's preference for remaining veiled in public, as Virginia Woolf characterized it in *A Room of One's Own*.[41] It was Lawrenson's letter to Acland, appearing in the "Corner's" February 10, 1883 column, that initiated the formation of the Women's Cooperative Guild. Lawrenson failed to claim authorship of that letter in the public space of the "Corner" until 1885.[42] Eventually she went on to hold Guild offices at the local and national levels, and to become one of that organization's most beloved and engaging speakers. Yet she had signed the February 10, 1883 letter with her initials and many, though not all, subsequent contributions to the "Corner" either with "M.L." or "Woolwich," her home town. She made a special point of cultivating anonymity when she wanted to comment on gender issues, as the following illustrates:

A few days ago a temperance advocate was addressing an open-air meeting at W———. He asked the opinion of his auditors as to how much "he" could honestly spend on beer. "For," said he, "I earn 25s. a week. I have a wife and three children. Do you say 4s. 6d. would be too much for rent? That leaves me 20s. 6d. Now we have five hats, gowns, coats, pairs of boots, etc.; say 6d. each. Tell me if I am putting it too high! Now, I have 18s.—say 2d. each for breakfast; 2d. each for dinner; can't afford supper, so say 2d. tea, etc.; total 17s. 6d.; leaving me 6d. That 6d. would be better invested in a benefit society than in a publican's till." "Yes," said a woman in the crowd; "but where are the coals, soap, wood, etc. to come from?" That man would have done well to leave the calculating, together with the 24s. 6d., to his wife. M.L.[43]

Since cooperators of both sexes were often temperance advocates, because they acknowledged that drink could undermine the household economy of the working-class family thereby compromising its prospects for security and up-ward mobility, it may be assumed that some of them failed to appreciate the cocky tone of Lawrenson's concluding sentence, even if they conceded the working-class wife to have expertise in the area of household economy.

Ellen Ross has revealed that working-class men had a reputation for being poor shoppers and willingly delegated to their wives the management of the housekeeping money.[44] However, control of the housekeeping money was not necessarily a source of power for the wife. The research of Jane Millar suggests that management of the money in a poor household was and remains today a difficult chore.[45] Anne Phillips's findings support Millar's. Phillips concludes that the working-class wife's customary control of the housekeeping money was "not power."[46] The only sort of power a working-class wife might be able to claim was what Elizabeth Roberts refers to as "moral force" authority[47]: she was often able to shame her husband and working children into turning over their wages to her. Mary Lawrenson was accustomed to having moral force authority because she was a working-class wife. She decided to use it to report what had happened to the temperance speaker at Woolwich. Moreover, she was herself a temperance advocate and may have concluded she could make fun of a fellow ally in the cause of working-class improvement if he happened to say something ill-considered.[48] In fact, it is a fair guess that she was the "woman in the crowd" who had heckled the temperance speaker for his simple-minded calculations. She constructed her comments in the "Corner" as boasts about the way an anonymous woman had publicly humiliated the speaker and she signed only with her initials in an attempt to conceal her identity. But she must have known she was fooling no one by using her initials. By 1887, when this appeared in the "Corner," Lawrenson was already well known within the Cooperative move-ment due to her activities on behalf of the Guild. Indeed, at that time she was leader of the Women's Cooperative Guild, serving as its general secretary. Yet she did not have the courage to sign her name in full when speaking on this gender issue about which she as an anonymous woman seemed to comment so confidently.

When Lawrenson spoke on cooperative issues in the "Corner," she was less concerned with protecting her identity. She always used her name when report-ing in her capacity as an official of the Guild, whether it be at the branch or na-tional level. When speaking from those positions, she even felt free to admonish male cooperators for failing to recognize the many contributions the Guild made toward enriching the social life of the movement and furthering its educational activities.[49] Lawrenson especially believed that women were free to speak their minds on matters pertaining to cooperation's involvement in areas traditionally considered suited to women's work, such as advocacy on behalf of children or the oppressed.[50] Unfortunately for her, she eventually discovered how limited that freedom was.

Lawrenson was a proponent of employee profit-sharing and worker-controlled workshops.[51] She considered such schemes especially useful as remedies for the abuses suffered by women workers in the sweated trades.[52] On January 12, 1889, she reported in the "Corner" her visit to a Christmas party given by some entrepreneurs for their female employees. These men had pooled their capital to buy the business where the women worked and were planning to introduce employee profit-sharing now that they had begun to realize a return on their investment. During the course of her article, Lawrenson mentioned that they had retained as manager the former owner of the establishment, who had been responsible for sweating the workers there.[53] On February 23, a letter from Fred W. Phillips, secretary of the concern whose Christmas party Lawrenson had visited, appeared in the "Corner." He wanted an opportunity to defend the reputation of the man who, he claimed, had been incorrectly characterized as a "sweater" by Lawrenson.[54] He argued that the man had been "a perfectly honest and fair employer of labour," and had "paid the best wages of anybody in the neighbourhood."[55] He demanded the column retract its allegations by publishing his letter.

Amy Sharp, who by 1889 was single-handedly editing the "Corner" (Acland retaining contact with it only as coordinator of its essay contests), published the letter, but added to it the comment that there was nothing to retract since Lawrenson's report was not "an editorial article, but . . . a signed contribution from a correspondent."[56] One month later there appeared in the "Corner" a letter from Lawrenson announcing her intention to sever her "*official* connection with the guild" at the end of "this financial year, April 30th."[57] Lawrenson learned the hard way who controlled the public utterances and activities of women in the Cooperative movement. What is more, she discovered that female editors and fellow women activists were willing to meet the requirements of the men in charge of the movement, if only to retain what space and voice they permitted.

Although the Guild served as an organization to express the needs and interests of married working-class women, Lawrenson and Annie Jones, who was married to Arthur Acland's friend Ben Jones, were the only such women in national leadership positions in 1889. While Jones's self-effacing personal style made it easy for her to get along with the middle-class women who then dominated the Guild, the outspoken Lawrenson refused to behave deferentially toward them. She believed working-class women should speak for themselves rather than through middle-class interpreters.[58] In particular, a personal animosity had developed between her and Amy Sharp, whom Lawrenson bluntly accused of requiring that she behave like a "humble obedient servant."[59] Lawrenson also had philosophical differences with a clique of young, unmarried, middle-class women who were emerging as the second generation of Guild leaders. These women included Catherine Webb, Margaret Llewelyn Davies, and her friend Rosalind Shore Smith. Webb, Llewelyn Davies, and Shore Smith came to reject employee profit-sharing and worker-controlled workshops. Moreover, they wanted to change the direction of the Guild. While Lawrenson had focused the efforts of that organization on the education of children and cooperative issues, the emerging leaders wanted to concentrate on the education of adult women and women's issues.[60] Recognizing that the men in control of the Cooperative movement might resist such an alteration in the Guild's functions, Webb, Llewelyn Davies, and Shore Smith handled any male opposition they encountered diplomatically. When Lawrenson faced male opponents, her tone was strident and her message direct.[61]

It is possible to conclude from the wording of Lawrenson's resignation letter that the *News* feared a costly libel suit from the man she had accused of sweating. In her letter she stresses that she would cease "*official*" work for the Guild at the end of the fiscal year, rather than when her term of office actually expired—at the annual Guild meeting usually held in June. Pressure from Sharp, who, as editor of the "Corner," would have been named in the suit, helped to force Lawrenson's resignation. Two weeks after the letter from Phillips appeared in the "Corner," Sharp wrote to Lawrenson on another matter, characterizing the general secretary's behavior as potentially "disastrous" for the Guild and urging her to resign on the grounds of overwork.[62]

No doubt the fear of episodes such as the one just described was one reason Samuel Bamford positioned the "Woman's Corner" at the back of the *News*. He figured that women inexperienced with public affairs would, in his opinion, misspeak occasionally and compromise the paper's commitment to expressing "good sense and a capacity for concert and progress." He gambled that men would ignore the column if it was not prominently placed. However, many felt compelled to read the "Corner" to police women's speech.

On an earlier occasion, no less a personage than Thomas Hughes, best known as the author of *Tom Brown's School Days*, found material chosen for discussion in the "Corner" so objectionable that he protested. This episode resulted in the imposition of a code of censorship on the "Corner" that would last for two decades. Correspondents to the column would be forbidden to speak about the statute laws and social mores governing the institution of marriage until after the turn of the century. Cooperative men defended the household patriarchies over which they presided and consequently found the topic of marriage a contentious one, pushing it from the pages of the *News* even though it was a topic frequently discussed in many other popular publications from the 1880s onward.[63]

On March 14, 1885, a woman who signed herself "One of the Degraded" wrote to the "Corner" in response to an article entitled "Wives and Money." She complained that her husband refused to give her any more housekeeping money now than "when I got married, though I have had five children, two of whom I have lost."[64] One of the Degraded may have lived in the London area, as the research of Ellen Ross indicates that working men there did not follow the practices of Lancashire men.[65] In London and its environs men customarily paid their wives whatever they deemed the women needed for weekly household expenses. These wives had no way of knowing how much their spouses actually earned. Nor were their allowances necessarily increased when children were born. Working men considered a new baby a "woman's expense" to be met as best a wife could from whatever her husband gave her.[66] Since participants in the Cooperative movement came from what one scholar of the movement has called "the cream of the working class,"[67] these men could have afforded to give their wives decent allowances. However, they monopolized for themselves the better parts of the "family wages" they were paid. As Jane Millar has pointed out, the concept of the family wage is based on two erroneous assumptions: that everyone in the family shares the income equally, and that the wage earner does not claim possession over any portion of what he contributes.[68] Clearly, One of the Degraded was married to a man who refused to share, and who claimed the better part of his wage for himself. One of the Degraded was therefore left in poverty. She regretted that she could not "even join the Women's Guild, for I should be depriving my dear little ones of something."[69] She observed that her husband, however, always had plenty of money for outings and dinner with his shopmates, and for dues to the Freemasons.[70] She closed by expressing the hope that young men would read her letter to the "Corner" and "think things over before subjecting her whom they love most to such degradation."[71] Her concluding remark is an intriguing one for two reasons. Supposedly, working-class marriages were complex systems of reciprocal obligations designed to provide economic and emotional support to the marriage partners and their offspring. Romance did not usually enter into them.[72] However, One of the Degraded mentions love. Also, she fails to concentrate her resentment toward her husband on his having forced poverty on the children. Scholars of working-class family relationships have noticed that women refused to forgive husbands who starved the children, but that those women rarely complained that they too suffered.[73] Yet One of the Degraded closes by asserting that she, herself, had been subjected to "degradation." This sentiment was perceived as "selfish" by some of the "Corner's" readers, several of whom wrote to the column to condemn her. One blamed wives when husbands failed to provide sufficient money, arguing that such wives had probably not proved they could manage the economy of their households.[74] Another expressed dismay that One of the Degraded would complain about mistreatment, since the moral force of suffering in silence was the only way to impress a husband into kind behavior.[75] It is interesting that these women dared to sign their names, whereas those who wrote in support of One of the Degraded did not. Her critics apparently felt protected by their traditionalist opinions.

Two weeks after the appearance of One of the Degraded's letter, a letter by a woman who signed herself "A Member of the Guild" appeared in the "Corner." She asserted that "if men cannot trust us with the money they ought not to marry us."[76] She compared married and single life for women and described the latter as "blessedness."[77] She also argued that now that working men had the vote, working-class women needed "to work for their own enfranchisement," because contrary to the claims of the men leading the Cooperative movement, women did not "have all the advantages . . . enjoyed by men" whether inside or outside of the movement.[78] This letter prompted a lengthy epistle from "A.D.," which the "Corner" published in two installments, on April 11 and 18. A.D. suggested that the solution to the problem of providing wives with sufficient money was a prenuptial agreement:

[I]t is generally known that, in high life, monetary arrangements play a most important part in matrimonial engagements. . . . Would it not be advisable for the parents of a young girl in other than the higher spheres of life to suggest some sort of arrangement which would preclude all possibility of any future disagreement arising?[79]

A.D. then gave an example of a plan "adopted by two of my acquaintances who commenced housekeeping at a very early age on a guinea a week."[80] The plan required that the couple consult "each other on every point, and allowed a certain amount to all things proportionately, to their mutual satisfaction, not forgetting a certain equal sum allowed to each for pocket money, which some men think a woman never requires."[81]

A.D.'s proposal was designed to guarantee what feminists came to call a wife's right to maintenance. As Susan Pedersen observes, feminists debated how best to ensure this right.[82] Some, like Anna Martin, wanted legislation to make a portion of the husband's income the legal property of the wife.[83] Equal rights feminists, on the other hand, wanted to remove restrictions on women's work so that women could support themselves independently of their husbands. But new feminists realized that equal rights feminists were ignoring the fact that most women were full-time housewives and mothers and that it was women's unpaid labor in the home that caused their poverty.[84] Consequently, many new feminists concluded that the only possible solution to the problem of women's economic dependence was the state endowment of motherhood. They argued that a woman's domestic labor in the home earned her a right to maintenance.[85] Most cooperative women, especially those involved with the Guild, agreed with this assessment. They resented what Eleanor Rathbone came later to identify as the "Turk complex" of the male breadwinner.[86] Wally Seccombe has outlined the rights to which working men felt entitled if they were able to earn a family wage.[87] Such men believed they had the right to take their spending money off the top of the pay packet regardless of the family's expenses for any given week. They considered themselves the owners of any consumer durables purchased for the family, even when the wife had bought them. They believed that under no circumstances should they personally experience scarcity, and that their jobs were done when they arrived home. Hence the home should be a quiet site for male leisure. Many cooperative women had no patience with such men. However, there is also evidence that others were either unwilling to speak out against such male behavior or that they were thankful to be married to men, no matter how selfish, who could support them without their having to undertake the double shift of domestic and paid labor. Women like the ones who chastised One of the Degraded wanted the "Corner" to devote itself to hints for maintaining the home on a budget.[88] Like male cooperators, they were made uncomfortable by talk in the column about the patriarchal nature of marriage.

By late spring the discussion of "Wives and Money" in the "Corner" had petered out and was replaced by debate over the propriety of women speaking in public. Then, on August 15, a certain D. London reopened the discussion with a letter that Thomas Hughes found too threatening to ignore. Noticing that no resolution had been reached concerning the matter of "Wives and Money," D. London suggested that the Guild sponsor an essay contest "on the 'Business Basis of Marriage,' and then let the Guild draw up a model 'Deed of Partnership' from the material supplied."[89] D. London understood the Guild had limited funds for the awarding of prizes to the contest winners, so she suggested that the Cooperative Newspaper Society should fund the contest and then print the winning essays in the main body of the *Co-operative News*.[90] Her suggestions presumed more of the Cooperative Newspaper Society than it was willing to give either to women or to controversial topics, but that was not the quarter from which objection came. Thomas Hughes, a lawyer who had come to the advocacy of cooperation by way of his earlier commitment to Christian Socialism, refused to countenance an essay contest involving an institution held sacred by the laws of God and man.

How Hughes communicated his objection to the D. London letter is unclear. No letter from him appeared anywhere in the *News*. Perhaps he spoke with his Christian Socialist associate E. V. Neale, who was on the Newspaper Society's board. Perhaps he talked with Bamford, or even Sharp, whose home was in Rugby, near to Hughes. In any case, judging from the text of the "Corner's" response to his concern, he feared Owenism's legacy to the Cooperative movement—with its reputation for experimentation in the matter of sexual relationships—was rearing its head.[91] As Barbara Taylor has observed, the Owenites knew patriarchy in marriage was sustained by women's economic dependence.[92] The Owenites anticipated the thinking of Eleanor Rathbone who, in the early twentieth century, concluded: "The economic dependency of the married woman is the last stronghold of those who, consciously or unconsciously, prefer women in subjection."[93] Hughes was determined to uphold patriarchy in marriage by insisting on the continuation of married women's economic dependence.

Acland and Sharp replied immediately to Hughes, expressing concern because they worried that his "alarm may . . . be shared by other readers."[94] They asserted that the opinions of correspondents with the "Corner" did not represent the opinions of the column's editors. They claimed the Guild and the "Corner" had nothing to do with one another, that "the guild only makes use of the 'Corner' as its best means of reaching its members," and assured their readers that D. London was not even a member of the Guild.[95] This desperate attempt by the editors to dissociate themselves from the Guild clearly shows the depth of the crisis generated by Hughes's objections. Both Acland and Sharp served as officers in the Guild's national organization. Acland was then its president and Sharp was running for a seat on its Central Committee. If the "Corner" and the Guild were actually as distinct as they claimed, it should have been necessary for them to have resigned one or the other of their positions to prevent a conflict of interest.

The editors of the "Corner" closed their response to Hughes by promising that the Guild was planning no "revolutionary attacks on the marriage laws."[96] Further reassurance on this point was provided in October, when Sharp published a two-part article on married women's property in the "Corner."[97] Timed to coincide with Hughes's scheduled return from a trip to America on which he had left before Acland and Sharp's clarification appeared,[98] this article also signaled to the men in charge of the newspaper that the women understood what the parameters were with respect to any future discussion of the institution of marriage.

Sharp's article spelled out the rights of wives under the married women's property laws currently on the books and concluded that no future legislation was necessary. She admitted that money problems, such as those described earlier in the year by correspondents with the "Corner," continued to exist under the current laws, but argued "no compulsory scheme" for solving them should be imposed.[99] Hence phrases "which have a ring of compulsion about them," like those suggested by D. London, including "deed of partnership" and "business basis of marriage" should be dropped from future use.[100] In sum, the editors of the column agreed that any future discussion of gender issues such as a woman's rights in marriage would avoid using legal language, which only men were empowered to employ. Several years later, Sharp actually found an opportunity to spell out in print for the column's readers more details about the agreement she and Acland had reached with the men in charge of the *News*. The occasion of this revelation was one of Acland's essay contests, whose theme in the autumn of 1889 was how to improve the "Corner."

The women who contributed essays recommended that the column increase in size. It had already grown from one page to two, but the coverage it gave to the burgeoning Guild often forced out articles on health care and fashions, or the sharing of cleaning tips and recipes by its readers. The essayists resented this.[101] But Sharp had to admit that she was unable to convince Bamford to give women's concerns more space. She said, "The last time I asked for [Bamford's] opinion on 'Corner' matters, he said the only remark he had to make was that they *couldn't* spare more space."[102] However, a woman signing herself "A.B.C.," who wrote to comment on the recommendations of the essayists, was not so much interested in the expansion of the "Corner's" space as in its use. She did not want more on fashions or cooking; she wanted discussion of "Women's Rights."[103] In particular, she believed "we ought to know a little more about the laws concerning ourselves . . . and . . . women's opinions of how they could be altered."[104] One of the topics she wanted discussed was: "Is it Right for Mothers to Persuade their Daughters to Marry, or not?"[105] Sharp replied by spelling out the understanding she and Acland had reached with the Cooperative Newspaper Society as a result of the Hughes episode. She said the discussion of gender issues had to be limited because "the *News* is devoted to the furtherance of interests common to both men and women."[106] Moreover, since "the 'Corner' is granted by the courtesy and kindness of men, it could not gracefully be turned to that use!"[107] As to information about the laws governing women and marriage, she said she would be happy to supply any information that "is likely to be useful to our readers."[108] She then reminded her audience that she had already done that in her series on the married women's property laws.[109] The men in charge of the *News* refused to allow the female editor of the "Corner" jurisdiction over its space. They feared that granting a woman such authority in the public sphere might jeopardize male authority in the private. Women might begin to "insist that marriage should be on equal conditions," as J. S. Mill observed would happen if women were given freedom of expression.[110]

Until her resignation as editor in 1896, Sharp was careful to ensure that the material published in the "Corner" conformed to the requirements of Bamford and the men on the Cooperative Newspaper Society's board of directors, as illustrated by a controversy that occurred in 1890 due to reader response to an essay entitled "Women's Influence," written by someone under the pseudonym "Narcissus" for the February 15, 1890 column. The week after its appearance, a reader who signed herself "Mary" wrote to protest what the essay had recommended. Narcissus had suggested that no matter how hectic her day had been, a wife had a "sacred" duty to greet her husband on his arrival home with a warm dinner and a cheery smile, since the poor man had been shut away all day in an "ugly, dismal work place."[111] Mary responded:

Now, madam, I've got seven children, the eldest barely nine, and the youngest just three months. . . . I ask you, when the blessed evening does come, which has most right to be "hungry and tired"—I, after my day of being cook, housemaid, laundress, nurse, governess, playmate, sewing-woman, and mother all in one; or my husband, after his day of sawing planks and drawing plans in a workshop full of mates who, whatever their faults may be (and I'm not denying they have plenty), don't suddenly take to howling at the top of their voices at every minute when it's ruination to what you have in hand to stop and see what's the matter?[112]

In the following weeks, correspondents responded so enthusiastically to Mary that the situation threatened to start a protracted as well as heated discussion of the patriarchal nature of marriage arrangements. Sharp soon realized she had opened the "Corner" to a forbidden topic and pulled back. She publicly admitted to editing the more sensitive portions of correspondents' letters.[113] She terminated discussion of "Women's Influence" on March 29, 1890, with a letter by "Esmeralda," who boasted: "When my husband comes home, I am always ready for a walk, read, and a good laugh. When I told him I was writing to you, he told me to sign myself 'one of England's best and truest wives.' "[114]

In return for Sharp's conscientious conformity to the code of censorship, the paper began to feature more news about women's concerns, but Sharp had no power to select the items and the "Corner" was not increased in size. For instance, in 1892 Bamford ran a special supplement to the paper and devoted a portion of it to "Co-operation Among Women," written by Beatrice Potter, later to become the wife of Sidney Webb.[115] Potter had undertaken the task of writing a history of the Cooperative movement, but guildswomen considered her unqualified to speak on women in cooperation because she was not a member of the Guild and refused to believe the Guild had yet made significant inroads on male hegemony in the movement.[116] So, in the following weeks, Bamford published Catherine (no relation to Potter's future husband) Webb's criticism of Potter's perceptions, along with Potter's rejoinder, in the space devoted to letters to the editor.[117] Also, throughout the 1890s, he either printed supplements to the *News* for the Women's Cooperative Guild at the time of their annual congresses,[118] or gave those events coverage in the main body of the paper. But the nature of the remarks made about Guild congresses in the paper's main body reveals his ambivalence to women's public activism.

Several months before Catherine Webb's report on the proceedings of the 1895 Guild Congress noted at the beginning of the chapter, an announcement in anticipation of that meeting appeared in the *News*'s column "Notes of the Week." It read:

No movement now-a-days worthy of its name is complete without its annual gathering. It would be strange indeed, then, if the Women's Co-operative Guild—which, though part of the great co-operative body, is essentially a movement in itself—did not boast such an assembly.[119]

Here the reporter clearly casts the organization representing women cooperators as "other." It is true that in terms of governance structure, the Guild was an aux-iliary body to the consumers' movement that consisted of a network of stores serviced by two wholesale outlets, but to go to the trouble of pointing that out in a piece that merely purported to announce the fact of an upcoming meeting is revealing.

The reporter then went on to add that few—understood to mean men—would pay attention to the forthcoming gathering because it was less important than the preparations being made for the impending general election, which was more significant than a cooperative women's meeting even in the minds of male cooperators:

It is to be regretted, however, that the . . . annual meeting of the guild, which takes place in London next week, should have fallen amidst the throes of a political crisis, for this must necessarily have the effect of lessening the publicity which would otherwise doubtless have been given to the proceedings.[120]

The reporter next commended the Guild for its efforts in spreading aware-ness about cooperation, tackling issues which affect women workers, and se-curing "for women opportunities for their fuller social development . . . which shall fit them to take a more active and useful share in public affairs."[121] In other words, the women were praised for confining their activism to issues which did not threaten male hegemony and for not daring to enter public space until they had been sufficiently trained to do so. Men, on the other hand, were never con-sidered to require training before they entered the public arena as activists. They were thought to have a right to do so regardless of their qualifications. And, of course, the requirement that a woman first be "fit[ted]" for "public affairs" might provide a pretext for excluding her even after she considered herself pre-pared. As Sonya O. Rose has observed, men created the public culture of protest and excluded women from it.[122] Cooperation was a working-class movement that was part of that culture and its men were determined to restrict women's efforts to participate in it.

In closing, the reporter cited statistics, noting that the Guild now had 182 branches, with a membership exceeding 8,000. He concluded: "A body of 8,000 women united in aim is not a force to be ignored. The guild has long since 'lived down' whatever prejudice existed against it."[123] This quotation hints that the men in charge of the Cooperative movement, which was 1,273,883 strong in 1895, were intimidated by 8,000 "united" women.[124] Moreover, it admits that opposition to the Guild existed. Though it encourages readers to believe that opposition had been overcome, the astute will wonder to what extent the rhetoric reflected reality. Finally, the wording of the quotation attributes any decrease in opposition to the Guild to its efforts to operate within the established parameters, thereby making the prejudiced less uncomfortable with its activities. In all, it was up to the Guild to "live down" fears about its possibilities, not up to the men to have a change of heart about women's place in the Cooperative movement.

Bamford, for one, never had a change of heart. He considered the "Corner" his property. In 1893, dissatisfied with Sharp's inability to convince Bamford to increase the "Corner's" size, the leaders of the Women's Cooperative Guild entered into their own negotiations with him. They asked him to provide regular supplements to the *News* for the reporting of their organization's activities.[125] They did not want a new, separate paper, such as some cooperative men were prepared to give them, because they were afraid that it would contribute to the further marginalization of women's concerns within the movement.[126] Bamford's response was to turn over a portion of the "Corner" to a biweekly feature called "Notes from the Guild," written by Catherine Webb, without first consulting Sharp about his decision. Sharp, upset by this development, published letters from "Corner" readers complaining about the intrusion of so much news about the Guild. But she was forced to desist and concede in print that the "Corner" needed to appeal to Guild members and not just to nonmembers whose tastes and interests differed from those of guildswomen.[127]

In 1898 Samuel Bamford died, leaving his editorial position at the *News* to his son, William. Two years before, Rosalind Shore Smith, now going by her married name of Nash, had become editor of the "Corner." She and her friend, Margaret Llewelyn Davies, who had replaced Lawrenson as general secretary of the Guild in 1889, kept in tandem the interests of the column and of the organization which used it. Under Llewelyn Davies's leadership the Guild expanded its concerns beyond those of the Cooperative movement to extramural women's issues, as evidenced by the coverage of Guild activities in the "Corner." During Nash's tenure as editor, the column devoted its space to Guild efforts to assist in the organization of trade unions for women, to secure the passage of legislation which would prohibit women from working in "dangerous" trades,[128] and especially to Llewelyn Davies's pet project of using the Guild's middle-class members as settlement house workers in order to extend the benefits of cooperation to the working poor.[129] None of these concerns were threatening to male authority, even though the men in the Cooperative movement were often unenthusiastic about them. And while it is true that the "Corner" shows the Guild had taken an interest in the women's suffrage question, in getting women elected as poor-law guardians and appointed as factory inspectors, and in agitating for women's right to run for election to the committees that governed the cooperative stores, none of these campaigns for women's rights involved the taboo issue of a wife's rights in marriage and what either the law or social practice mandated about them. That topic was still banned.[130]

Although male cooperators might not relish the prospect of women becoming citizens equal to themselves in the public sphere, it was difficult for them to counter the Guild's relational feminist arguments that domesticity and motherhood qualified women to speak, and perhaps even to vote, on public matters affecting the home and children. Male cooperators believed domesticity and motherhood were natural conditions for women and they had come to define their manhood according to whether their wages were sufficient to support non-wage-earning wives. Sonya O. Rose has correctly noticed that working men did not seek domesticity for their wives out of a desire to emulate the middle class. Rather, domesticity for working-class wives "signified" status for their husbands in the male wage-earning community.[131] And, as Ellen Ross has shown, since the boundary between "rough" and "respectable" was so porous, working-class wives who aspired to respectability, as the wives of the well-paid workers who participated in cooperation did, similarly came to define their status by upholding female domesticity.[132]

The Guild's variety of feminism brought it certain advantages in terms of winning from male cooperators the right to speak on citizenship issues. Since the Guild's relational feminism defined women as mothers and homemakers, it meant the Guild did not encourage women to enter into competition with working men for jobs. Sonya O. Rose has show that male trade unionists attempted to erect defenses to forestall women's incursions into their trades when they felt threatened by female competition.[133] The Guild posed no threat to male monopolies in the workplace since it was an early advocate of "protective" legislation to restrict women's access to jobs that could be defined as inappropriate for women.[134] The Guild's position on women's employment won it toleration from male cooperators worried about female competition in the workplace. In addition, cooperative men interpreted the relational feminism of the Guild as relatively unthreatening to the patriarchal prerogatives of husbands in the home because it did not appear to them to challenge the traditional division of gender roles. Barbara Brookes has suggested that for working men "who had little authority outside the home, power in sexual relationships was perhaps a means of asserting their masculinity."[135] Working-class men consequently demanded to rule their homes like kings, since outside of the house they felt less powerful. The Guild's feminism did not appear to them to undermine that rule. Of course, rigid gender role separation among the working class may also be attributed to factors other than male egotism. As Brian Harrison has observed, if a working-class family aimed to stay out of poverty, it needed a good household manager, and the working class found it sensible to delegate that job to the woman of the house.[136] Jane Millar agrees, observing that a woman's management of the household often determined whether and/or how a family experienced poverty.[137] In either case, so long as women cooperators agreed not to challenge patriarchal marriage, male cooperators could concede them some latitude when they wanted to speak on citizenship issues.

In 1904 William's sister, Annie Bamford Tomlinson, who had long been involved with the Women's Cooperative Guild, replaced Rosalind Nash as editor of the "Woman's Corner." Bamford Tomlinson was the first professional journalist to edit the column. A shared commitment to professional journalism functioned as a bond between the Bamford siblings. They both felt that objectivity in reporting was essential and censorship inappropriate among professional journalists. This caused them to interpret the purpose of the *Co-operative*

News differently from their father. Samuel had believed any topic that made cooperation look deficient in any way should not receive coverage in the *News*. The Bamford siblings, on the other hand, thought the only way to keep cooperation true to its ideals was to publicize its failings so they could be corrected. In this context Samuel's aversion to covering the criticisms that *cooperative* wives had of their *cooperative* husbands' conduct within their *cooperative* households is understandable. Cooperation was supposed to create abundance for those who participated in it, but these criticisms showed that some of the movement's women did not have enough housekeeping money despite their loyalty to shopping at the movement's stores. Cooperative stores attracted clientele from the ranks of the lower middle class and the so-called respectable working class. Recent studies of the standards of living of the mid- and late-nineteenth-century working class by Ellen Ross and Sonya O. Rose have shown that all manual workers were liable to experience periods of economic hardship.[138] Rose has reckoned that 80% of the male manual workers earned so little their families could survive only if their wives engaged in waged labor either inside or outside the home.[139] She has asserted that even the 10 to 20% of the relatively well-paid skilled laborers experienced occasional hardships that forced their wives to resort to paid employment as a temporary strategy for family survival.[140] Paul Johnson's study of the saving and spending habits of the working class corroborates these statistics for those participating in the Cooperative movement.[141] He has found that "few co-operators were really needy," but most faced temporary fluctuations in their incomes, which they hoped to negotiate in part by relying on the "divi."[142] These realities proved cooperation had a way to go before it could be said to have delivered economic security to its participants, and the Bamford siblings recognized this.

Cooperation was also supposed to work a character transformation for its participants, focusing them on others, as Peter Gurney points out in *Cooperative Culture and the Politics of Consumption in England*.[143] But the criticisms of cooperative husbands that had threatened to find their way into the "Woman's Corner" proved that such men continued to think of themselves before their families. For Annie and William, the poverty of wives and the selfish conduct of husbands represented failings within the cooperative community that needed to be exposed so they could be corrected. As Jane Lewis observes, it was a popularly held conception that the "fecklessness" of working-class men could be as responsible for their families' poverty as their wives' mismanagement of the household economy.[144] The Bamford siblings clearly thought so. Therefore, during their tenure as editors, discussion of the issue of marriage reform was permitted in the "Corner."

In 1907 a Middlesbrough County Court judge ruled that a wife was not entitled to keep as her own any money she had saved from housekeeping expenses, because her husband had been the earner of that money. Since working-class wives saved by strenuous economizing that often involved stinting themselves,[145] cooperative women became interested in the court case. The leadership of the Guild argued that working-class wives worked for their savings no less than their husbands worked for wages.[146] As Susan Pedersen has pointed out, working-class wives did not see themselves as unemployed parasites as middle-class feminists often judged housewives to be.[147] They considered that they worked for a living and deserved recompense. The court ruling had revived for cooperative women the old issue of "Wives and Money," and what was more, added a demeaning complication because "The crux of the situation turns on whether the money is saved with the knowledge of the husband. That is to say, a wife must have her husband's permission to save, and should that permission have been withheld, the wife's savings may be taken from her."[148] In sum, the ruling upheld couverture and a married woman's dependence on her husband in all matters. Further, the ruling created particular problems for participants in the Cooperative movement.

Although married women were theoretically able to subscribe to the stores in their own names, most cooperative societies enrolled a wife under her husband's name and permitted no other members of the household to join, often excluding even adult children living at home. The Guild had tried to change this policy by lobbying for what it called "open membership" beginning in the late 1890s. By 1907, little headway had been made with that campaign and, in any case, given the nature of the court decision, open membership would have made little difference since the wife would have used money from her husband's earnings to take out the membership in her own name.

To the credit of cooperation, store managers since the early days of the movement had had a policy of treating a wife's investment in the stores as her own property even when the membership was in the husband's name.[149] As Sidney and Beatrice Webb commented, this policy had turned the cooperative store into the working-class woman's bank.[150] But good business practices rather than feminism had motivated the managers to adopt this policy. They knew that they depended on the custom of the wife and could not afford to alienate her. The movement's ideology of thrift and saving, combined with the communal atmosphere provided by the neighborhood "co-op," gave further foundation for the managers' policy. Since they knew the families who shopped at their stores, they were aware of which ones were troubled by alcoholism, which were saving to buy homes, and which had recently experienced illnesses and had to pay doctor's bills. Any mysterious or sudden requests for withdrawals would have aroused their concern, and would have been denied if they came from a husband with a reputation as an alcoholic or a spendthrift, even if the membership was in his name.[151] Finally, store managers were working-class husbands in the habit of letting their wives have authority over household expenditures and therefore considered that authority to be a help to the home, not a threat to their manhoods. As one man put it, "A good wife [is] the best help a man could have. The wife should always be cashier, because she could make a shilling go as far again as a man. What a woman worked for ought to be legally her own."[152]

Bamford Tomlinson covered the "Wives' Savings" issue for a year in the "Corner." Moreover, her brother opened his editorial column to letters on the topic and made no secret of his sympathy for the Guild's efforts to secure legislation to guarantee a wife's right to her savings. For instance, on January 18, 1908, he printed a letter from a correspondent who signed himself "A Mere Man." This writer alleged that the Guild was run by old maids and unhappily married women who stirred up trouble about domestic issues like "Wives' Savings" and then filled the "Corner" with their "absurd and illogical gush[ings]."[153] Bamford followed this with several weeks of letters from men and women attacking A Mere Man in the main pages of the *News*, while his sister did the same in the "Corner."[154] Clearly, Bamford's interpretation of the *News's* mission to function as "the flag of [the] party . . . the sign by which the world knows it" was different from his father's.

William Bamford was sympathetic to the women's movement, though he was no feminist.[155] He had reservations about the Guild's involvement in too many noncooperative agitations,[156] and had no desire to increase the size of the "Corner" beyond the extra page he had given it when he succeeded his father.[157] His journalistic policy was to maintain the *News's* objectivity and independence in order to keep the Cooperative movement true to its ideals. He once wrote that

the *Co-operative News* to-day is the most democratically owned of any newspaper published, and being governed by a representative society separate from the two Wholesales and the Union, it remains in a position of independence, and holds the power to criticise either through articles or letters, wherever and whenever such criticism is considered necessary in the interests of the movement.[158]

The "representative society" to which Bamford referred was the Cooperative Newspaper Society, whose directors were elected by the cooperative stores that had taken shares in the Society, voting for candidates according to the number of shares they owned.[159] When Bamford took over from his father, he began the practice of publishing in the *News* the minutes of the Newspaper Society's board meetings. Generally, these are unrevealing; the board members seem more concerned with return on investment than editorial policy, rarely linking editorial policy and circulation. At the spring 1914 board meeting, for instance, when the directors did take the time to comment on the paper's content, all agreed that Bamford's editorship had improved the quality of the paper, and consequently its circulation.[160] This endorsement of Bamford's leadership came at a significant juncture for the *News* and its women's column, as both were in the midst of covering the Guild's struggle with the Cooperative Union over its right to agitate for divorce law reform.

It is customary to attribute the "Corner's" discussion of and the Guild's involvement with gender issues, like the 1907 court judgment or divorce law reform, to a change in leadership of the Guild, the replacement of Lawrenson by Llewelyn Davies in 1889.[161] But surely if Llewelyn Davies's leadership had been entirely responsible for the greater latitude given women in their public utterances and activities with respect to the marriage issue, some evidence of it would have appeared sooner than twenty years into her tenure as the Guild's general secretary.

The contributions of Llewelyn Davies are reassessed in chapter four, where it is found that contrary to the standard interpretation of her career as contributing to the broadening of opportunities for married working-class women, an argument can be made that she actually assisted in the restriction of possibilities for them. As has been observed by Judy Giles in *Women, Identity and Private Life in Britain*, middle-class women like Llewelyn Davies often became the means by which the wants and dreams of married working-class women were represented to the world, and their interpretations of these contributed to a reaffirmation of the stereotype that such women led dreary and unsatisfying lives, which was not necessarily so.[162] Further, Llewelyn Davies confirmed the Guild in its narrow focus on *married* working-class women, a focus which tended to ensure that the traditional roles of wife, mother, and consumer were the only ones considered appropriate for women of that class. Indeed, during her lifetime she was criticized for this reason when she directed the Guild in agitations in support of protective labor legislation for working women, since such legislation removed many possibilities for their employment outside the home.[163]

It is more reasonable to attribute the advent in the "Corner," at least, of open discussion of gender issues to a generational changing of the guard in the newspaper's leadership than to Llewelyn Davies's influence as the head of the Guild. This thesis is further confirmed by the actions taken against the Guild by the Cooperative Union in 1914. The Union, the national body that represented the interests of the movement, punished the Guild for its support of divorce law reform by withholding the annual grant of money it customarily gave the Guild. The "Corner," on the other hand, suffered no consequences for its airing of the debate over divorce. The era of Thomas Hughes was over at the newspaper because the men in charge of it had determined that it should be so. The men of the Cooperative Union, however, remained uncomfortable with discussion of and activity on behalf of gender issues. For example, when the Liberal government introduced its plan for national insurance in 1911, the Guild set to work to make sure that maternity benefits were included and that they would be paid to the mother rather than the male head of household. The "Corner" covered the Guild's efforts. Meanwhile, the overly sensitive men in control of the Cooperative Union objected to the use in public of the word "maternity," as it referred to a delicate condition about which it was impolite to speak.[164] It is no wonder then that the Union was displeased with the Guild's commitment to divorce law reform.

The Guild had turned its attention to the divorce laws when Prime Minister Asquith appointed a royal commission to investigate them in 1909. The organization collected information about working-class marriage situations from its members and was invited to present its findings to the commission.[165] The Guild concluded that the laws needed to be amended to provide equal access to inexpensive divorce for men and women, and to include mutual consent as a ground for divorce. A number of guildswomen, especially in Lancashire with its large Catholic population of Irish descent, objected to the organization advocating such liberalization of the grounds for divorce, although they were ready to accept cheaper divorce and equal access to it for women and men.[166]

When the royal commission published its findings in 1912, its majority report endorsed the Guild's positions, excepting that of mutual consent as a ground for divorce. On November 16, both the Bamford siblings applauded the Commission's conclusions in editorials.[167] William said that

it would be idle to deny that it would be better for human progress, for the moral welfare of the nation, and for the healthy outlook of children, if easier means were provided for the dissolution of some marriages . . . one would have thought it did not require a Royal Commission to convince us of this.[168]

He was especially pleased by "the declaration that women would be put on the same level as men as regards the power to secure divorce," and that the working class would have greater access to divorce because facilities for it were to be made cheaper.[169] He concluded:

People of all classes should be taught that marriage, in spite of the religious symbols about it, should not be used for a cover for life-long cruelty and immorality. There is more danger to the ethical progress of the nation in this state of affairs than there can be in making divorce easier of achievement.[170]

An Anglican minister wrote to the *News* to protest Bamford's editorial, but Bamford refused to publish his letter.[171]

In 1913, the first signs of potential trouble between the Guild and the men in charge of the Cooperative movement appeared. At a quarterly meeting of the Cooperative Wholesale Society (CWS), a delegate protested the CWS's plan to grant £100 to the Guild because he believed that the women's agitation for divorce law reform was subversive to the religious institution of marriage.[172] Religion had always been a sensitive subject for cooperators. From its inception in the mid-1800s, the movement had had to restrict its discussion for the simple reason that cooperation attracted Owenites, secularists, Christian Socialists, as well as members of a variety of Christian sects. However, the Central Committee that governed the Guild had recently launched a "push the sales of CWS products" campaign in appreciation for the Wholesale Society's support of its efforts to win women employees of cooperative establishments a minimum wage.[173] The Central Committee understood that sales mattered to the men of the CWS. If they took seriously the complaint of the protesting delegate, it would be because they feared the loss of custom from churchgoers. The Guild was fortunate that its divorce law reform agitation coincided with its "push the sales of CWS products" campaign. The coincidence prompted another man at the meeting to silence the protestor by pointing out that "women could, and did, help the Wholesale very materially."[174]

Despite its favorable resolution, this episode illustrates well the subordinate position of the Guild when it came to controversial policy initiatives. It had to manipulate the men, after the fashion of a wife managing her husband, in order to embark on them unmolested. Moreover, there was never any guarantee that the Guild's machinations would be successful. The next year the Salford Catholic Federation sent its protest about the Guild's advocacy of divorce law reform to that organization's Central Committee. It charged that the Guild was involving itself and the entire Cooperative movement in religious matters, which would force Catholics to abandon cooperation. The Central Committee dismissed the Federation's complaint; so the Federation took its case to the Cooperative Union. The Union chastised the Guild for its support of divorce law reform and recommended that it cease its work for the liberalization of the laws.

The "Corner" reported the protest of Guild branches that considered the Union's rebuke a threat to their organization's "independence."[175]

One of the jobs of the Cooperative Union was to organize the movement's annual congress. In 1914, that was scheduled to be held in Dublin, Ireland, an inauspicious site given the Guild's agenda. Each year at congress the Central Board of the Union authorized a generous monetary grant for the Guild to help subsidize that organization's educational work. The Guild needed that £400 because its only other major source of funds was the 2d. per member per annum each local branch of the Guild was constitutionally mandated to subscribe to the central fund. That amounted only to £230 9s. 4d. in 1914.[176] At its Dublin meeting the Central Board received a deputation from the Salford Catholic Federation, which put its case that Catholic cooperators would withdraw from the Cooperative movement if it appeared to sanction divorce by subsidizing the Guild.[177] Except for Mrs. Gasson, the only woman on the board, who argued the Guild had never made divorce a religious question, the board members wanted to avoid jeopardizing the allegiance of Catholic cooperators.[178] So it was resolved to make the renewal of the Guild's grant contingent upon its dropping the agitation on behalf of divorce law reform, and to require that it never again take up any work disapproved by the Cooperative Union.

The Guild responded immediately by launching a fund-raising campaign to maintain its independence. This was clearly a "Wives and Money" issue for the Guild, whose leaders and most members believed that once the "pay packet" had been turned over to them, the manner of its disposal was a Guild decision. The men on the Central Board felt differently. As the "wage providers," they demanded the final say in how the money was spent, just as men in working-class households might insist that the family income be spent to guarantee their own standards of comfort.[179]

The Union and the Guild remained at odds for four years, with the "Corner" covering every detail of the women's struggles. In their space in the official newspaper of the Cooperative movement, women could speak freely because they were under the protection of the paper's general editor, whose policy happened to work in their interests. The CWS helped the Guild too, by increasing its subsidy to that organization to £150 by 1918. Since "women could, and did, help the Wholesale very materially," the men of the CWS wanted to encourage cooperative women to continue in their traditional roles as buyers. Finally, there were individual men and cooperative societies who supported the Guild in its fight with the Union. They did so because they saw the conflict as a struggle between the rank and file and the center, not as a gender issue. As one man put it:

I don't want to discuss at the moment whether they ought or ought not to have entered into the divorce controversy. . . . The greater question is whether they are to fashion their own destiny, or whether they shall always be tied to the apron strings of Annual Congresses of the Co-operative Union.[180]

Cooperators distrusted dictation from their leaders, valuing rule from the bottom up.[181] Under the combined pressure of men so motivated and the need for unity in the face of the threats to the movement's "profits" coming from the state's attempt to tax them, the Union restored the grant in 1918.[182]

On April 26, 1919, the last "Women's Corner" appeared in the *Co-operative News*; the column was being renamed. The next week "Our Women's Page" made its first appearance. Bamford Tomlinson had never been happy with the column's title.[183] In 1913, she had changed its name from "Woman's Corner" to "Women's Corner," though she failed to explain why she found the latter preferable to the former.[184] It is tempting to assume that she considered the singular noun, woman, too objectifying, or that she believed the plural to convey better the collective sisterhood of female cooperators. Similarly, in 1919, it might be supposed that she thought a wider sphere of activity had been opened for women both inside and outside of the Cooperative movement since the column's inception, and hence women's confinement to a tiny corner had ended. But on the occasion of the transition from the "Corner" to the "Page" she merely likened it to a move of house—a move to a larger house with less "restricted space."[185] The retitled "Corner" was part of a restructuring of the entire *News*. The first "Women's Page" on May 3, 1919 appeared in the context of a paper that was shorter (only twenty pages as opposed to thirty-plus), but physically larger (each page had four columns instead of two or three). Women were allotted two of those larger pages, starting on page fourteen.

Since the reason Bamford Tomlinson named the column "Our Women's Page" is a mystery, it is only possible to speculate that she included "Our" in the title to signify ownership. But the truth of the matter was that the column belonged to the general editor, and without the protection of his editorial policy neither Bamford Tomlinson nor correspondents to it would have been able to speak freely about such topics as marriage. Nor was the Guild any freer to determine its course than Bamford Tomlinson hers as the women's column's editor. Guildswomen needed the patriarchal protection of sympathetic men to finance their activities. To secure this support they had to appear eager to continue in their traditional roles as wives, mothers, and shoppers. Also, they often had to engage in manipulative behavior, timing their campaigns on behalf of women's rights to coincide with those guaranteed to benefit the Cooperative movement financially. Finally, from the placement of the new women's column in the *Co-operative News* it is evident that women still spoke from the margins of the Cooperative movement. "Our Women's Page" appeared at the back of the *News*, after the national, cooperative, and international news; after book reviews, serialized fiction, editorials, and letters to the editor; and sometimes after advertisements, personals, obituaries, and various announcements of upcoming cooperative activities. The men who controlled the Cooperative movement were unwilling to reconsider women's roles within it; so the women accommodated themselves to the restrictions put upon them as women have traditionally had to do.

NOTES

1. "Woman's Corner," *Co-operative News*, September 7, 1895.

2. Ibid.

3. Pat Thane, "Visions of Gender in the Making of the British Welfare State: The Case of Women in the British Labour Party and Social Policy, 1906–1945," in Bock and Thane (eds.), *Maternity and Gender Policies*.

4. Pat Thane, "The Women of the British Labour Party and Feminism, 1906–1945," in Smith (ed.), *British Feminism in the Twentieth Century*.

5. Waters, *British Socialism and the Politics of Popular Culture*, 167.

6. Koven and Michel, "Womanly Duties: Maternalist Politics and the Origins of Welfare States in France, Germany, Great Britain, and the United States."

7. Pedersen, "The Failure of Feminism," 86–110; Pedersen, "Gender, Welfare, and Citizenship in Britain during the Great War," 983–1006; Pedersen, *Family, Dependence and the Origins of the Welfare State*.

8. Rose, "Gender Antagonism and Class Conflict"; Jenny Morris, *Women Workers and the Sweated Trades* (Brookfield, VT: Gower Publishing Company, 1986); Seccombe, "Patriarchy Stabilized."

9. Rosemary Feurer, "The Meaning of 'Sisterhood': The British Women's Movement and Protective Labor Legislation, 1870–1890," *Victorian Studies* vol. 31 (Winter 1988), 233–260; Jane Humphries, "'. . . The Most Free Form of Objection . . .': The Sexual Division of Labor and Women's Work in Nineteenth-century England," *Journal of Economic History* vol. 47, no. 4 (December 1987), 929–949; Lewis and Rose, "'Let England Blush': Protective Labor Legislation, 1820–1940," in Wikander et al. (eds.), *Protecting Women*; Carolyn Malone, "Gender Discourses and the Making of Protective Labor Legislation in England, 1830–1914," *Journal of British Studies* vol. 37, no. 2 (April 1998), 166–191; Sonya O. Rose, "Protective Labor Legislation in Nineteenth-century Britain: Gender, Class, and the Liberal State," in Laura L. Fader and Sonya O. Rose (eds.), *Gender and Class in Modern Europe* (Ithaca: Cornell University Press, 1996).

10. Liddington and Norris, *One Hand Tied Behind Us*, chapter 9.

11. Webb, *The Woman with the Basket*.

12. Gaffin and Thoms, *Caring and Sharing*.

13. Beatrice Potter, *The Co-operative Movement in Great Britain* (London: Swan Sonnenschein & Company, 1895), 192–193; G.D.H. Cole, *A Century of Co-operation* (London: George Allen & Unwin, Ltd., 1944), 215–226; Gurney, *Co-operative Culture and the Politics of Consumption in England*, 232.

14. Gillian Scott, "'Working Out Their Own Salvation': Women's Autonomy and Divorce Law Reform in the Co-operative Movement, 1910–1920," in Yeo (ed.), *New Views of Co-operation*, 133–134.

15. Liddington and Norris, *One Hand Tied Behind Us*, 136.

16. Scott, "'Working Out Their Own Salvation,'" in Yeo (ed.), *New Views of Co-operation*, 134.

17. Kobayashi, "The Paradox of Difference and Diversity," in Jones et al. (eds.), *Thresholds in Feminist Geography*.

18. *Co-operative News*, September 2, 1871.

19. Ibid.

20. This particular Bamford was no relation to the Lancashire poet and radical, Samuel Bamford, nor to the Rochdale pioneer, James Bamford.

21. Bonner, *British Co-operation*, 492.

22. "Woman's Corner," *Co-operative News*, January 6, 1883. In the "Woman's Corner" for January 20, 1883, a correspondent (Eleanor Allen) wrote that she too hoped that the new column would increase the paper's circulation.

23. Ibid.

24. Ross, *Love and Toil*, 76–77.

25. Bonner, *British Co-operation*, 492.

26. Llewelyn Davies, *The Women's Co-operative Guild*, 108.

27. Gurney, *Co-operative Culture and the Politics of Consumption in England*, 171–180.

28. In fact, the idea for a children's column came from Annie Jones, who followed Acland as president of the Guild. See "Woman's Corner," *Co-operative News*, February 7, 1885.

29. Kobayashi, "The Paradox of Difference and Diversity," in Jones et al. (eds.), *Thresholds in Feminist Geography*, 6.

30. Glenda Laws, "Women's Life Courses, Spatial Mobility, and State Policies," in Jones et al. (eds.), *Thresholds in Feminist Geography*, 52.

31. Those familiar with the etymology of the term "distaff" with respect to women will know it dates back to much earlier times when the wife's side of a family was referred to as the distaff side because the distaff was an implement used by women in the spinning process.

32. "Women's Lives," *Co-operative News*, October 21, 1882, illustrates well the sort of public activism Acland envisioned for women. It focused on concerns suited to women's traditional roles as homemakers and caregivers to the young.

33. "Woman's Corner," *Co-operative News*, June 26, 1886.

34. "Woman's Corner," *Co-operative News*, March 31, 1883.

35. "Woman's Corner," *Co-operative News*, June 2, 1883.

36. "Woman's Corner," *Co-operative News*, August 2, 1884.

37. Loeb, *Consuming Angels*, 152.

38. "Woman's Corner," *Co-operative News*, December 29, 1883, June 21, 1884, February 14, 1885, represent several such unanswered pleas on the part of the editors.

39. Letters that discussed religion or party politics, as well as letters that offered opinions in strident tones about employee profit-sharing in cooperative stores and workshops, were frequently signed with initials.

40. "Woman's Corner," *Co-operative News*, November 23, 1889.

41. Virginia Woolf, *A Room of One's Own* (London: Granada, 1981), 49.

42. "Woman's Corner," *Co-operative News*, August 15, 1885.

43. "Woman's Corner," *Co-operative News*, September 24, 1887.

44. Ross, *Love and Toil*, 51.

45. Jane Millar, "Women, Poverty and Social Security," in Christine Hallett (ed.), *Women and Social Policy* (New York: Prentice Hall, 1996), 57.

46. Phillips, *Divided Loyalties*, 57.

47. Roberts, *A Woman's Place*, 110.

48. "Woman's Corner," *Co-operative News*, January 12, 1889.

49. "Woman's Corner," *Co-operative News*, August 9, 1884, February 7 and 14, 1885, August 15, 1885.

50. "Woman's Corner," *Co-operative News*, January 2, 1886.

51. Employee profit-sharing and worker-controlled workshops were highly controversial issues within the Cooperative movement in the last two decades of the nineteenth century. They divided the movement into two camps, the individualists and the federalists. The advocates of the former backed them; the latter opposed them and preferred to concentrate on the consumer rather than the producer in their efforts at working-class amelioration. See Philip N. Backstrom, *Christian Socialism and Co-operation in*

Victorian England: Edward Vansittart Neale and the Co-operative Movement (London: Croom Helm, 1974), 161–185.

52. "Woman's Corner," *Co-operative News*, March 24, 1888.

53. "Woman's Corner," *Co-operative News*, January 12, 1889.

54. "Woman's Corner," *Co-operative News*, February 23, 1889.

55. Ibid.

56. Ibid.

57. "Woman's Corner," *Co-operative News*, March 23, 1889.

58. "Woman's Corner," *Co-operative News*, August 9, 1884.

59. Mary Lawrenson Collection, Cooperative Union Library, Manchester, draft of an 1888 letter to Amy Sharp from Lawrenson.

60. "Woman's Corner," *Co-operative News*, June 4, 1887.

61. A comparison of Lawrenson's and Webb's relations with the men at the stores to which they belonged may be obtained by consulting "Woman's Corner," *Co-operative News*, February 7 and 14, 1885 vis-à-vis March 7, 1885.

62. Mary Lawrenson Collection, Cooperative Union Library, Manchester, February 1889 letter to Lawrenson from Sharp.

63. Kent, *Sex and Suffrage*, 101.

64. "Woman's Corner," *Co-operative News*, March 14, 1885.

65. Ross, *Love and Toil*, 76–77.

66. Ibid., 77–78.

67. Gurney, *Co-operative Culture and the Politics of Consumption in England*, 159–160.

68. Millar, "Women, Poverty and Social Security," in Hallett (ed.), *Women and Social Policy*, 54.

69. "Woman's Corner," *Co-operative News*, March 14, 1885. The annual dues were 6d. per annum, although some branches charged more, and over the years dues increased, reaching as much as 4s. in several branches by the 1920s; see Webb, *The Woman with the Basket*, 144.

70. "Woman's Corner," *Co-operative News*, March 14, 1885.

71. Ibid.

72. Lewis, citing the work of Ellen Ross, "The Working-class Wife and Mother and State Intervention, 1870–1918," in Lewis (ed.) *Labour and Love*, 106–107.

73. Ross, *Love and Toil*, 29.

74. "Woman's Corner," *Co-operative News*, April 18, 1885.

75. Ibid.

76. "Woman's Corner," *Co-operative News*, March 23, 1885.

77. Ibid.

78. Ibid.

79. "Woman's Corner," *Co-operative News*, April 11, 1885.

80. Ibid.

81. Ibid.

82. Pedersen, *Family, Dependence and the Origins of the Welfare State*, 44.

83. Lewis, "The Working-class Wife and Mother and State Intervention, 1870–1918," in Lewis (ed.) *Labour and Love*, 113.

84. Millar, "Women, Poverty and Social Security," in Hallett (ed.) *Women and Social Policy*, 58.

85. Thane, "The Women of the British Labour Party and Feminism," in Smith (ed.), *British Feminism in the Twentieth Century* says (132) this was the position of the Independent Labour Party women. Pedersen, *Family, Dependence and the Origins of the Welfare State*, observes that this was the position of Independent Labour Party women and the members of the Fabian Women's Group with respect to women with small chil-

dren, but that they and the Fabian women felt the equal rights feminist position that women should have equal access to opportunities for waged labor was appropriate when women had no small children (44–45).

86. Pedersen, "Eleanor Rathbone 1872–1946," in Pedersen and Mandler (eds.), *After the Victorians*, 108.

87. Seccombe, "Patriarchy Stabilized," 57–58.

88. "Woman's Corner," *Co-operative News*, November 9 and 23, 1889.

89. "Woman's Corner," *Co-operative News*, August 15, 1885.

90. Ibid.

91. Taylor, *Eve and the New Jerusalem*, provides the best overview of the challenge presented to traditional marriage arrangements by Owenite principles.

92. Ibid., 196.

93. Land, quoting Rathbone's 1924 comments, "Eleanor Rathbone and the Economy of the Family," in Smith (ed.) *British Feminism in the Twentieth Century*, 121.

94. "Woman's Corner," *Co-operative News*, September 5, 1885.

95. Ibid.

96. Ibid.

97. "Woman's Corner," *Co-operative News*, October 17 and 24, 1885.

98. The *Co-operative News* for August 29, 1885, gave Hughes's travel plans.

99. "Woman's Corner," *Co-operative News*, October 24, 1885.

100. Ibid.

101. "Woman's Corner," *Co-operative News*, November 9, 1889.

102. "Woman's Corner," *Co-operative News*, November 23, 1889. The Guild, in particular, was dissatisfied with the size of the "Corner" and throughout the 1890s complained to Bamford. See, for example: Women's Cooperative Guild, *Thirteenth Annual Report of the Women's Co-operative Guild* (Manchester: Cooperative Wholesale Society's Printing Works, 1896), 26–27 and Women's Cooperative Guild, *Fourteenth Annual Report of the Women's Co-operative Guild* (Manchester: Cooperative Wholesale Society's Printing Works, 1897), 10.

103. "Woman's Corner," *Co-operative News*, November 23, 1889.

104. Ibid.

105. Ibid.

106. Ibid.

107. Ibid.

108. Ibid.

109. Ibid.

110. Quoted by Kent in *Sex and Suffrage*, 191.

111. "Woman's Corner," *Co-operative News*, February 15, 1890.

112. "Woman's Corner," *Co-operative News*, February 22, 1890.

113. "Woman's Corner," *Co-operative News*, March 29, 1890.

114. Ibid.

115. Supplement to the *Co-operative News*, February 20, 1892.

116. *Co-operative News*, March 5, 1892.

117. *Co-operative News*, February 27 and March 5, 1892.

118. The first such supplement appeared in 1892 in honor of the Guild congress held in Manchester to celebrate the formation of its one-hundredth branch. It should also be noted that in the 1890s women's activities and concerns found their ways into other segments of the cooperative press. In 1896, for instance, the Cooperative Wholesale Society began publication of the *Wheatsheaf*, which had no women's column but did cover Guild activities. Also, a number of local cooperative societies published *Records*, as they were called, which had their own versions of the "Woman's Corner." See Women's Cooperative Guild, *Thirteenth Annual Report of the Women's Co-operative Guild*, 13; and

Women's Cooperative Guild, *Fourteenth Annual Report of the Women's Co-operative Guild*, 20.

119. *Co-operative News*, July 6, 1895.

120. Ibid.

121. Ibid.

122. Rose, *Limited Livelihoods*, 142.

123. *Co-operative News*, July 6, 1895.

124. Gurney, *Co-operative Culture and the Politics of Consumption in England*, 241.

125. Minute books of the Central Committee, January 23 and 24, 1893, meeting, items 6 and 7.

126. Ibid. Also see pages 110–111 of Llewelyn Davies's *The Women's Co-operative Guild*.

127. "Woman's Corner," *Co-operative News*, March 11 and 18, 1893.

128. The Guild had been involved with the Women's Trade Union League since the early 1890s, and with that organization had worked for the unionization of women and legislation to protect them from exploitation by their employers. For more on the Women's Trade Union League see Sally Alexander, "'Bringing Women into Line with Men': The Women's Trade Union League, 1874–1921," in Alexander, *Becoming a Woman and Other Essays in 19th and 20th Century Feminist History*; Norbert C. Soldon, *Women in British Trade Unions, 1874–1976* (Dublin: Gill and Macmillan Ltd., 1978); Gladys Boone, *The Women's Trade Union Leagues in Great Britain and the United States of America* (New York: Columbia University Press, 1942).

129. From 1901 to 1904 the "Corner" was preoccupied with reporting the activities of the Guild's experiment with the Sunderland Cooperative Society to bring cooperation to the poor.

130. In 1897, the Guild devoted its sectional conferences to the women's suffrage question, as noted in the April 17 issue of the "Corner." Women's suitability as factory inspectors and poor-law guardians were discussed respectively in papers by Llewelyn Davies and by a Mrs. Green and reprinted in the January 16, 1897, and the March 19, 1898, editions of the "Corner." Finally, the "Corner" frequently took the position that women were more to blame than men for opposing women's election to store commitees, a position which was sure to mollify men on the watch for anti-male sentiment; see the July 22, 1899, and July 14, 1900, editions of the "Corner."

131. Rose, *Limited Livelihoods*, 123.

132. Ross, *Love and Toil*, 12.

133. Rose, "Gender Antagonism and Class Conflict," 191–208.

134. From June 23 to August 24, 1883, the "Corner" ran a series of articles advocating such legislation. And in the 1890s, when the Women's Trade Union League switched its policy from trying to create a level playing field for men and women to the advocacy of protective legislation for women, the Guild joined with it in common cause.

135. Barbara Brookes, "Women and Reproduction, 1860–1939," in Lewis (ed.), *Labour and Love*, 159.

136. Harrison, *Prudent Revolutionaries*, 314.

137. Millar, "Women, Poverty and Social Security," in Hallett (ed.) *Women and Social Policy*, 57.

138. Ross, *Love and Toil*, 45; Rose, *Limited Livelihoods*, 76.

139. Rose, *Limited Livelihoods*, 76–79.

140. Ibid.

141. Paul Johnson, *Saving and Spending: The Working-class Economy in Britain, 1870–1939* (Oxford: Clarendon Press, 1985), 139–140.

142. Ibid.

143. Gurney, *Co-operative Culture and the Politics of Consumption in England*, chapter 2.

144. Lewis, *Women in England*, 46–47.

145. Pedersen, *Family, Dependence and the Origins of the Welfare State*, 39.

146. "Woman's Corner," *Co-operative News*, August 21, 1907.

147. Pedersen, *Family, Dependence and the Origins of the Welfare State*, 32.

148. "Woman's Corner," *Co-operative News*, August 21, 1907.

149. This policy was applauded in the "Woman's Corner," *Co-operative News*, November 9, 1907.

150. Sidney and Beatrice Webb, *The Consumers' Co-operative Movement*, 11.

151. See Llewelyn Davies's *The Women's Co-operative Guild* (99) for confirmation of this practice's existence.

152. "Woman's Corner," *Co-operative News*, December 7, 1907.

153. *Co-operative News*, January 18, 1908

154. *Co-operative News*, January 25, February 1 and 8, March 14, 1908.

155. *Co-operative News*, November 11, 1908.

156. *Co-operative News*, June 24, 1916.

157. The discussion that appeared in the "Woman's Corner" between August 6 and September 10, 1910, makes clear William Bamford's lack of enthusiasm for increasing the size of the column and his sister's inability to persuade him otherwise.

158. *Co-operative News*, February 6, 1915.

159. This was contrary to voting practices within the cooperative stores, where all members had one vote regardless of the number of shares they owned.

160. *Co-operative News*, May 30, 1914. It should be noted that it is impossible to compare the minutes which appeared in the paper with the originals as the originals no longer exist.

161. Gaffin and Thoms, *Caring and Sharing*, 54–81; Scott, *Feminism and the Politics of Working Women*, chapters 3 and 4.

162. Giles, *Women, Identity and Private Life in Britain*, 1–3.

163. Women's Cooperative Guild, *Handbook of the Annual Meeting* (Manchester: Cooperative Printing Society, Ltd., 1895), xxviii, offers a defense of that organization's position on protective legislation against its critics.

164. Women's Cooperative Guild, *Thirty-fifth Annual Report of the Women's Co-operative Guild* (Manchester: Cooperative Wholesale Society's Printing Works, 1918), 6.

165. Women's Cooperative Guild, *Working Women and Divorce* (New York: Garland Publishing, Inc., 1980).

166. "Women's Corner," *Co-operative News*, April 9, 1913.

167. *Co-operative News*, November 16, 1912.

168. Ibid.

169. Ibid.

170. Ibid.

171. The Reverend T. S. Hudson later complained about this during the debate over the Guild's support for divorce law reform held at the annual Cooperative Congress of 1915. The Cooperative Union Limited, *The Forty-seventh Annual Co-operative Congress* (Manchester: Cooperative Union Ltd., 1915), 523.

172. *Co-operative News*, June 21, 1913.

173. Women's Cooperative Guild, *Thirty-first Annual Report of the Women's Co-operative Guild* (Manchester: Cooperative Wholesale Society's Printing Works, 1914), 4.

174. *Co-operative News*, June 21, 1913.

175. "Women's Corner," *Co-operative News*, April 18, 1914.

176. Women's Cooperative Guild, *Thirty-first Annual Report of the Women's Co-operative Guild*, 46.

177. The Cooperative Union Limited, *Forty-sixth Annual Co-operative Congress* (Manchester: Cooperative Union Ltd., 1914), 13.

178. Ibid., 14.

179. Pedersen, *Family, Dependence and the Origins of the Welfare State* notes that men claimed a disproportionate share of the wages they turned over to their wives by either expecting or demanding that the housekeeping budget be spent to keep them well fed, 159–160.

180. *Co-operative News*, June 14, 1914.

181. Gurney, *Co-operative Culture and the Politics of Consumption in England*, chapters 8 and 9.

182. The Cooperative Union Limited, *The Fiftieth Annual Co-operative Congress* (Manchester: Cooperative Union Ltd., 1918), 636–638. Although the grant was restored, the question of the independence of auxiliary bodies like the Guild remained unresolved as the Cooperative movement became increasingly centralized in the interwar period.

183. "Women's Corner," *Co-operative News*, January 11, 1913.

184. Ibid.

185. "Women's Corner," *Co-operative News*, April 26, 1919.

Chapter 2

The Gendered Geography of the Cooperative Movement

Virginia Woolf was one of the first feminists to think in spatial terms. Her assertion that women need rooms of their own if they are to write fiction articulated the connection between female subordination and the male domination of space and its allocation. Within the English working-class movements of the late nineteenth and early twentieth centuries, women's subordination often manifested itself as prohibitions on female access to places and spaces. The situation among male trade unionists serves as a case in point.

Male trade unionists advocated protective labor legislation for women to keep them in the home, as Carol Dyhouse has pointed out.[1] Wally Seccombe and Sonya O. Rose have shown that male trade unionists insisted on the breadwinner wage in an effort to maintain male dominance, not for the sake of family survival as Jane Humphries mistakenly suggested.[2] Male hostility toward women in the workforce came from the fear of female competition.[3] Because women were paid significantly less than men, they undercut men's wages. This served to reduce a man's status at work, and therefore also his self-esteem. Harold Benenson has argued that Lancashire men were particularly hostile to women who continued to work for wages outside the home after marriage.[4] This may at first sight appear to be quite surprising since it was not unusual for women to continue in employment after marriage in the textile districts of Lancashire. However, women's continued employment after marriage allowed employers to rationalize paying men less. Weavers, in particular, were never able to convince employers to pay them a breadwinner wage because their wives also worked at the trade.[5] Men so "victimized" felt they had good reason to support restrictions on female employment.

Since Lancashire was the home of the Cooperative movement, it is important to understand the attitudes that prevailed in that county with respect to gender. Historians such as Philippa Levine, Jane Lewis, Brian Harrison, Diane Gittens, Jill Norris, and Jill Liddington have presumed that the concept of separate

A TYPICAL GROUP OF MEMBERS OF A NORTHERN GUILD BRANCH, ABOUT 1889.

Reproduced courtesy of the Co-operative Women's Guild.

spheres took little root in Lancashire because married women there so frequently worked outside the home for wages.[6] They argue this resulted in greater independence for women, as illustrated by the fact that female textile workers represented the majority of unionized women at the turn of the century and that so many of them were suffragists. Lewis, Gittens, Norris, and Liddington, in particular, are impressed by evidence that the husbands of women textile workers helped with the housework, inferring that this exception to the rules governing the gendered division of labor somehow made such women more equal to men.[7] Unfortunately, the result of women's greater presence in the workforce in Lancashire may have been a greater male insistence on restricting women's public influence. The county's skilled male workers were especially interested in maintaining the sexual division of labor.[8] Had the men wanted to protect themselves without compromising women's right to work, they would have supported the formation of trade unions for women rather than restrictive legislation. But the Trades Union Congress never paid anything more than lip service to efforts to organize women,[9] and, in the Lancashire weaving trade, men even attempted to restrict trade union membership to the male head of household in families where both the husband and wife were employed.[10]

Without doubt, the working class throughout England had developed by the middle of the nineteenth century very clear ideas regarding appropriate spatial separation for males and females at work. As Sonya O. Rose and Sally Alexander have argued, these ideas contributed to the creation of separate spheres among the working class at play and in the home as well.[11] Ellen Ross has commented on the separation of physical space within working-class homes, observing that the parlor belonged to the wife and the best chair to the husband.[12] Jane Humphries notes that the rigid maintenance of separate spheres between the genders among the working class may have helped to discourage unwelcome sexual intimacies.[13] This devotion to the maintenance of strictly defined gender roles would, as Jane Lewis has argued, lead to the creation of a division of labor between men and women in the public sphere when women were eventually conceded some space therein.[14]

In the English Cooperative movement men strove to maintain the boundaries of gendered space. Like trade unionists, male cooperators sought to control women's participation in the movement by restricting their access to positions deemed appropriate only for men. They considered women unsuitable either for membership on committees with authority over the finances of cooperative societies or for election to the national executive of the movement. Lancashire's male cooperators became particularly notorious among female cooperators for their dedication to the limitation and control of women's participation in the movement.

Paradoxically, the distributive cooperative movement begun in 1844 by the Rochdale Pioneers drew its strength from the concept of mutuality between the sexes. The survival of a working-class family required the married couple to combine their efforts to make their household income stretch. The cooperative stores were designed to help them in that endeavor. At the stores, couples were assured of value for their money and fair dealing. In addition, their purchases accumulated a dividend that could be used in times of unemployment or illness

to tide the family over. Cooperative stores attracted clientele from the ranks of
the lower middle class and the so-called respectable working class. Peter Gurney
characterizes the men drawn to cooperation as people who earned regular,
though not necessarily high, wages.[15] The wives of such men would not have
needed to work outside the home for wages, but they may have had to supplement their husbands' earnings on occasion by doing waged labor within the
home. This would have been particularly true when their children were young
and extra money was needed, and it may have continued until the children were
old enough to begin bringing in wages of their own to help the family.[16] Anec-
dotal evidence collected by the Women's Cooperative Guild about its members
confirms these generalizations. Margaret Llewelyn Davis observed in her 1904
history of the Guild that most of its members did not go out to work full-time.[17]
They tended to be the wives of men who made between 20s. and 30s. per
week.[18] They rented their houses and few of their dwellings had such amenities
as bathrooms.[19] Their families were large and, consequently, these women had
been unable to join the Guild until they were middle-aged.[20] Their children's
waged labor or departures from home had made it possible by then for the
women to have the time and money for involvement with the Guild.

The recent investigations of historians into the lives of women of the respectable working class shed further light on what female cooperators were like.
They suggest that the wives of securely employed working men interpreted female emancipation as domesticity[21]—freedom from the necessity of having to
pull the double shift of waged labor and housework.[22] Judy Giles argues that
such women saw the home as a site of fulfillment; they did not feel constricted
by their household responsibilities, as many middle-class feminists presumed
they should.[23] They considered that there was status to be had from the "professional" execution of housewifery,[24] which explains why the "Woman's Corner's" tips for running the home were always so popular among its readers. Jane
Lewis argues that working-class housewives "derived a sense of self-worth from
their domestic responsibilities and authority."[25] Ellen Ross observes that since
working-class families were so dependent upon the wise management of limited
resources, the caring services working-class wives and mothers performed "carried even more emotional resonance" for women in the late nineteenth and early
twentieth centuries than they do for women today.[26] Indeed, this was the reason
so many working-class women were unwilling to surrender to the welfare state
their domestic obligation of providing for their families, and hence opposed the
institution of such "benefits" as schools meals.[27]

The women who shopped at the cooperative stores valued domesticity for
women, and this had consequences for those who hoped to coax them into joining the Women's Cooperative Guild. Martin Pugh has argued for a later period
that the comforts of domesticity can dampen any drive to activism.[28] The leaders
of the Guild certainly found this to be true among the cooperative women they
attempted to organize.[29] In addition, what Patrick Joyce has described as the
deferential and traditionalist culture of the working class limited the Guild's
leaders in their efforts to create the preconditions necessary for the establishment of the Cooperative Commonwealth to which they aspired.[30] Few cooperative women either imagined or desired a society without status distinctions. In

fact, the working-class families with incomes regular enough to enable them to shop at cooperative stores, where prices were inflated so that high dividends could be returned, strove to separate themselves from those with fewer resources. Involvement with cooperation for them functioned as "status confirmation."[31] Theirs was a culture which Chris Waters has characterized as elitist.[32] Cooperators were keen to maintain boundaries between the "rough" and the "respectable." Since one of the prime indicators of respectable status was women's domesticity, cooperators of both sexes upheld the gendered division of labor into separate spheres for men and women. This resulted in the economic dependence of cooperative women on their husbands. The women of the Cooperative movement consequently lacked the other requirement Virginia Woolf highlighted as essential to women's freedom besides a room of their own—an income of their own.

Dependent on their husbands' wages, cooperative wives were acknowledged by their husbands as the household managers. Their husbands delegated to them the responsibility of ensuring that the family expenditures did not exceed income. In their effort to maintain the separate spheres that would guarantee women's financial dependence, some cooperative men claimed women had a "natural" talent for managing the household budget, which no man could equal.[33] But as was noted in the previous chapter, such responsibility brought women more pressure than it did power. In Lancashire, the delegation to the wife of jurisdiction over the domestic budget resulted in it becoming customary for the husband to turn over to his wife each week his entire wage packet for the household expenses. She would then give him some spending money for the week.[34] In the London area, on the other hand, wives often did not know how much their husbands made. The custom there was for husbands to pay their wives from the wage packet whatever they deemed necessary for the week's household expenses.[35] In both areas, wives who were cooperators spent their husbands' wages at the cooperative stores, even though most were not shareholding members in their own names. Out of the 1,454 cooperative societies in existence throughout Britain in 1902, only 145 permitted what was known as "open membership," which enabled wives to become members.[36] Societies in Lancashire were especially reluctant to permit anyone except the male head of household from becoming a shareholding member. Of the 145 societies with open membership in 1902, only 35 were located in the northwest, while 59 were in London and the home counties.[37] Directors of societies in Lancashire defended their resistance to open membership by claiming that such membership was prohibited to avoid the accumulation of excess share capital.[38] But the Guild's leaders knew that restrictions on membership merely served to exclude women, "shutting out the people whose loyal support is the foundation of financial prosperity."[39] The result of restrictions on membership was that wives were prohibited from attending the quarterly meetings of the societies, from running for positions on either the educational or management committees of the stores, and sometimes even from using any reading room or library a society might have. Thus the Cooperative movement relied on the wives of regularly paid working men, but all that was expected of the women was that they should "come and *buy*."

By the 1870s, the shopping of financially dependent women had turned the Pioneers' experiment into a nationwide network of distributive and productive societies organized into the Cooperative Union, supplied by an English and a Scottish Wholesale Society, and governed by an annual congress attended by well over a thousand delegates. Men, some from the working and some from the middle class, ran the societies, the Union, the wholesale societies, and the congress. Then, in the early 1880s, some male cooperators began to think women should have the opportunity to become propagandists for the cause. They imagined both sexes working to convince the unconverted that cooperation would be the agency for the transformation of the entire socioeconomic system. They envisioned women helping men in the campaign to create a more moral economy than that operated by the competitive capitalist system, taking retail sales out of the control of the profit-mongers and putting them into the hands of the consumers. They looked forward to the more equal distribution of wealth and power that these changes would institute. These men desired, in particular, to use women to teach their sisters who shopped at the stores that the movement was about more than accumulating a dividend, and to ensure that the next generation, the children, were instructed in the sharing ideals for which cooperation stood.[40] So it was that Alice Acland came to edit a weekly women's column in the official newspaper of the movement in 1883. Within four months of the column's inauguration, its editor and its regular readers had managed to form a club to coordinate their efforts to propagandize the movement, the Women's League for the Spread of Cooperation.[41] This organization was renamed the Women's Guild for the Spread of Cooperation in 1884.[42] Originally envisioned as a separate sphere in which women could have meetings, readings, and discussions of their own, the Guild soon became a mechanism for feminine incursions into male space within the Cooperative movement.[43] Its leaders also began to make demands on the movement's financial resources.

The Guild's founders had not initially imagined that their organization would lead women to trespass on male turf. Alice Acland, the Guild's first general secretary, advised guildswomen not to imitate men or push "themselves into positions which have been filled by men hitherto. Women gain nothing in matters of this kind by entering into competition with men. The thing to be done is to see whether there is not special work which can be done, not only best by women, but which can be done by women only."[44] However, teasing out women's work from men's within the Cooperative movement proved difficult, as Acland quickly discovered. In her original outline of objectives for Guild work, the first three she listed were already the province of the educational committees, which most cooperative societies had affiliated to them, and on which only men sat:

1. To spread a knowledge of the *advantages* of co-operation.
2. To stimulate among those who know its advantages a greater interest in the *principles* of co-operation.
3. To stir up and keep alive in ourselves, in our neighbours, and in the rising generation, a more earnest appreciation of the value of co-operation to ourselves, our children, and to the nation.
4. To improve the condition of women all over the kingdom.[45]

This tendency for the Guild to duplicate the activities of the educational committees created jurisdictional problems that were aggravated by the fact that the Guild was in no way affiliated to the Cooperative Union, the umbrella organization that presided over the movement. The new women's group was a separate auxiliary body over which the Union technically had no control, even though three of the Guild's functions duplicated those of the Union's Central Education Committee. The Acland-Jones circle, which had aimed to organize cooperative women so that they might educate one another and their children, had neglected to consider that issues of control and overlapping of functions might become a problem. They had failed to consider that possibility because working-class organizations had had women's auxiliaries in the past without such problems arising. As Anna Clark observes of such auxiliaries, it was understood that they would remain dependent on the main organization, which was run by men.[46] Thus, to paraphrase Barbara Taylor's conclusions about female auxiliaries, they were designed to reproduce in the public sphere the patriarchy of the household.[47]

Acland desired to avoid challenging the patriarchy which controlled the Cooperative movement, so she sought to define an area of work that could be done "by women only." When that proved difficult, the first meeting of the Guild at the 1883 Cooperative Congress found itself spending ninety minutes discussing whether it was worthwhile for an organization of women cooperators even to exist.[48] The women present at the meeting eventually concluded that as long as they proceeded by the motto "Study to be quiet, and do your own business," cooperation was women's business, since it had to do with provisioning the home.[49] However, their decision had revolutionary potential as far as the men in charge of the Cooperative movement were concerned. In *Feminist Lives in Victorian England*, Philippa Levine describes how middle-class ladies revolutionized gender relationships by reconfiguring, indeed collapsing, the boundaries between the private and public spheres.[50] The men in charge of the Cooperative movement came to interpret the guildswomen's decision as having potentially similar consequences within cooperation. The guildswomen had concluded that the male-managed business of cooperation was part of their female-managed private sphere and had inadvertently collapsed the two separate spheres. This situation would prove intolerable for male cooperators who refused to acknowledge that the Rochdale Pioneers had created a movement capable of destroying the boundaries between the public and private because of its dependency on female consumers making purchases for the provisioning of the home.

In the contentious endeavor of renegotiating the boundaries of gendered space within the movement, female cooperators used what were considered women's natural roles as guidelines to reassure the men that the women had no interest in subverting traditional gender roles. As homemakers, the women requested a say in what the stores stocked; as mothers, they claimed a voice in the education of the young. Theoretically, no man need feel emasculated by the granting of concessions such as these, since they merely helped women in the performance of their appropriate gender roles. Nonetheless, these concessions were not easily won, because their exercise involved women's physical presence in places where they had never before ventured—the quarterly business meetings of cooperative societies and the meetings of the educational committees. Margaret Llewelyn Davies in her history of the Guild commented that women who dared to attend quarterly meetings were "looked on as strange beings with an ulterior motive."[51] She added that male opposition was "especially roused when women see there is something more for them to do than buy loyally at the Store."[52] The first women who dared to trespass on male turf in the Cooperative movement bore testimony to the accuracy of Llewelyn Davies's observations.

Mary Lawrenson, co-founder of the Guild with Acland, was one of the first women to dare to attend a business meeting, at the Woolwich Cooperative Society where her husband was director.[53] She sensed the male discomfort immediately and strove to assure the men they need not feel threatened by the appearance of women in formerly male preserves, because of the complementary nature of the sexes. Drawing on one of Benjamin Franklin's metaphors, "that man and wife are like the two sides of a pair of scissors," she asserted that "husbands and wives are alike interested in this business of Co-operation, each having a share in the work suited to their powers."[54] Nevertheless, the men felt business decisions were not "suited to women's powers." They resented guildswomen sending deputations to store managers to make recommendations as to what sort of items should be stocked. For instance, the women of the Guild branch at Hebden Bridge took it upon themselves to advise their store manager that if the drapery and millinery departments were improved, more women would shop at the store.[55] Store managers began to complain to the Guild's national leadership about this unwelcome interference, so Acland had to counsel the women "to make quiet representations" to the men.[56] Thus a compromise was arranged; women could speak about business matters with the men in control of the stores as long as they did so deferentially and did not presume to speak with confidence and authority. A different compromise was reached on the matter of education, and it was one consonant with the prevailing conceptions of women's natural roles.

In 1884, Mary Lawrenson and one of her friends became the first women ever elected to an educational committee.[57] There is no record of whether Lawrenson's husband had exerted his influence as the director of the Woolwich Cooperative Society to guarantee the return of the women, but there is evidence that their presence was not welcomed by the men on the committee. Lawrenson recounted that some men were pleased that women had not ventured into the business end of Cooperation by running for positions on management committees: "let them stick to the educational work; that's their place."[58] But she said other men remarked that "when women take up educational work, it's time to stop them."[59] Some such men served on the Woolwich Society's educational committee. They patronized their female colleagues. For instance, when Lawrenson tried to use her position on the committee to win some of its funds to support the educational activities her Guild branch planned to sponsor, the committee readily agreed, but four months later, her branch was still waiting for the money.[60] Also, she tried to talk the educational committee into funding singing classes because she, like most guildswomen, believed it was as important for cooperators to recreate as to trade together if a family-like community was going to be built among them.[61] However, the men on the committee vetoed her proposal.[62]

Lawrenson was not the type of person to be deterred by opposition; her Guild branch started the classes on its own with its meager funds collected from branch member dues. On another occasion, she lectured the Braintree Cooperative Society for banning women from its library and reading room on the grounds they were not voting members of the society, since they were enrolled under their husbands' names.[63] Ultimately, she even went so far as to assert, "Educational work we claim as specially suited to women," and remained confident the men would eventually grant them "some monetary help" for their efforts at the branch level.[64] At the national level, she was responsible for securing the Guild's first monetary grant from the Cooperative Union. She and her husband were friendly with E. V. Neale, the former Christian Socialist and first general secretary of the Union. In 1886, he began, with a grant of £10, the Union's practice of donating funds annually to finance the Guild's educational work.[65] Lawrenson became so emboldened by her success in carving out a niche for women in the space of cooperative education that she began to boast she could get elected to a management committee if she ran.[66] Other women also felt empowered by the men's concessions to them of a place on the educational side of the movement and began to push for more influence on its business side. Annie Jones, the second president of the Guild, imagined the day when women would become buyers for the drapery departments of cooperative stores.[67] However, the men who controlled the Cooperative movement would remain ever reluctant to grant women positions of authority over pounds and pence. The Guild kept statistics on the number of guildswomen serving on both educational and management committees. Table 1 compares for a thirty-year period the number of guildswomen serving on educational committees with those on management committees.

These figures show that between 1890 and the onset of war in 1914 guildswomen managed to increase their representation on educational committees from 42 to 408, but their representation on management committees lagged far behind, growing only from 0 to 93. During and immediately after the war, guildswomen's representation on management committees improved, owing perhaps to a greater tolerance caused by the war for women's incursions into hitherto male arenas. Nonetheless, for every three women on educational committees there was only one on a management committee by 1920.

It may be argued that women felt less prepared to handle balance sheets than syllabi, and this rather than male opposition accounts for the smaller numbers of women on management committees, fewer of them bothering to run for such positions in the first place. However, the Central Committee that governed the Guild realized as early as 1887 that women would need training in bookkeeping and accounting before they could expect to function competently on management committees,[68] and in 1891, began a concerted effort to instruct guildswomen in the reading of balance sheets.[69] Moreover statistical evidence and the testimonies of defeated female candidates suggest that male opposition functioned as a greater cause of the women's failure to secure election to management committees than female reluctance to present themselves as candidates.

Table 1
Committee Membership Distribution[70]

Year	Educational Committees	Management Committees
1890	42	0
1891	57	6
1892	73	6
1893	65	15
1894	60	6
1895	72	9
1896	101	16
1897	115	22
1898	124	19
1899	158	12
1900	163	21
1901	159	30
1902	180	39
1903	191	37
1904	238	30
1905	251	31
1906	306	40
1907	286	35
1908	314	44
1909	334	47
1910	314	49
1911	346	50
1912	373	67
1913	397	75
1914	408	93
1915	413	89
1916	431	111
1917	469	136
1918	539	172
1919	624	204
1920	662	220

For several years the Guild kept records of the number of women who ran for either management or educational committees and lost (see Tables 2 and 3). These show that although fewer women did indeed put themselves forward as candidates for management committees, those who were both qualified to serve the business side of the Cooperative movement and bold enough to run for such offices lost elections in higher proportions than did women who ran for positions on educational committees. Anywhere from 20 to 53% of the women who ran for positions on management committees failed to get elected, whereas the failure rate for women candidates for positions on educational committees never exceeded 14% and typically hovered around 10%.

Table 2
Female Candidacies for Management Committees[71]

Year	Successful Candidates	Unsuccessful Candidates	Failure Rate*
1897	22	17	43.59
1898	19	8	29.63
1899	12	9	42.86
1900	21	11	34.38
1901	30	14	31.82
1902	39	14	26.42
1903	37	19	33.93
1904	30	9	23.08
1905	31	22	41.51
1906	40	10	20.00
1907	35	19	35.19
1908	44	29	39.73
1909	47	38	44.71
1910	49	45	47.87
1911	50	57	53.27
1912	67	48	41.74
1913	75	61	44.85
1914	93	56	37.58
1915	89	57	39.04

*Failure rate represents the percentage of unsuccessful female candidates out of the total number of women running for any particular year.

Historians have generally assumed that male opposition to women's greater involvement in the Cooperative movement was quickly and easily overcome. For instance, Jean Gaffin and David Thoms, in *Caring and Sharing*, and Jill Norris and Jill Liddington, in *One Hand Tied Behind Us*, dismiss the evidence for opposition without much comment.[72] And those scholars who admit to its continued existence dismiss it without investigating either its nature or its impact.[73] In many respects, they are reading the evidence the way late nineteenth- and early twentieth-century Guild leaders hoped they would. Margaret Llewelyn Davies, general secretary of the Guild for the thirty-two year period from 1889 to 1921, insisted in her 1904 history of the organization on the ease with which guildswomen overcame the reluctance of male cooperators to give them a place and a voice in the movement.[74] Her vision of the Cooperative Commonwealth to come motivated her to de-emphasize the existence of male opposition. Llewelyn Davies imagined both sexes participating equally in the governance of that future Commonwealth. Indeed, she asserted that the existence of separate organizations for women, like the Guild, would be unnecessary there.[75] She was thus unwilling to prejudice the eventual cooperation of the sexes by dwelling on those occasions when guildswomen encountered male opposition. She seemed to sense that rhetoric can create reality, not simply reflect it, and what was left unspoken might therefore cease to exist. Yet there are passages in her history which invite an alternative reading of women's experiences in the Cooperative movement.

Table 3
Female Candidacies for Educational Committees[76]

Year	Successful Candidates	Unsuccessful Candidates	Failure Rate*
1897	115	9	7.26
1898	124	17	12.06
1899	158	5	3.07
1900	163	13	7.39
1901	159	19	10.67
1902	180	15	7.69
1903	191	19	9.05
1904	238	10	4.03
1905	251	17	6.34
1906	306	20	6.13
1907	286	33	10.34
1908	314	43	12.04
1909	334	56	14.36
1910	314	35	10.03
1911	346	39	10.13
1912	373	51	12.03
1913	397	66	14.25
1914	408	61	13.01
1915	413	68	14.14

*Failure rate represents the percentage of unsuccessful female candidates out of the total number of women running for any particular year.

In commenting on the unavailability of space for women to hold Guild meetings, Llewelyn Davies wrote:

Branch meetings are usually held on Co-operative premises, sometimes in hired rooms. But the only place available may be a loft, with flour bags to sit on. We get such contrasts as these in letters from Branch Secretaries:— From S.: "We have only a very small room to meet in. If there are twenty in it we are too crowded to move, so you will see we have no convenience for lectures or anything else." From B.: "We have got a nice room—fine, and all up to date—and we are enjoying ourselves. We have got 91 members, and keep getting two or three more every week."[77]

This passage is as much a complaint about the insufficiency of the resources allocated to women as it is a boast about women's capacities for making do with what little they are given. More to the point, it prompts the reader to ask why women had to put up with sitting on flour sacks in lofts while men monopolized the boardrooms.

Llewelyn Davies's ambivalence about whether to conceal or reveal the extent of male opposition encountered is also evident in the collection of reminiscences of guildswomen she assembled in 1931, entitled *Life As We Have Known It*. In that volume a felt hat worker named Mrs. Scott recollected the "awful" abuse received by women who dared to run for management committees at the turn of the century.[78] She remembered how her candidacy had prompted someone to send her husband poison-pen letters. She concluded her testimony with the following equivocation: "Now women take their place alongside the men, but there still remains much to be done."[79] Despite the reticence on the part of the Guild's leadership to speak of the opposition encountered by guildswomen, the experiences of the women who dared to invade male space within the Cooperative movement have not been entirely erased from history.

The intrepid Mary Lawrenson never bothered to stand for a management committee; her goals for herself and her sex were grander. Moreover, she achieved them, becoming the first woman ever elected to the Central Board of the Cooperative Union, in 1894, when she stood as a candidate for its Southern Section. To secure this post she had had to win the votes of a majority of men, on a majority of management committees, governing the cooperative societies in the Southern Section of the Union. Cooperators had divided the country into five sections in 1873: the Scottish, Northern, North-Western, Midland, and Southern Sections. Over the years, as cooperation grew, the men added sections or divided ones that had gotten too big. For instance, a Western Section was created in 1878, a South-Western in 1895, and an Irish one evolved between 1889 and 1895. The Central Board of the Cooperative Union was composed of men elected from each of the sections, and numbered between sixty and seventy individuals at the turn of the century. One of the reasons Lawrenson was able to gather sufficient male support to win a seat on the Southern Section of the Central Board was that she was an advocate of profit-sharing in worker-owned and -controlled workshops. The advocates of this position were a powerful minority in the Cooperative movement, and they predominated in the south, in particular the London area. To them, Lawrenson was an ally in their battle against the supporters of consumer-based cooperation, in which no profits were shared with employees. Her friendship with E. V. Neale, the most prominent of the employee profit-sharing advocates, certainly helped her campaign as well.

Lawrenson left no record of her impressions of what it was like to serve as the only woman on a committee of more than sixty men, but Catherine Webb did. Webb was elected to the Southern Section of the Central Board in 1895, the year after Lawrenson, but Lawrenson was not returned that year. Webb described herself as feeling like "a very thin edge of the wedge of equality," and as being relieved the next year when Lawrenson again won a seat on the Southern Section of the board and was there to provide some female companionship.[80] Webb was naive and starstruck by the opportunity to serve on the board at the same time as George Jacob Holyoake, the grand old man of the Cooperative movement. Holyoake is reputed to have been a feminist, but his behavior toward Webb calls this reputation into question.[81] She recounts that he could never remember her name or the reason why she was at a meeting of the Central Board. On one occasion he even went so far as to insult her by confusing her with a representative of a firm of private traders, the dire enemies of cooperation.[82] It is true Holyoake was in his late seventies when he first met Catherine Webb on the

Central Board, and it is tempting to attribute his behavior to senility. However, he is reputed to have remained mentally spry until his death in 1906, as evidenced by his continued production of histories of the Cooperative movement and tracts advocating profit-sharing among cooperative employees.[83]

Unlike Lawrenson, Webb eventually abandoned the cause of employee profit-sharing. Perhaps that explains Holyoake's behavior toward her. Nonetheless, her success in gaining election to the Central Board provides further insight into the gendered geography of the Cooperative movement. It illustrates the fact that men in the Southern Section, the so-called "co-operative desert" where stores were few in number and rarely prosperous,[84] were more willing to concede a place to women on the business side of the movement than were men in the other sections of the country. In fact, the North-Western section, which included the West Riding and Lancashire—the birthplace and headquarters of cooperation—became notorious among guildswomen for its opposition to granting women any place at all within the movement. Llewelyn Davies bluntly stated in the Guild's 1897 annual report: "We know that . . . the remains of masculine prejudice against us are to be found more in the north than in the south."[85] What was more, over the years she compiled statistical evidence to support her observation about the geographical distribution of male opposition to expanding the scope of women's participation in the Cooperative movement. Her figures indicate that women who ran for positions on management committees in the North-Western Section failed on average 63% of the time, while in the Southern Section the failure rate of women candidates averaged only 24%. Opposition to women candidates for educational committees in the North-Western Section was much less, with failures averaging 18%. However, in the Southern Section women who ran for educational committees failed only on the average of 5%. Tables 4 and 5 provide more detailed statistics. It therefore appears that in Lancashire and the West Riding the voting members of cooperative societies, who were by and large men because of resistance to open membership, were more reluctant than cooperators in the Southern Section to elect women to positions of authority even when those positions supposedly suited women's natural roles, as was the case with their candidacies for educational committees.

The figures compiled by Llewelyn Davies also show that many more women came forward as candidates for both management and educational committees in the Southern than in the North-Western Section. The explanation for this is two-fold. First, the Guild was very much a London-based organization, unlike the rest of the Cooperative movement. Even today, what remains of the once prosperous enterprise built by nineteenth-century cooperators is headquartered in Manchester, while the Guild has its national offices near the capital. Women needed the support and encouragement offered by the Guild before they dared to advance themselves as candidates for cooperative offices of any sort. Consequently, where the Guild was weak, few women ran for either management or educational committees.

In 1889, when Llewelyn Davies became general secretary, she recognized the numerous and prosperous cooperative societies of Lancashire and the West Riding as fertile ground for the establishment of Guild branches.[86] She toured these societies from her home in the Lake District to stir up interest in forming

Guild chapters among the women who shopped at the stores. Beginning in 1893, she appointed a series of branch organizers to assist her in this work. Her efforts paid off. There were soon more branches of the Guild in the northwest than there were in the south. What was more, the branches in the northwest were larger in terms of membership totals. By 1900, the Guild had 273 branches nationally with a total membership of 12,809.[87] Eighty-seven of those branches were in the organization's Southern Section and had a membership of 3,151, while 106 were in the North-Western Section where membership totaled 6,579.[88] Table 6 presents further statistical evidence of the growth of Guild branches and membership in the northwest. However, even the increased presence of the Guild was insufficient to guarantee that women would come forward to run for cooperative offices in Lancashire and the West Riding, as the numbers of women candidates shown in Tables 4 and 5 never kept pace with the growth of the Guild in that section of the country.

Table 4
Female Candidacies for Management Committees by Section[89]

Year	Southern Section	North-Western Section	Failure Rate Southern	Failure Rate North-Western
1897	*22/8	0/3	26.66	100.00
1898	13/3	0/2	18.75	100.00
1899	8/0	0/1	0.00	100.00
1900	17/1	1/3	5.55	75.00
1901	22/5	1/2	18.51	66.66
1902	25/4	6/5	13.79	45.45
1903	26/5	3/3	16.12	50.00
1904	19/1	4/4	5.00	50.00
1905	20/5	4/3	20.00	42.85
1906	27/6	4/1	18.18	20.00
1907	24/7	2/4	22.58	66.66
1908	29/15	4/7	34.09	63.63
1909	25/16	3/9	39.02	75.00
1910	31/24	2/11	43.63	84.61
1911	27/23	5/10	46.00	66.66
1912	37/20	11/8	35.08	42.10
1913	34/19	17/14	35.84	45.16
1914	47/17	13/17	26.56	56.66
1915	46/16	19/12	25.80	38.70

*The first number in each series represents successful women candidates, the second unsuccessful.

The increasing strength of the Guild in the northwest could not overcome women's ineligibility for office. As long as open membership was resisted, it remained impossible for women to have direct representation on the committees of cooperative societies. The Guild's branches were urged by the Central Committee to push for open membership, but the Guild's annual reports are not conscientious about charting the course of this campaign in hard numbers. Perhaps seeing the data in black and white would have been too depressing, so it was omitted. Also, it is doubtful that guildswomen were truly committed to the campaign because, as Llewelyn Davies admitted, "Guild members are very loth to deprive their husbands of rights, however much they desire to exercise their own."[90] But in 1902 the Guild did publish the results of a survey of its branches as to whether the cooperative societies to which they were affiliated permitted open membership. Of the 293 branches in existence that year, 205 responded (results are shown in Table 7).

Table 5
Female Candidacies for Educational Committees by Section[91]

Year	Southern Section	North-Western Section	Failure Rate Southern	Failure Rate North-Western
1897	*76/3	11/2	3.79	15.38
1898	78/2	15/7	2.50	31.81
1899	100/3	18/0	2.91	0.00
1900	103/3	17/2	2.83	10.52
1901	101/5	12/4	4.85	25.00
1902	100/6	17/5	5.66	22.72
1903	98/6	19/7	5.76	26.92
1904	119/3	34/4	2.45	10.52
1905	130/2	41/5	1.51	10.86
1906	162/11	36/3	6.35	7.69
1907	158/6	36/11	3.65	23.40
1908	183/10	37/10	5.18	21.27
1909	176/13	45/12	6.87	21.05
1910	148/12	50/10	7.50	16.66
1911	182/9	51/17	4.71	25.00
1912	204/12	65/11	5.55	14.47
1913	210/26	68/14	11.01	17.07
1914	216/16	72/20	6.89	21.73
1915	230/12	70/18	4.95	20.45

*The first number in each series represents successful women candidates, the second unsuccessful.

It should be noted that unlike the Cooperative Union, the Guild did not have a Scottish Section. It had planned for one when it had divided itself into sections and districts on the model of the Union in 1890. But the Scottish Women's Cooperative Guild, which emerged in Glasgow in 1889, never affiliated with the English women's organization. Sidney and Beatrice Webb maintain that the Scottish Guild encountered greater male opposition than the English.[92] Evidence in the "Woman's Corner" of the *Co-operative News* confirms their impressions. As one Scotswoman wrote cryptically to that column, "Ours is an adventure that has to be very delicately dealt with."[93] Branches of the Scottish Guild were under the jurisdiction of the educational committees of their cooperative societies. In England, Guild branches were independent, which left them without guaranteed funding but with what many guildswomen considered greater latitude when it came to pursuing causes men were reluctant to support, like the singing classes Mary Lawrenson's Guild branch wanted to establish.

Table 6
Guild Membership[94]

Year	Southern Branches/Members	North-Western Branches/Members	National Totals Branches/Members
1895	60/1872	61/3899	182/8004
1896	76/2426	64/4231	200/9093
1897	79/2551	81/5195	223/10,555
1898	84/2789	87/6404	237/12,103
1899	87/2906	100/6600	262/12,537
1900	87/3151	106/6579	273/12,809
1901	88/3142	109/6881	284/13,278
1902	83/3183	117/7399	293/14,136
1903	88/3513	132/8622	322/16,140
1904	104/4293	146/9781	359/18,556
1905	118/5016	153/10,458	395/20,460

The Guild's survey of open membership confirms that the northwest, the home of the Cooperative movement, lagged behind the south with respect to the inclusion of women as members of cooperative societies. The report on open membership even commented, "The actual effect of any restriction of member-ship is to exclude women . . . shutting out the people whose loyal support is the foundation of financial prosperity. The position is worst in the North-Western Section."[95] Interestingly, the report pointed out, "Open membership exists in many of the largest and most progressive societies."[96] However, because the noncompliant cooperative societies in the northwest were large, they could af-ford to ignore the Guild's reprimands. They needed to curry no favor from their female customers to make them regular shoppers at the stores; cooperative shopping was already a habit among women there.

It may therefore be concluded that a second explanation for the higher inci-dence of women seeking office in the south, and for their success, existed and that it was of greater consequence than the Guild's association with London and its environs. Namely, the men in the south were more tolerant of women's ac-tive presence in the movement than were men in the northwest. The simple ex-planation for this male tolerance was the movement's poverty in the south, which made southern men more appreciative of what women could do on its behalf. It certainly made directors of cooperative societies in the south less re-sistant to open membership, as struggling stores needed as much share capital as they could accumulate. In the northwest, on the other hand, the movement was well established; the habit of shopping at the "co-op" was engrained. There was no need for men there to concede women any space or voice in cooperation either to guarantee that they would "come and *buy*" or to maintain the fiscal solvency of their societies.

Table 7
1902 Guild Survey[97]

Section	Open	Either Husband or Wife & Children	Joint Membership & Children	One Member per Household	Misc.	Total
Midland	31	1	1	1	-	34
Northern	8	5	1	2	-	16
North-West	35	8	10	20	4	77
Southern	59	1	-	3	-	63
West & S.W.	12	1	-	2	-	15

The story of branch formation during the first few years of the Guild's existence amply illustrates the tolerant attitudes of men in the south and the reasons for them. Men there were eager to see Guild branches established in as many cooperative societies as possible. Although the statistics charting the Guild's development in its early years are sketchy, Llewelyn Davies maintained that when she became general secretary in 1889, only seven of the organization's fifty branches were located in the northwest.[98] Most other branches were in London and the home counties, and many of them had been formed at the instigation of men.[99] The southern men were quite frank about their motivations for supporting the Guild. As the secretary of the Tottenham Industrial Society's Guild branch reported, they wanted help with the "arduous task of building up this struggling society."[100]

However, whether "struggling" or prosperous, cooperative societies often offered very little to their Guild branches in terms of rooms for meetings, not to mention space for educational work or social activities. Of the 29 branches existing in 1887, twenty-one gave information on various occasions between 1884 and 1886 in the "Woman's Corner" of the *Co-operative News* regarding their meeting sites: eleven met in the rooms ordinarily used by the management or educational committees of their societies, one was given the society's lecture hall when it was not in use, two others were permitted the use of their societies' reading or assembly rooms, and six had to go off cooperative premises to meetings arranged at members' houses, coffee houses, or hired sites. Only one Guild branch had a room of its own, in Wallsend-on-Tyne, where the management committee had graciously "fitted up" a cottage for its use.[101]

In 1887, when Mary Lawrenson was the Guild's general secretary, she drew attention to the issue of space in her address to a conference held by the southern branches of the Guild. She pointed out that "want of a suitable room" stood in the way of branches starting the children's classes so many had desired to initiate.[102] She hoped that, "as time goes on the guild will acquire the use of rooms on all store premises, in which to hold meetings, classes, etc."[103] She stressed that when cooperative societies build new buildings or make additions to existing structures, they should remember "a room for the ladies."[104] But "a room for the ladies" was rarely remembered. Her successor as general secretary, Margaret Llewelyn Davies, was destined to struggle with the issue of space throughout her thirty-two years in office.

Like Virginia Woolf, Llewelyn Davies linked the issues of space and money, and with good reason: some cooperative societies actually charged Guild branches for their use of rooms "on Co-operative premises." What was worse, some of these would only give their branches money from their educational funds because they expected to get it back in room charges. As Llewelyn Davies observed:

The great majority of branches have the use of co-operative meeting rooms free, and in twenty-two cases where there is no room belonging to the store, the society or educational committee pays the rent of one. But in forty-four branches a large proportion, sometimes the whole of the grant or donation received, is swallowed up in the hire of a room, and in seven the cost is more than the grant. There are . . . ten branches where no money is received, and where the branch has to pay for their room. [There were 359 branches in 1904 when Llewelyn Davies wrote this.][105]

Because she knew being guaranteed "£500 a year" was as important as having "a room of one's own" if one hoped to do meaningful work for the Co-operative movement, Llewelyn Davies kept track of the number of branches receiving any aid at all from their societies. In the Guild's annual report for 1896, for instance, she recorded that there were 200 branches, one of which received £48 a year, three £40, one £20, two £12, eight £10, and forty from £1 to £10.[106] There were also nine branches that had their delegates' fares to the Guild's annual congress paid, and one or two that were guaranteed "expenses of all lectures and classes."[107] However, "the rest (about 50 or 60) of the branches report that they only receive help in the way of room and light, except a few, which are not even supported in this way."[108] In 1899, Llewelyn Davies began the practice of providing tables in the annual reports, showing how many branches were supported and by how much. It was then she discovered that many more than "a few" branches were not supported at all, while others had to share their funds. Sometimes large cooperative societies would have several stores and, consequently, several Guild branches, which would all have to make do on one grant. She lamented that women were "continually in the position of beggars for all their different needs."[109] Table 8 provides information regarding grants to Guild branches until 1921, the year Llewelyn Davies left office as general secretary and the keeping of such statistics ceased.

While these figures show that the percentage of Guild branches receiving annual grants more than doubled over the course of Llewelyn Davies's tenure as general secretary, they also indicate the men were hardly generous to the women. More than 30% of the branches in 1921 still could not count on regular annual grants from the societies to which they were affiliated, and most of those that could had to work with less than £10. Surprisingly, however, nowhere in the Guild's reports is it described how poverty curtailed branch work. Rather, one comes away with the impression that the guildswomen were pleased they managed to do so much with so little, like the house-proud working-class wives they were.

Table 8
Grants to Guild Branches[110]

Year	Total Number of Branches	Total Receiving Grants over £10	Total Receiving Grants under £10	Total Number Receiving Grants	Percentage Receiving Grants
1899	262	25	55	80	30.5%
1900	273	32	69	101	36.9%
1901	284	33	73	106	37.3%
1902	293	35	80	115	39.2%
1903	322	39	86	125	38.8%
1904	359	44	97	141	39.2%
1905	395	52	107	159	40.2%
1906	424	54	124	178	41.9%
1907	452	56	135	191	42.2%
1908	495	61	166	227	45.8%
1909	509	62	195	257	50.4%
1910	521	62	201	263	50.4%
1911	525	69	194	263	50.0%
1912	537	75	229	304	56.6%
1913	558	81	264	345	61.8%
1914	591	86	277	363	61.4%
1915	611	95	267	362	59.2%
1916	609	100	308	408	66.9%
1917	630	89	329	418	66.3%
1918	666	102	331	433	65.0%
1919	716	112	372	484	67.5%
1920	784	140	406	546	69.6%
1921	905	194	426	620	68.5%

The annual reports of the Guild are litanies of causes behind which cooperative women threw their energies each year, including, for example, campaigns to extend cooperation to the poor and for a minimum wage for female cooperative employees, as well as for the vote and national maternity health care benefits. However, reading between the lines it becomes abundantly clear how the poverty in which male cooperators kept the women warped the development of the Guild. The Guild prided itself on being a democratic organization, governed by the decisions made at its annual congresses, not from the top down by its Central Committee. Each branch was entitled to send delegates to congress, one for every twenty-five members. But without branch funds, these working-class women delegates had to pay their own way, resulting in low percentages of branches sending representatives to annual congresses, as illustrated in Table 9.

Table 9
Branches Sending Delegates to the Annual Congresses[111]

Year	Total Number of Branches	Number Sending Delegates	Percentages
1899	262	125	47.7%
1900	273	123	45.0%
1901	284	166	58.4%
1902	293	163	55.6%
1903	322	119	36.9%
1904	359	169	47.0%
1905	395	183	46.3%
1906	424	235	55.4%
1907	452	218	48.2%
1908	495	255	51.5%
1909	509	290	56.9%
1910	521	315	60.4%
1911	525	296	56.3%
1912	537	291	54.1%
1913	558	307	55.0%
1914	591	302	51.0%
1915	611	404	66.1%
1916	609	360	59.1%
1917	630	385	61.1%
1918	666	216	32.4%
1919	716	420	58.6%
1920	784	438	55.8%
1921	905	483	64.4%

Branch poverty also undermined the Guild's claim to be a democratic organization in another way: it made it difficult for rank-and-file members to rise to positions of national leadership within the Guild. A review of the names of the women serving on the Guild's Central Committee each year reveals much repetition despite the rule prohibiting service beyond three consecutive years for everyone except the general secretary. This rule had been put in place in 1888 to ensure that everyone who so desired would have an opportunity to serve the organization on the national level.[112] However, it appears only a very limited number of working-class women had the personal financial resources, not to mention the time, to spend climbing up through the ranks of branch, district, and sectional service, thereby becoming well enough known to win a seat on the Central Committee. Members of the committee were elected annually by the branches from lists of nominees submitted by them. Successful candidates were those who had built up reputations through years of service as district or sectional secretaries. Since the official position of the Guild was that service should be voluntary, no salaries were paid.[113] Women without sufficient spending money of their own therefore needed to rely on funding from their branches. But few branches were wealthy enough to provide the financial support their members required.

Insufficient funds not only made it difficult for working-class women to rise within the Guild, it also limited their prospects for gaining national offices within the Cooperative movement. Male opposition to women holding such positions was at the root of the men's miserliness. Mary Cottrell realized how fatal was the combination of poverty and male prejudice. In 1919 she became only the second woman the Guild managed to get elected to a seat on a section of the Central Board of the Cooperative Union other than the Southern. She sat for the Midland Section. Cottrell also earned another distinction during her career in the service of the Guild and the Cooperative movement. In 1921 she became the first woman ever elected as a director of the English Cooperative Wholesale Society. She knew it took money to promote a candidate and bring her into enough prominence for her to win an election. She wrote to Llewelyn Davies with respect to women running for national offices in the movement, "It is quite useless just to nominate a 'nice capable woman' from a management committee unless a great deal of time and effort is given to making her well known."[114]

Llewelyn Davies became particularly frustrated by the Guild's inability to place a woman on the North-Western Section of the Central Board. She had made the cultivation of that area of the country her special concern as general secretary. In 1895, she announced in the annual report that the Guild was promoting the candidacy of Miss Sarah Reddish for a position on the board for that section.[115] Someone more suited to represent that area of the country would have been difficult to find. Reddish was from Bolton. She had worked in textile manufacturing since the age of eleven, eventually rising to the position of forewoman in a hosiery mill. She was the first Guild organizer Llewelyn Davies had hired to stimulate the development of branches in Lancashire and the West Riding; she served in that position for two years, from 1893 to 1895. Reddish had long been involved with the Guild. Her Bolton branch had been founded in 1886 and was one of the few outposts the Guild then had in Lancashire. She served as president of the branch from 1886 until 1901, and on the Guild's Central Committee in 1889, and in the year she was the organization's president, 1897.[116] She was also involved in organizing women's trade unions and fighting to secure female employees a minimum wage. She wrote papers for the Guild on cooperation and on women's suffrage. Moreover, she was a confident public speaker with considerable abilities as an administrator, becoming responsible for the formation of the North of England Society for Women's Suffrage in 1903.[117] Jill Norris and Jill Liddington make considerable mention of her activities in their history of working women's suffrage agitation in Lancashire.[118] But despite this impressive resume, she never won election on any of the five occasions she ran for a seat on the North-Western Section of the Central Board.

Ironically, it was precisely this impressive resume which prevented her election. Given the reluctance of male cooperators in the northwest to concede to women any roles much beyond that of shopping at the stores, it was to be expected that such men would oppose a feminist who insisted on women's right to a place and a voice in public spheres such as the workplace and Parliament. Mike Savage's study of the domination maintained by men over working women in the Preston weaving trade demonstrates that a male network of fathers, husbands, and factory overseers controlled women's employment opportunities.[119] It makes clear that such women were not free agents determining the course of their lives without male supervision. Sarah Reddish, however, lived free from male control, rose to an overseer's position, and pursued a career as a public agitator. It is therefore not surprising that her candidacies fell victim to a male backlash against women's independence. However, opposition to the election of women to national offices within the Cooperative movement was so entrenched in the northwest that even candidates whose feminism was not as overt as Reddish's fared no better than she. In 1900, Mrs. Bury made her first of seven consecutive attempts to secure a seat on the North-Western Section of the board. Since she was married, a mother, and no longer worked for wages outside the home, she should have been more acceptable to voters desirous of maintaining either separate spheres or the patriarchal control of public women. Yet none of her bids for office were successful.

The intractability of the male opposition to the candidacies of Reddish and Bury frustrated Llewelyn Davies because the rhetoric of the Cooperative movement claimed there was no gender discrimination within it. She observed in the pages of the Guild's annual report for 1920:

It is always said there is equality of opportunity for men and women in the movement. Certainly, most of the doors are open. But the seats are full, and possession is nine-tenths of the law, so that in reality the opportunity is not equal, and seats are hard to win.[120]

In the northwest, in particular, the seats were full. Men there did not see the inclusion of women as necessary to the survival of the Cooperative movement, as did the men in the south. Consequently they were unwilling to open up to women spaces and places hitherto off limits to them.

The Women's Cooperative Guild never managed to establish a branch at every store. In 1904, Llewelyn Davies observed that there were 364 Guild branches affiliated to 272 cooperative societies, but that there were 1481 cooperative societies in Britain.[121] To some extent male opposition accounts for the Guild's failure. It would have been very difficult for a wife to become involved with a branch if her husband was opposed to her doing so. In fact, because the working-class household was so dependent on the services of the wife/mother, the entire family was liable to resent her having outside interests.[122] She would have been unable to sneak out of the house for meetings, and indeed, she, herself, may have not wished to "waste" the household money on branch dues, even if they were only 6d. a year.[123] Evidence suggests that women who became involved with the Guild had supportive husbands.[124] Unfortunately for the Guild, fewer such men appear to have lived in the northwest, where cooperators were most numerous and the possibility for the most extensive branch development existed. Table 10 illustrates further the extent of the Guild's failure to organize the women of the Cooperative movement, giving figures for ten-year intervals around the turn of the century.

Just as the Guild failed to establish a branch at every store, it failed to convince the majority of women who shopped at the stores that the Cooperative movement was about more than the "divi." Despite the efforts of historians like

Gillian Scott to argue otherwise,[125] few female cooperators bothered to join the Guild and become involved in its efforts to foster the revolutionary and idealistic ends to which cooperation supposedly tended. As Paul Johnson has observed, the majority of women who shopped at the stores were practical-minded, "more interested in money than social development; it was the dividend and the uses to which it could be put in managing a family's finances that was the real inducement to co-operate."[126] The Guild's leaders often represented a point of view that such women opposed. For example, the leaders condemned the high store prices that brought the high dividends.[127] They argued that high prices excluded the poor from participating in cooperation. Most women cooperators found that sort of idealism too costly to take seriously.[128] Hence they never entertained the notion of joining the Guild; they had so little in common with the perspective of its leaders. The Guild estimated that even without open membership half of the shareholders in the Cooperative movement at any given time were women.[129] If that is so, 45,539 Guild members out of the more than two million female cooperators for the year 1920 represents a poor showing.[130] It is likely that every woman who shopped at a cooperative store had heard of the Guild, but only a small fraction of them ever joined it.

Table 10
Cooperative Societies and Guild Branches[131]

Year	Number of Societies	Number of Shareholders	Number of Guild Branches	Number of Guild Members
1890	1240	962,000	54	1,402
1900	1439	1,707,000	273	12,809
1910	1421	2,542,000	521	25,942
1920	1379	4,505,000	784	45,539

As time passed, the Guild's leadership became increasingly left-of-center with respect to certain political and women's issues. It supported a negotiated peace during World War I, adult suffrage, and divorce law reform. Even some Guild branches had difficulties with such advanced views, and interestingly, those that did tended to be in the northwest. Mrs. Bury's branch at Darwen in Lancashire fought with the Central Committee over its stand on adult suffrage and divorce law reform. Eventually, the Darwen branch seceded from the national organization.[132] The northwest was the stronghold of the Cooperative movement, but the opinions of the Guild's leadership alienated women there as much as the organization's very existence worried some men, thus stunting the Guild's growth.

Finally, the conditions of a working-class woman's life made involvement with the Guild either difficult or unattractive. There were children to bear and care for, and housework to do. Those activities were extraordinarily time consuming a century ago. Working-class houses had few amenities that would make housework easier,[133] and the high birthrates among the working class guaranteed that most married women were frequently pregnant and had little ones demanding attention.[134] Moreover, a cooperative woman, even though she was married to a well-paid man with a secure job, may still have had to supplement the family income on occasion. There would consequently have been little time for the Guild. Indeed, evidence suggests that women who did join the Guild, especially those who rose to leadership positions like Mrs. Bury, had no need to work for wages, had grown children, and had devised a "system" for doing their housework so that it did not interfere with Guild activities.[135]

Then, too, there were pleasures associated with domesticity that could lead a working-class wife to prioritize homemaking over public activism on behalf of the Guild and its causes. Thankful that she was married to a good provider rather than to a drunk or a libertine like so many other working-class women, she gloried in her role as a wife and mother. Since cooperation drew its strength from this respectable portion of the working class, it is not surprising that so few female cooperators were attracted to the Guild despite their commitment to the stores and the dividends they produced.

The gendered geography of the Cooperative movement at the turn of the century was thus a product of the interplay of several forces. Male prejudice against women in certain public arenas prompted the men to attempt to control women's activities by restricting the Guild's access to meeting rooms and funding, and to oppose women's election to managerial positions within the movement. In the northwest, the prosperity of cooperative societies reinforced male prejudice, while in the south the men were more tolerant because they depended on women to help them in the pioneer work of establishing stores in the "co-operative desert." Finally, the circumstances of working-class women's lives made many female cooperators either unable or reluctant to use what the Guild referred to as their "basket power" to demand a voice or place beyond that which was permitted them. In sum, the factors that kept cooperative women fiscally and spatially impoverished were embedded in the socioeconomic realities of working-class life that shaped cooperative culture.

NOTES

1. Carol Dyhouse, *Feminism and Family in England, 1880–1939* (New York: Basil Blackwell, 1989), 83.

2. Seccombe, "Patriarchy Stabilized," 55; Rose "Gender Antagonism and Class Conflict," 191–192. Rose mentions Humphries's thesis here.

3. Rose, *Limited Livelihoods*, 6; and Rose, "Gender Antagonism and Class Conflict," 198–202

4. Benenson, "The 'Family Wage' and Working Women's Consciousness in Britain," 77.

5. Seccombe, "Patriarchy Stabilized," 64. Further, Patrick Joyce notices in *Work, Society and Politics: The Culture of the Factory in Later Victorian England* (New Brunswick, NJ: Rutgers University Press, 1980), that the absence of a breadwinner wage caused weavers to assert their dominance over women at work in other ways, e.g., by forbidding them to tune their own looms (112–113).

6. Levine, *Feminist Lives in Victorian England*, 9; Lewis, *Women in England*, 49; Gittens, *Fair Sex*, 130–133; Harrison, *Prudent Revolutionaries*, 127–128; Liddington and Norris, *One Hand Tied Behind Us*, 54.

7. Lewis, *Women in England*, 19–20, 28; Gittens, *Fair Sex*, 133; Liddington and Norris, *One Hand Tied Behind Us*, 54. Elizabeth Roberts, however, realizes that sharing housework did not make wives their husbands' equals, see "Working Wives and Their Families," in Barker and Drake (eds.), *Population and Society in Britain*, 152–153.

8. Seccombe, "Patriarchy Stabilized," says men in skilled trades other than weaving were more often protectionists (73).

9. Sally Alexander notes this about the TUC during the WTUL's phase of advocating the organization of trade unions for women rather than protectionism: Alexander, "'Bringing Women into Line with Men': The Women's Trade Union League, 1874–1921," in Alexander, *Becoming a Woman*, 69.

10. Savage, "Capitalist and Patriarchal Relations at Work: Preston Cotton Weaving, 1890–1940," in Murgatroyd et al. (eds.), *Localities, Class and Gender*, 183.

11. Rose, *Limited Livelihoods*, 142; Alexander, "'Bringing Women into Line with Men': The Women's Trade Union League, 1874–1921," in Alexander, *Becoming a Woman*, 61.

12. Ross, *Love and Toil*, 79–80.

13. Jane Humphries, "'. . . The Most Free Form of Objection . . .': The Sexual Division of Labor and Women's Work in Nineteenth-century England," 930.

14. Lewis, *Women in England*, x–xi.

15. Gurney, *Co-operative Culture and the Politics of Consumption in England*, 18.

16. Elizabeth Roberts in "Working Wives and Their Families," in Barker and Drake (eds.), *Population and Society in Britain* notes that women would be relieved of the obligation to contribute to income when their children became old enough to work (143).

17. Llewelyn Davies, *The Women's Co-operative Guild*, 148.

18. Ibid., 150.

19. Ibid., 151.

20. Ibid., 150.

21. Roberts, "Women's Strategies, 1850–1940," in Lewis (ed.), *Labour and Love*, 238.

22. Taylor, *Eve and the New Jerusalem*, 112.

23. Giles, *Women, Identity and Private Life in Britain*, 3, 19.

24. Ibid., 20.

25. Lewis, "The Working-class Wife and Mother and State Intervention, 1870–1918," in Lewis (ed.), *Labour and Love*, 108.

26. Ellen Ross, "Labour and Love: Rediscovering London's Working-class Mothers, 1870–1918," in Lewis (ed.), *Labour and Love*, 74.

27. Lewis, "The Working-class Wife and Mother and State Intervention, 1870–1918," in Lewis (ed.), *Labour and Love*, 112.

28. Martin Pugh, "Domesticity and the Decline of Feminism," in Smith (ed.) *British Feminism in the Twentieth Century*, 153 .

29. Llewelyn Davies complains about the difficulty of luring working-class women away from domesticity in *The Women's Co-operative Guild*, 38–39.

30. Joyce, *Work, Society and Politics*, 116.

31. Waters, *British Socialism and the Politics of Popular Culture*, 160–162.

32. Ibid.

33. "Woman's Corner," *Co-operative News*, December 7, 1907.

34. Ross, *Love and Toil*, 76–77.

35. Ibid.

36. Statistics are available for 1902 because of a survey the Guild compiled that year. Women's Cooperative Guild, *The Nineteenth Annual Report of the Women's Co-operative Guild* (Manchester: Cooperative Wholesale Society's Printing Works, 1902), 7.

37. Ibid.

38. "Woman's Corner," *Co-operative News*, May 30, 1903. In this article the director of the Oldham Cooperative Society offers this as well as other excuses for the prohibition on open membership.

39. Women's Cooperative Guild, *The Nineteenth Annual Report of the Women's Co-operative Guild*, 8.

40. "Woman's Corner," *Co-operative News*, May 12, 1883.

41. "Woman's Corner," *Co-operative News*, April 14, 1883.

42. "Woman's Corner," *Co-operative News*, August 2, 1884.

43. "Woman's Corner," *Co-operative News*, January 6, 1883.

44. "Woman's Corner," *Co-operative News*, February 17, 1883.

45. "Woman's Corner," *Co-operative News*, May 12, 1883.

46. Clark, *The Struggle for the Breeches*, 218.

47. Taylor, *Eve and the New Jerusalem*, 268.

48. "Woman's Corner," *Co-operative News*, May 26, 1883.

49. Ibid.

50. Levine, *Feminist Lives in Victorian England*, 171.

51. Llewelyn Davies, *The Women's Co-operative Guild*, 100. She also mistakenly claims here that the Guild managed to change this way of looking at women attending quarterly meetings.

52. Ibid., 161.

53. Since nonmembers were not permitted entry to quarterly meetings and membership was usually in the husband's name, Woolwich must have had open membership, which permitted women to become members in their own names and therefore to attend quarterly business meetings and run for cooperative offices.

54. "Woman's Corner," *Co-operative News*, March 8, 1884.

55. Ibid.

56. "Woman's Corner," *Co-operative News*, June 7, 1884.

57. "Woman's Corner," *Co-operative News*, September 6, 1884.

58. "Woman's Corner," *Co-operative News*, April 4, 1885.

59. Ibid.

60. "Woman's Corner," *Co-operative News*, February 7 and 14, 1885.

61. "Woman's Corner," *Co-operative News*, August 15, 1885.

62. Ibid.

63. "Woman's Corner," *Co-operative News*, November 7, 1885.

64. "Woman's Corner," *Co-operative News*, April 4, 1885.

65. "Woman's Corner," *Co-operative News*, December 4, 1886.

66. "Woman's Corner," *Co-operative News*, June 16, 1888.

67. "Woman's Corner," *Co-operative News*, July 10, 1886.

68. "Woman's Corner," *Co-operative News*, December 3, 1887.

69. Catherine Webb, whose father had instructed her in the business side of the movement, being himself the manager of the Battersea and Wandsworth Cooperative Society and later a director of the Cooperative Wholesale Society, was commissioned by the Guild's Central Committee to write a pamphlet on how to read a balance sheet. The pamphlet was used by the branches for classes on the subject for their members.

70. These figures are taken from the annual reports of the Women's Cooperative Guild, available at the Hull University Library and the London School of Economics.

71. Ibid.

72. Gaffin and Thoms, *Caring and Sharing*, 6; Liddington and Norris, *One Hand Tied Behind Us*, 40.

73. For example, in *Feminism and the Politics of Working Women*, Gillian Scott concedes that the Guild was kept underfunded by male cooperators yet refuses to acknowledge that this enabled the men to control women's activities (18).

74. Llewelyn Davies, *The Women's Co-operative Guild*, 21.

75. "Woman's Corner," *Co-operative News*, July 7, 1894.

76. These figures are taken from the annual reports of the Women's Cooperative Guild, available at the Hull University Library and the London School of Economics.

77. Llewelyn Davies, *The Women's Co-operative Guild*, 39.

78. Margaret Llewelyn Davies, *Life As We Have Known It*, (New York: W. W. Norton & Company, Inc., 1975), 96.

79. Ibid.

80. "Woman's Corner," *Co-operative News*, June 6, 1896.

81. Webb certainly felt he was a feminist and portrayed him as such despite his behavior toward her; see her tribute to him for the hundredth anniversary of his birth, "Women's Corner," *Co-operative News*, April 21, 1917. More recently, Barbara Taylor has portrayed him as a feminist in *Eve and the New Jerusalem*.

82. "Woman's Corner," *Co-operative News*, June 5, 1897.

83. Among the publications Holyoake produced in the last decade of his life are: *Bygones Worth Remembering*, *The Co-operative Movement Today*, *Essentials of Co-operative Education*, a new edition of his *History of Co-operation in England*, *The Jubilee History of the Leeds Industrial Co-operative Society*, *The New Party of Profit Seizers*, *Robert Owen the Precursor of Social Progress*, and *Sixty Years of an Agitator's Life*.

84. Bonner, *British Co-operation*, 99.

85. Women's Cooperative Guild, *The Fourteenth Annual Report of the Women's Co-operative Guild*, 17.

86. Llewelyn Davies, *The Women's Co-operative Guild*, 28.

87. Women's Cooperative Guild, *The Seventeenth Annual Report of the Women's Co-operative Guild* (Manchester: Cooperative Wholesale Society's Printing Works, 1900), 10.

88. Ibid.

89. These figures are taken from the annual reports of the Women's Cooperative Guild, available at the Hull University Library and the London School of Economics.

90. Llewelyn Davies, *The Women's Co-operative Guild*, 99.

91. These figures are taken from the annual reports of the Women's Cooperative Guild, available at the Hull University Library and the London School of Economics.

92. Sidney and Beatrice Webb, *The Consumers' Co-operative Movement*, 176–177.

93. "Woman's Corner," *Co-operative News*, March 1, 1890. Also see the May 31, 1890, edition of the "Woman's Corner" for a report of a discussion about merging the two guilds at the Cooperative Union congress held in Glasgow that year.

94. These figures are taken from the annual reports of the Women's Cooperative Guild, available at the Hull University Library and the London School of Economics.

95. Women's Coopertive Guild, *The Nineteenth Annual Report of the Women's Co-operative Guild* (Manchester: Cooperative Wholesale Society's Printing Works, 1902), 8.

96. Ibid.

97. Ibid., 7.

98. Llewelyn Davies, *The Women's Co-operative Guild*, 28.

99. Information about the founding of individual branches can be found in the branch reports that appeared regularly in the "Woman's Corner" of the *Co-operative News* during the middle to late 1880s.

100. "Woman's Corner," *Co-operative News*, May 7, 1887.

101. "Woman's Corner," *Co-operative News*, May 2, 1885. By 1914, however, Wallsend-on-Tyne had lost access to the cottage and was meeting in the boardroom of the store; see "Women's Corner," *Co-operative News*, August 8, 1914.

102. "Woman's Corner," *Co-operative News*, February 26, 1887.

103. Ibid.

104. Ibid.

105. Women's Cooperative Guild, *The Twenty-first Annual Report of the Women's Co-operative Guild* (Manchester: Cooperative Wholesale Society's Printing Works, 1904), 14.

106. Women's Cooperative Guild, *The Thirteenth Annual Report of the Women's Co-operative Guild*, 17.

107. Ibid.

108. Ibid.

109. Women's Cooperative Guild, *The Sixteenth Annual Report of the Women's Co-operative Guild* (Manchester: Cooperative Wholesale Society's Printing Works, 1899), 9.

110. These statistics were compiled from the annual reports of the Women's Co-operative Guild, available at Hull University Library and the London School of Economics.

111. Ibid.

112. Llewelyn Davies, *The Women's Co-operative Guild*, 51.

113. Ibid., 58; and Webb, *The Woman with the Basket*, 47.

114. London School of Economics, coll. misc. 268 m363, vol. I, item 47, folio 148.

115. Women's Cooperative Guild, *The Twelfth Annual Report of the Women's Co-operative Guild* (Manchester: Cooperative Wholesale Society's Printing Works, 1895), 18.

116. Llewelyn Davies, *The Women's Co-operative Guild*, 28.

117. Olive Banks, *The Biographical Dictionary of British Feminists, vol. 1, 1800–1930* (Brighton: Wheatsheaf Books Ltd., 1985), 169.

118. Liddington and Norris, *One Hand Tied Behind Us*, for example 163, 224, 291.

119. Savage, "Capitalist and Patriarchal Relations at Work: Preston Cotton Weaving, 1890–1940," in Murgatroyd et al. (eds.), *Localities, Class and Gender*.

120. Women's Cooperative Guild, *The Thirty-seventh Annual Report of the Women's Co-operative Guild* (Manchester: Cooperative Wholesale Society's Printing Works, 1920), 2.

121. Llewelyn Davies, *The Women's Co-operative Guild*, 4–6.

122. Norris and Liddington in *One Hand Tied Behind Us* (217) maintain this resentment was often present.

123. By the 1920s, dues had risen to as much as 4s. per year in some branches; see Webb, *The Woman with the Basket*, 144.

124. Llewelyn Davies, *The Women's Co-operative Guild*, 61.

125. Gillian Scott, "'Working Out Their Own Salvation': Women's Autonomy and Divorce Law Reform in the Co-operative Movement, 1910–1920," in Yeo (ed.) *New Views of Co-operation*, 132.

126. Johnson, *Saving and Spending*, 127.

127. Ibid., 130.

128. Ibid., 143.

129. "Women's Corner," *Co-operative News*, January 26, 1918.

130. The Scottish Guild fared no better. About one million of the four and a half million cooperators in Britain in 1920 were Scottish, and there were only a little over 17,000 women in the Scottish Guild. The figure for Scottish Guild membership is extrapolated from information found in the "Women's Corner" of the *Co-operative News* for May 25, 1918.

131. Statistics for the Cooperative Movement are taken from Gurney, *Co-operative Culture and the Politics of Consumption in England* (241–242) who relies on G.D.H. Cole. The figures for the movement as a whole include England, Scotland, and Wales. The Guild's statistics include England and Wales only. Generally speaking, Scotland's number of shareholders may be computed by factoring 20% out of the totals for all three countries.

132. Hull University Library, DCW 1/7, Minute books of the Central Committee, April 25 and 26, 1918.

133. Roberts, *A Woman's Place*, chapter 4.

134. Ibid., chapter 3.

135. Llewelyn Davies, *The Women's Co-operative Guild*, 151–152.

Part II

Angels in the Store

The Late Miss GREENWOOD,
Vice-President (Rochdale).

Mrs. M. LAWRENSON
(Woolwich).

The Late
Mrs. B. JONES
(Norwood).

Mrs. ACLAND, *President*.

Miss SHUFFLEBOTHAM
(now Mrs. Trotman),
Treasurer (Coventry).

The Late
Mrs. HELLIWELL
(Hebden Bridge).

Miss ALLEN (now Mrs. Redfearn),
General Secretary (Manchester).

FIRST CENTRAL COMMITTEE, 1884.

Reproduced courtesy of the Co-operative Women's Guild.

Chapter 3

The Early Leaders of the Women's Cooperative Guild

Mary Lawrenson knew what it was like to be alone in the world. In 1872, she took a teaching position in a small village far from her home. She was only twenty-one and missed her family so much that she "was constantly looking out for letters from home."[1] This brought her into contact with the village postmistress, known among the villagers as "the owd humpty woman" because of deformities caused by rheumatic fever.[2] This poor woman was a widow and none of her six children had survived to adulthood. Shunned by the villagers because of her physical disabilities, she had not a friend in the world until Lawrenson entered her life. The two spent Christmas together that year. Had they not had one another, each would have been alone for the holiday. Lawrenson judged the woman to be "the kindest, most lovable, and most improving acquaintance" she had ever had the "good fortune to make," and considered it a shame that none of the villagers had ever taken the time to get to know the crippled postmistress.[3] "She lived only one or two doors off the co-operative store—and, had there been a branch of our guild" the situation would have been different.[4] A community of women would have existed to support one another, and this lonely woman would have been included.

Mary Lawrenson was one of the founders of the Women's Cooperative Guild and served as its general secretary from 1885 to 1889. Along with its other early leaders, she worked to make the Guild an organization on which cooperators could depend to construct an environment which would further the movement and help build the future Cooperative Commonwealth. Accordingly, these early leaders made it their business to teach the women who shopped at the stores that cooperation was about more than accumulating dividends. They stressed that it had as its objective the creation of a more moral economy—one based on association, and not on competition like capitalism's. The early leaders encouraged the formation of children's classes to introduce the next generation to cooperation's principles and objectives at as young an age as possible. Also, they hosted recreational activities for youths and families to discourage the teenagers from becoming involved in public house and music hall culture and to show families that cooperation could meet more than just their need for groceries. However, they also hoped that the Guild would help women as women. When Alice Acland declared as the fourth objective of the Guild "[the improvement] of the condition of women all over the kingdom,"[5] she had in mind using the Guild as a support group for housewives. The Guild's meetings would give them an opportunity to gather outside their homes at least one night a week to share their concerns, interests, and worries with one another. They would talk about cooperation, but they would also become interested in one another and form friendships so that no one need feel as though she were alone in the world. Judging by Lawrenson's comments about the possibility of the Guild including "the owd humpty woman," she would have kept the organization's community of women open even to non-cooperators. Single women rarely made enough to be able to participate in the movement. So the widowed postmistress was probably too poor to be a shopper or a shareholder at a cooperative store. However, she was not to be excluded by guildswomen. Women like her would become adopted members of the cooperative family.

Because the Guild's leaders hoped to use their community of women to create a cooperative family on which men, women, and children could depend for support, it is questionable as to whether they saw themselves as acting in the public sphere. They may have considered the Cooperative movement to be as much a part of the private sphere as their homes, and therefore an appropriate arena for women's efforts.[6] On the other hand, they may have been acting within the tradition of Victorian feminists, whom Susan Kingsley Kent has observed trying to moralize the public sphere by infusing it with womanly values from the private.[7] Or perhaps cooperation and feminism were for them so similar that the two had become merged in their minds.

The Guild's early leaders operated from a relational feminist perspective, although most of them would have classified themselves as cooperators not feminists. However, there were certainly similarities between the cultural projects upon which cooperators and feminists were embarked. As Peter Gurney has maintained, cooperators were involved in the construction of a new way of life—a revolutionary new culture that would function as an alternative to capitalism's consumer culture.[8] This entailed a transformation of individual behavior analogous to what Victorian feminists hoped to achieve, because cooperators sought to imbue individuals with such values as selfless caring for others, values usually regarded as more natural to women and the private sphere than to men and the public. Thus the cooperative objectives at which the Guild's early leaders aimed were compatible with feminism's. Cooperation's Owenite roots also contributed to making the movement's cultural objectives similar to feminism's. Barbara Taylor observes of the Owenites that they sought to develop alternative styles of recreation, for instance. These would be family-centered and include women and children, in contrast to the male-dominated leisure activities of working-class culture.[9] Similarly, cooperators sponsored entertainments of an improving sort aimed at families.[10] Their objective was the same as that of their Owenite forebears and that of feminists—the creation of a social environment capable of inculcating associative values appropriate to life in the better world that their movement would create. In this spirit the early leaders of the Guild worked to make a cooperative family that would be a safe haven from the competitive, capitalist world and its immoral popular culture. This family would be entirely separate from the public world of capitalism, as several Guild leaders spoke of instituting associated homes for cooperators, cooperative holiday resorts, cooperative schools, reading rooms, libraries, and choral societies, as well as cooperative factories and farms to supply the cooperative stores.

Because the cooperative world was a sphere apart from the capitalist world, the early leaders of the Guild thought it appropriate for women to help men in its construction. They believed there existed tasks uniquely suited to women in that regard. For instance, Alice Acland, co-founder of the Guild with Lawrenson, advised female cooperators to be "the sunbeams, the encouragers."[11] The angels in the house thus became the angels in the store. But on the construction site of the Cooperative Commonwealth, the guildswomen encountered difficulties. There were no precise guidelines for defining what it meant to be a "sunbeam" or an "encourager." So guildswomen began to trespass on territories men had reserved for their own work within the movement, which, of course, produced male resistance. Also, it proved difficult to create a community of mutually supportive women in a society riven by class divisions. Class-generated personal animosities and ideological differences consequently poisoned guildswomen's relationships with one another. Moreover, they began to realize that some of their objectives were mutually conflicting. How, for example, was one to reconcile the goal of creating associated homes, where women would be freed from the obligation to perform household duties, with the desire of so many cooperative women, whether Guild members or not, for a private, but reformed, domesticity wherein housewives would be valued for their skills as homemakers and mothers? There could be no Cooperative Commonwealth until these difficulties were overcome, and unfortunately, attitudes and behaviors engendered by the Old Immoral World tended to make that impossible. Both the Women's Cooperative Guild and the Cooperative movement were caught in the trap that had ensnared so many utopia builders before them: the only way to create a more perfect world is to have one already. If, as Owenite-influenced utopians in particular presumed, the individual's personality is a product of nurture more than nature, the creation of a perfect environment for the nurturing of individuals becomes problematic without there already being exceptional individuals present to create it. There must be in existence an elite group of people who have escaped the negative influence of the environment, who have seen a vision for a better future, and who have become able to actualize it within their own lives. These people are naturally gifted, unlike the masses who are slaves to their environments. Hence they undermine the environmentalist position, and any hope that the future utopia will inaugurate a less class-stratified society as well, since they prove that it is natural for some to be superior to others.[12]

Alice Acland hoped the "Woman's Corner" might unite "the great band of co-operative womankind in England" so that they would no longer be divided, "but all co-operate together, each lending a helping hand to help all others."[13] She tried to use the column to extend assistance across the divide separating her from working-class women cooperators. Comfortably situated in the world, her idea of helping the working-class women in the movement centered on providing household and cooking hints so that their husbands would not be "driven from their own firesides to . . . the public-house" for comfort and food.[14] Often the "Corner" stressed that the wife was to blame if her husband was a drunkard because she had failed in her domestic responsibilities. So too if her children were out on the streets. Acland therefore provided her readers with suggestions for home entertainments to amuse the children within the house.[15] Acland felt that respectability was accessible to everyone, regardless of income level. All that was needed was the housewife's determination to overcome the circumstances of her situation. The research of historians has shown that it was possible for some women to accomplish this miracle. Ellen Ross has found working-class women living in the worst of conditions who nevertheless maintained respectable behavior in their own and their families' dress, speech and conduct.[16] Anne Phillips speaks of impoverished middle-class women who preserved a veneer of respectability despite their circumstances.[17] Acland undoubtedly was personally acquainted with women cooperators from both classes whose determination had enabled them to overcome the obstacles presented by their environments.

Like Acland, the middle-class Edith Wilson, who was active in the Guild and became a frequent correspondent to the "Woman's Corner," offered advice to her working-class sisters on how they should conduct their affairs. For instance, she once suggested that classes be run for working-class girls on Saturdays to train them in domestic duties so that "they are helped into situations as servants" and, once married, know "the arts that make a home comfortable."[18] She had a truly limited ability to conceive of working-class women doing anything other than housework, and she acknowledged that the limitations of her imagination were class based. She confessed her "experience in economy [was] drawn from housekeeping on several hundreds a year, paid yearly"; so she could not imagine what it must be like to have to stretch "less than £100 a year paid in weekly instalments."[19] She therefore suggested that housewives, who had experienced provisioning families on "an income of say 20s. a week" send their tips for economizing to the "Corner" for publication."[20]

Wilson attributed poverty to the working-class housewife's ignorance, not to insufficient wages. In this respect, she was in step with the thinking of many middle-class observers of the working class.[21] On one occasion she happened to be "in a small grocer's shop . . . in a small street of a new workmen's suburb" talking to the daughter of the owner, with whom she was friendly, when "a child came in with an inarticulate murmur, laid down a halfpenny, and retired with a single candle."[22] She could not understand why anyone would buy only one candle when it was cheaper to buy four for three half-pence. She concluded: "Either there is [a wife] . . . who is never three half-pence ahead of the world . . . or she is someone who never looks forward so much as four days."[23] Wilson could not believe that the former was a possibility: "Is such poverty credible?" she asked.[24] So it had to be the housewife's inability to manage her husband's wages that had put the family into the position of wasting what money it had.

The wealthy Wilson was not alone in her lack of understanding of the behaviors of the destitute. Working-class guildswomen, who managed on "less than £100 a year paid in weekly instalments," led comfortable lives when compared to their poorer sisters who sent their children to buy one single candle. They might fear that the illness or death of their husbands would plunge them into situations which the Edith Wilsons of the world found hardly "credible," but generally they congratulated themselves on having it better than those trapped in chronic poverty. Often, they professed, the poor had only themselves to blame for their circumstances. Like true cooperators, they believed self-help was in everybody's reach, expressing an element in the cooperative creed which stood in stark contrast to the Owenite environmentalism that also informed the movement. Hence they believed there must be some innate moral failing in the characters of those trapped by poverty. Articles Acland ran in the "Corner" helped to confirm them in this misconception about those who led "rough" lives. For instance, the life of a London laundress named Mrs. Blackwell was once featured in the column because Acland felt guildswomen might want to know more about "the condition of the London poor," a topic about which "much interest has been lately excited in many journals"[25] Such people were clearly as much another species to the working-class rank and file of the Guild as they were to Acland and Wilson. But Acland either found or created a laundress with whom her readers could identify—one who proved that individual determination could triumph over adverse circumstances, thereby reinforcing her readers' prejudices about the role of self-help in the making of respectability.

Mrs. Blackwell lived "in a small London street, rather dirty and noisy, and with very bad smells in hot weather; but still not too unwholesome."[26] She always had regular employment because of her extraordinary skills as a washer and ironer. She worked for "a kind, thoughtful" mistress and was married to a mason, who, "though a good workman, [was] often out of work."[27] In other words, Mrs. Blackwell worked hard, but in decent conditions, and only engaged in waged labor outside the home because of the unfortunate circumstances which occasionally befell her otherwise reliable husband.

Mrs. Blackwell had seven children. The oldest girl had gone into service (Edith Wilson was probably pleased to read this), and the oldest boy had been apprenticed to learn a trade so that he could one day "support himself comfortably."[28] The other children all went to school and were in the Band of Hope at the temperance union to which she belonged. Mrs. Blackwell read books that she borrowed from her clergyman and sometimes went "to the theatre or to a concert."[29] She was saving for a holiday by the sea and for retirement. So, it appears this London laundress was neither too poor to have some discretionary income for "improving" amusements nor too poor to help herself by saving. Her children had grown and flourished despite their neighborhood environment. The impression the reader was supposed to gather was that this was due to their mother's influence. She had introduced them to temperance, reading, and religion. The article concluded: Mrs. Blackwell "is quite contented, and enjoys the life which has been allotted to her of a London laundress."[30] Readers were thus encouraged to question the accuracy of the more horrific depictions of the "condition of the London poor" which had "lately excited" some journals, as well as any rumors that the poor were discontented. But above all they were supposed to come away persuaded that any degraded people who might exist had only themselves to blame. After all, if Mrs. Blackwell could maintain herself and her family in decency, anyone could.

Although it was always possible that some unexpected economic calamity could reduce the weekly incomes the husbands of guildswomen provided, these women felt confident that they would be able to weather that storm with as much dignity as Mrs. Blackwell lived her life. In fact, they were less worried by the possibility of being reduced to her circumstances than they were of being left behind by their children, for whom they and their husbands had provided opportunities for upward social mobility. The Guild's early leaders were aware of this rank-and-file concern, and that was one reason they pushed for the working-class housewife's right to have at least one night a week for attending a Guild meeting designed to stimulate her intellectually and set her on the road to self-improvement. Annie Jones, the second president of the Guild, wanted to educate cooperative women "so that their children should not be ashamed of them."[31] At one of the first sectional conferences held by the Guild, Elizabeth Tournier, a middle-class woman who served several terms of office on the Central Committee that governed the organization, related a story about a poor widow woman, which she felt sure would motivate guildswomen in their studies. It seems this woman had one son who wanted to go to college; so she "strove and slaved" to make that possible.[32] But in the course of her efforts "her own little stock of knowledge through disuse dwindled away, and she gave herself no time to keep it up."[33] Her son became ashamed of her and told any of his college friends who visited him that his mother was his washerwoman. One day, on accidentally overhearing this, "the poor woman turned like stone, and in two days was dead."[34] The Guild's leaders considered it vital that women cultivate their minds to prepare them to function in the sorts of unfamiliar situations in which their children's social mobility might land them. Therefore, neither guildswomen nor their leaders were prepared to ignore class distinctions or to imagine their elimination either in the community of women they were building or the larger Cooperative Commonwealth to come. Indeed, they were bent on the perpetuation and cultivation of social stratification in order to demarcate themselves as separate from and better than those less fortunate.

Many of the early leaders of the Guild were as conservative on gender issues as they were about class. Their insistence on the maintenance of separate work for men and women on behalf of cooperation stands in illustration. Alice Acland told guildswomen to attempt no platform speaking and reminded them they were only to assist the men in propaganda work for the movement by helping with tea parties.[35] She did not think women should run for election either to the educational or management committees of cooperative societies, but only make polite suggestions to them and encourage their husbands to serve on them.[36] Even those leaders who found Acland's limitations too confining and believed they could dare to do more were circumspect in their recommendations. They declared that they had to be careful that "the Women's Guild does not lift up a banner with 'Women's Rights' inscribed on it in large red letters, and forthwith proceed to make war upon co-operative mankind."[37] Annie Jones and Mary Lawrenson are two examples of such cautious leaders. Both believed that if the home remained the focus of whatever they undertook as individuals or an organization, men might permit them to do work which had hitherto been denied to women and reserved only for men. For Jones and Lawrenson, home was the locus of women's power.[38] However, in their estimation, this did not necessarily limit women's abilities to effect change, so they did not consider themselves as operating from "exclusion and lack" but from "difference and power."[39] As Jane Lewis points out, women who chose what some may consider "limited" roles did not perceive themselves as having embraced limitations,[40] and this was certainly true of both Jones and Lawrenson.

All the Guild's early leaders lived close enough to London to convene meetings there. Jones lived in London because her husband was director of the City's branch of the Manchester-based Cooperative Wholesale Society. However, she was originally from Lancashire and, unlike any of her colleagues in the Guild's national leadership in the 1880s, had worked in a factory as a girl. Perhaps it was her experience as a waged laborer that gave her the self-confidence to ignore Alice Acland's prohibition on platform speaking.[41] After Acland retired from the Guild's presidency, owing to ill health, in 1886, she took over her position. Jones had a knack for deftly handling male concerns about Guild activities, unlike Mary Lawrenson who served with her on the Guild's Central Committee. At Norwood's cooperative store, to which Jones belonged, the men supported her efforts to establish a library and a newsroom.[42] Lawrenson at Woolwich, however, encountered resistance when she asked for funding for her Guild branch.[43] There are a number of possible explanations for the differences in the ways male cooperators related to these two women, and all of them shed light on the gender politics operating within the Cooperative movement.

Annie Jones's physique may have enabled her to disarm male opposition. She was a petite woman, who consequently took up little physical space. She therefore appeared as nonthreatening to men. Her size may even have stirred their protective instincts. Lawrenson, on the other hand, was more powerfully built. She was also animated, assertive, and direct, as opposed to the more reserved and soft-spoken Jones. Male cooperators who believed respectable women held their tongues undoubtedly considered Lawrenson "rough"; one can imagine their outraged shocked when she boasted about heckling the temperance speaker as reported in chapter one. To make matters worse, she and another Woolwich guildswoman became the first women to intrude themselves on male space when they got elected to the educational committee of the cooperative society there. Jones as much as Lawrenson believed women should sit on educational committees because education, especially the instruction of children, was woman's work.[44] They also both thought women could be useful on the management committees that ran the stores, since women could make more informed decisions about groceries, millinery, and drapery than men.[45] But Jones never offered herself as a candidate for any of these positions; Lawrenson did. In fact, Jones made a point of never advising "anyone to take up cooperative work and neglect household duties."[46]

Jones often spoke about the Guild's "desire to raise the condition of women, and to promote the good of our fellow human beings . . . by meeting and making efforts together to teach one another how to make our homes more comfortable and more happy."[47] Her constant references to women's home duties in her public utterances disarmed the men. Jones also mollified them by publicly professing to accept male stereotypes of women as grumbling, gossiping, and prone to "petty jealousies."[48] Lawrenson, on the other hand, tended to lecture men about their shortcomings as leaders. She maintained that if cooperative women were too focused on the "divi," it was the men's fault because they set the tone for the movement. She pointed out that male cooperators were too preoccupied with returns on their investments as shareholders, preventing cooperators from spending money on living up to the movement's ideals. For instance, it annoyed her when the male leaders of the movement turned their backs on the institution of worker-owned cooperative workshops and profit-sharing because such schemes were too expensive.[49] Regardless of their cost, she believed founding and funding such concerns was the right thing to do. She also lectured the men for their miserliness with respect to funding recreational activities for youths and classes for children.[50] Referring to Dickens's *Hard Times*, she told the men they were "all in a muddle" like Stephen Blackpool and his fellow weavers.[51] In sum, Jones and Lawrenson had similar ideas regarding the sorts of activities appropriate to women's efforts on behalf of cooperation. However, their personal styles were radically different, and the result was that men found Jones much less threatening.

Lawrenson was a scold. Perhaps that was due to the fact she was a schoolteacher by profession, or to the fact she had been the oldest child in a family of eleven. In either case, it prompted her to reprimand the male leaders of the movement as though they were selfish boys who had refused to share their toys with others. She was resented for that. Accordingly, male cooperators did not trust her when she claimed that the Guild was not stepping outside of women's "mission" to be merely the "companions and 'helpmeets'" of men, and that all she was asking was for them to give women "a little help and encouragement" in the execution of their traditional roles as homemakers and caretakers of the young and the marginalized.[52] They did not believe her because she accused the men of failing to carry "co-operation into your homes," of not treating their mothers, wives, and sisters fairly.[53] To the men it sounded as though she had "lift[ed] up a banner with 'Women's Rights' inscribed on it in large red letters." In particular, her pronouncement sounded like a challenge to the patriarchy that male cooperators so conscientiously maintained in their households.

Lawrenson had been raised in a family devoted to cooperation. Her father was a Lancashire printer who had settled in Woolwich with his wife and children. He had an enduring influence on her life, having taught her "to ponder the 'why' of poverty and distress."[54] He also had encouraged in her the development of a strong working-class identity. It is therefore no wonder she sometimes lost patience with her "social betters," like Amy Sharp at the "Woman's Corner" as reported in chapter one.[55]

As a poorly paid teacher, she had not been able to afford to become a cooperator. The prices at the store and the entrance fee were beyond her reach as a single woman. But as soon as she married, she joined a store.[56] She and her husband eventually settled in her former hometown of Woolwich, her husband becoming the director of the cooperative society there. She was a great admirer of

E. V. Neale, the Christian Socialist and first general secretary of the Cooperative Union. Like him, she believed consumer control was insufficient to ensure equity in the Cooperative Commonwealth. There had to be instituted worker-owned and worker-controlled productive concerns as well as employee profit-sharing in the enterprises managed by the Cooperative Wholesale Society. She looked to cooperative production as a solution to the problem of the sweated trades, which she believed degraded young women to the point of forcing them into prostitution. Lawrenson was a sexual puritan, like most working-class women. As Ellen Ross and Judy Giles have observed, maintaining the sexual innocence of young women was important to women of the working class who wanted to separate themselves from the rougher sort.[57] Consequently, any who joined the cooperative family Lawrenson aimed to create could look forward to having their activities strictly supervised. Decent wages would be given to the young, and sexually sublimating recreational activities provided for them in an effort to control their behavior. Peter Gurney characterizes cooperative culture as a culture of control, designed to exclude disorderly and spontaneous behavior.[58] Mary Lawrenson's attitudes certainly prove that his assessment of the situation is correct. They also show that cooperators resembled the nineteenth-century socialists studied by Chris Waters. These working-class activists were just as interested in "civilizing" their peers as were cooperators.[59]

Lawrenson, Jones, and Acland saw women as the custodians of cooperative ideals and accepted the Victorian stereotype that women were naturally more virtuous than men. Occupying such a moral pedestal was no limiting impediment in their opinion, however. Indeed, they believed it carried weighty responsibilities, and certain influential men in the Cooperative movement agreed. Those men believed such "angels" could be useful to the cause of cooperation provided, of course, the women operated within the parameters male cooperators established.

In 1884, J.T.W. Mitchell, the president of the Cooperative Wholesale Society, told guildswomen that "there was no power greater than that of woman when rightly exercised."[60] According to Mitchell, the right exercise of power for women in the Cooperative movement was to "revive" those who had become "lukewarm in regard to co-operation," to increase sales at the store, "not to talk too much at their meetings," and to form "a stronger attachment to the 'old house and home.'"[61] However, Mitchell's guidelines were not much help to either sex in establishing what the parameters of women's work should be. Encouraging lukewarm cooperators and increasing sales at the store might require platform speaking and running for election to educational and management committees. Moreover, in becoming more attached to their homes, women might find it was not enough merely to influence their husbands' votes in municipal or national elections; they might come to want the franchise for themselves.[62] As early in Guild history as 1885, at least one branch was already discussing women's suffrage.[63] It is certain Mitchell had not intended his remarks to be interpreted so as to advocate voting privileges for women; after all, he did say women should not talk too much, indicating that he was afraid of the powerful networks women created for themselves through "gossip."[64] His remarks therefore illustrate one of the problems faced by the Guild's early leaders in their efforts to make their organization useful both to women and to the Cooperative movement; they highlight how problematic was the distinction between public and private, men's work and women's.

In 1885, Acland ran a series of letters written by a certain E.B. in the "Woman's Corner." They were entitled "The Municipal Duty of Co-operative Women." E.B. began her first letter by asserting that "everybody sees that it is the duty of women to look after the welfare of the household."[65] But, she observed, there was one problem with that: "however much she may try to make her home healthy and happy, there are things beyond her control which work against her."[66] Those "things" included "nasty" water, poor drainage, small houses that force children to play in the streets where "they are thrown with bad children . . . and see bad actions and sights, and hear bad words."[67] Public houses "in every street," negligent landlords, insufficient numbers of police officers, "All the above evils, and many more, are municipal evils; that is they belong to the bad government of towns . . . [and] are all the fault of people living in towns, who will not attend to their municipal duties."[68]

E.B. argued that although most women could not vote in municipal elections because they were not householders, they had municipal duties nonetheless, and it was their obligation to fulfill them since the public sphere affected the private. Accordingly, "each wife . . . must use her influence to see that her husband gives his vote for an honest and just councilman."[69] This, of course, required each wife to keep abreast of town politics and interested in municipal issues. Like Acland, E.B. was conservative in her estimation of the means women should use; they must influence men from behind the scenes, be assistants, "sunbeams," "encouragers," not voters. However, despite her conservatism, she had blurred the line between private and public, proving how difficult it was to separate the two, and confusing both women and men in their efforts to define what woman's proper sphere was.

Catherine Webb's branch of the Guild at the Battersea and Wandsworth Cooperative Society was the one that had entered on discussions of women's suffrage in 1885. The year before, it had examined women's waged labor, a particular interest of Webb's.[70] In the 1890s that interest led her to become involved with the Women's Industrial Council (WIC), which grew out of Clementina Black's Women's Trade Union Association in 1894.[71] Webb was the WIC's general secretary from 1895 to 1902.[72] The WIC was closely linked with the Fabian Women's Group,[73] and was part of the radical and socialist London milieu in which the Guild's early leaders circulated. As an organization it was committed to the advocacy of protective labor legislation for women. In particular, it wanted to see such legislation extended to home workers.[74] Members of the WIC were educated middle-class women who wanted to help their working-class sisters.[75]

During the years Webb edited the Guild's "Notes" feature in the "Woman's Corner," she wrote as much about organizations like the Women's Industrial Council and Lady Dilke's Women's Trade Union League as she did about the Guild.[76] She believed that once all women workers were unionized, every worker's wage would increase because employers would no longer be able to use cheaper female labor to replace more expensive male labor.[77] She thought cooperators should collaborate with trade unionists to organize workers because until everyone earned decent wages, there would always be people too poor to afford to shop at cooperative stores.[78] She considered that guildswomen had a special role in this project. As shoppers, it was up to them never to buy items made by sweated labor and to make sure the cooperative stores stocked no such goods.[79] So, according to Webb, housewives could put sweat shopowners out of business by shopping wisely. She agreed with J.T.W. Mitchell that "there is no power greater than that of woman when rightly exercised." But her expansion of women's concerns as homemakers to include labor issues only served further to blur the boundaries between private and public.

Webb was the daughter of the manager of the Battersea and Wandsworth Cooperative Society. Her father had worked his way up from poverty through the Cooperative movement. By the time Catherine was born, he was so well situated that she was brought up like a middle-class girl. Consequently, there is some question as to the class with which she identified. She referred to herself as "a working-woman" before male cooperators.[80] Perhaps this was a concession to her father's class heritage. Lillian Faderman points out that women like Webb, who devoted themselves to public careers in the service of some humanitarian cause, tended to be molded by their fathers and overwhelmingly desired to please their male parents.[81] However, Webb felt unable to call herself working class before rank-and-file members of the Guild because, as she once confessed to them, she had never in her life done housework, unlike her "sisters in working-class homes."[82] Interestingly, a number of early Guild leaders who had never been housewives became staunch proponents of associated homes. These include the middle-class Catherine Webb and the working-class, but single, Sarah Reddish.

Carol Dyhouse in *Feminism and the Family in England* describes a number of schemes envisioned by middle-class reformers who aimed to institute collectivist living in an effort either to reduce labor for working-class women or to solve the problems created for middle-class women by the shortage of servants.[83] None of these schemes had any appeal for cooperators because they were designed to be run as for-profit enterprises by capitalists. Cooperative visions of associated homes were informed by Owenite ideology and modeled on Owenite attempts in the 1840s to found self-sufficient communes. Cooperative advocates of associated homes argued it was necessary to change the environment in order to transform human nature in preparation for the coming of the Cooperative Commonwealth. Like their Owenite forebears, they believed the competitive values of the Old Immoral World were inculcated into people by living in nuclear families in private households.[84] But unlike many of their Owenite predecessors, most cooperators never intended that associated homes would liberate women from their traditional roles.[85] In 1885, Annie Jones's husband, Ben, described what living in an associated home would mean for women as follows:

The work of women would be made much lighter by division of labour. In an associated home, one could cook, another could nurse, a third could act as chambermaid, a fourth could be a waitress, and so on. Those who wished to do nothing, and could afford the luxury, could pay their poorer or more energetic sisters to do the work for them.[86]

It is interesting to note that Jones failed to imagine the abolition of class as well as traditional gender roles in his vision of an associated home, leaving one to wonder how communal living might foster values that would be different from those of families living in the capitalist world.

E. V. Neale had a grand plan for the construction of associated homes, and Catherine Webb was captivated by it because she hoped that such living arrangements might free housewives from housework so that they could have public lives.[87] Neale imagined that a number of families could be brought together to live in a community where there would be houses with "large and gracious rooms for living in," separated from all the washing and cooking activities that can make a house unpleasant "by means of lifts and tramways (running under the groups of houses)."[88] These devices would remove "all refuse and dirty things . . . at fixed times to places where they were to be dealt with. Meals . . . could be brought in covered cars and placed on the tables of those who liked to eat in their own homes."[89] There would be a creche for children staffed by "kind, skilful nurses."[90] Women could elect to do their own laundry, cooking and child care if they wanted, but the presumption was they would not. Similarly, it was assumed that most residents would not want "to eat in their own homes." "Mutual service and social intercourse" would be preferred by the residents to "independent privacy."[91]

However, ordinary working-class women, as Judy Giles and Carol Dyhouse have pointed out, relished privacy and domesticity.[92] They were tired of sharing facilities and craved a private space where they could express themselves as housewives.[93] Most were uninterested in having a public life and preferred instead to define themselves through their homes. Indeed, no working-class wife could claim to be respectable if she failed to take pride in her home.[94] Alistair Thomson in his study of rank-and-file guildswomen's attitudes towards proposals for associated homes reveals that cooperative women felt no differently from their sisters outside of the movement.[95] However, this fact did not deter Guild leaders like Catherine Webb. She continued to push for associated homes, hoping they could be introduced piecemeal by first establishing cooperative laundries and kitchens. She believed that guildswomen could be persuaded to abandon at least the most laborious and time consuming of their domestic duties, clothes washing and baking.[96] The laundries found some favor, but not the kitchens.[97] As one woman put it:

I am afraid if we had a co-operative kitchen we should lose our homeliness. And a true woman likes to do her own cooking. In fact, my family prefer to come home to dinner every day sooner than have it elsewhere. I think we English, like no other country, enjoy our homes. . . . I for one think it a pleasure to cook my own dinner, and bake my own bread.[98]

This woman obviously considered that being a housewife was not necessarily a limiting experience for a woman. In addition, it should be noted that she went on to claim that it was possible for a woman to have a public career as an activist for the Guild and still be a homemaker. She argued all that was required was "good management,"[99] not associated homes as Catherine Webb thought. She concluded by saying she was "sure there are hundreds of others" who would agree with her about the pleasures of domesticity.[100] She was wrong about that; there were millions. The fictional Mrs. Littleton whose exploits were featured in the "Woman's Corner" was their heroine.

Fate could not deal Mrs. Littleton a household emergency that could defeat her skill and cunning as a homemaker. Once there was a fire at her husband's shop, where he worked with his brother at an unspecified artisanal trade. It affected the apartment above it, where her mother-in-law and sister-in-law lived. Mrs. Littleton was suddenly faced with having to house and feed her in-laws, in addition to caring for her own children and elderly mother. She had little food in the house, and not much money left to buy any because it was the end of the week and her husband had not yet given her the housekeeping money for the next week. But she made do, and the story of how she managed was told in fine detail. At the end of it all her husband paid her the best of all compliments: "My dear, I never knew your equal at housekeeping; we couldn't have had a better table if we had been expecting all those folk for a month."[101] In other words, he acknowledged her as a skilled worker whose contributions were valuable. Every cooperative woman wanted that sort of recognition from her husband, but of the Guild's early leaders only Annie Jones and Mary Lawrenson seemed to realize that. It was because, unlike Webb, Jones and Lawrenson were both married and working-class.

In 1889, the leadership of the Guild was about to be captured by a woman who, like Webb, was middle-class and unmarried—Margaret Llewelyn Davies. There is an unpublished history of the Women's Cooperative Guild that characterizes the organization as directionless until Llewelyn Davies came along.[102] In particular, it denigrates the leadership of Lawrenson. It exempted Jones presumably because Jones died before she and Llewelyn Davies arrived at any differences of opinion. Such was not the case with Lawrenson.

Llewelyn Davies became the Guild's general secretary upon the resignation of Lawrenson. Because of the embarrassing circumstances which had forced her resignation, Lawrenson curtailed her work for the Guild after it. Almost immediately, Llewelyn Davies and her associates, other middle-class single women like Catherine Webb, made it clear that the Guild would make its primary focus the education of women, not children.[103] This change of direction for the Guild eventually prompted Lawrenson to come out of her forced retirement and run for a seat on the Central Committee in 1891. Though she won the election, she was unable to convince the committee to resume efforts on behalf of the education of children in the principles of cooperation. So Lawrenson was forced to find another outlet for her interest in the young. She became involved in the movement's children's leagues.

In 1891, Lawrenson and Llewelyn Davies were at loggerheads over the issue of productive cooperation as well as children's education. That year the new general secretary had decided it was time for the Guild to take an official position in the dispute over worker-owned and -controlled workshops and profit-sharing which had riven the Cooperative movement for half a decade.

By the end of the 1880s, controversy over the place in the movement of worker-owned and -controlled workshops and of profit-sharing had split the men who controlled the movement into two camps. E. V. Neale, assisted by his fellow Christian Socialist, Thomas Hughes, and by the secularist and former Owenite, George Jacob Holyoake, argued for the institution of such workshops as well as for profit-sharing with the employees in those owned and run by consumers under the aegis of the Cooperative Wholesale Society. Interestingly, most such advocates were London-based and had come to the movement by way of either Christian Socialism or Owenism. Their opponents were Lancashire men, almost invariably of working-class origin, like their leader, J.T.W. Mitchell. Lancashire was the birthplace and center of the consumer-owned distributive cooperative movement. Each year at congresses convened by the Cooperative Union over which Neale presided, resolutions were passed supporting his position and, each year, their enforcement was ignored by Neale's opponents. In 1891, Llewelyn Davies aligned the Guild with the cause of consumer-owned distributive cooperation.

At a sectional conference held in London for the southern branches of the Guild, she read a paper arguing that "it might be more to the advantage of the worker to have good wages and shorter hours, than the doubtful chance of a share in [uncertain] profits."[104] This was a dissident point of view to argue in London, the center for the cause of worker control over production and of profit-sharing; so she had her minions there for self-defense, including her close friend Rosalind Shore Smith. Despite their support, her opponents managed to have the last word in the discussion which followed her presentation of the paper. A working-class woman asserted "that they as workers were more interested in productive workshops organised in the interests of the workers" than in consumer control.[105] Her remarks were greeted by a round of applause.

Mary Lawrenson had not attended the conference, but when she read its coverage in the "Woman's Corner," she was driven to write a lengthy defense of worker-owned workshops, which appeared in the "Corner" in two installments, on November 21 and December 12. She said she found it inaccurate to categorize people as either workers or consumers, as Llewelyn Davies had done in her paper, and then to argue that everyone is a consumer but may not be a worker. Looking at the Guild, she found every woman in it to be as much a worker as a consumer:

Our guild is one composed of women workers. A member may be a worker in a trade shop, or a worker who, as housewife and helpmeet to a recognised trade worker, as one skilled in her trade of house-keeping, "doubles the gains by her prudence and pains."[106]

Llewelyn Davies and her associates of course knew that what Lawrenson claimed for ordinary guildswomen was true; such women were workers because they were involved in the task of reproduction in the home. However, neither Llewelyn Davies nor the clique of single middle-class women who supported her had any personal experience of doing such work. They therefore tended to see the Guild's rank and file primarily as consumers. Only after long years of association with working-class women did Llewelyn Davies come to the opinion that such women were producers because of their efforts as mothers and house-wives. Her first opportunity to articulate her new position came between 1911 and 1913, during the Guild's campaign for the payment of the new state-sponsored maternity benefit directly to women rather than to their husbands.[107] However, later in her life she reverted to her original position. In the 1930s she claimed that the state should pay family allowances to housewives who did not work for wages outside the home, in order to enhance the purchasing power of married working-class women, not as pay for reproductive work.[108] This was consistent with many other interwar advocates for the endowment of mother-hood, as Susan Pedersen points out,[109] but not with the position of the Guild, which continued to argue for the endowment as pay for women's reproductive labors.[110]

Lawrenson's defense of worker-owned manufactories also highlights an-other difference between her and the second generation of Guild leaders exem-plified by Llewelyn Davies. The early leaders were less in touch with the busi-ness realities of the Cooperative movement than were their successors. In her defense of worker-owned manufactories, Lawrenson attempted to uphold the higher principles of the movement, which she believed both Llewelyn Davies and male cooperative leaders ignored. She argued such manufactories consti-tuted a "superior form of associative production" to the consumer-owned ones of the Cooperative Wholesale Society.[111] She believed all such manufactories' financial risks were worthwhile because they embodied the cooperative princi-ple "each for all, and all for each" through their incorporation of profit-sharing with employees.[112] In sum, she built her defense of worker ownership and profit-sharing on the foundation of moral principle. Llewelyn Davies, Lawrenson felt, had computed the cost-effectiveness of worker ownership and profit-sharing and had found they did not measure up to what a worker would gain by a mere in-crease in wages and a reduction in hours. It shocked Lawrenson that Llewelyn Davies had reduced ideals to pounds, just like the male opponents of worker ownership and profit-sharing.

The new general secretary did not bother to respond to her predecessor's case; the Guild's Central Committee agreed with her and not with Lawrenson.[113] Lawrenson thus found herself increasingly marginalized within the community of women she had helped to create. In 1893, she lost an election to the Central Committee and, thereafter, was never able to regain a seat on it. When she be-came the first woman ever elected to the Central Board of the Cooperative Un-ion, the Guild ignored her. Instead, attention was given to Catherine Webb and Sarah Reddish, two members of Llewelyn Davies's inner circle who were run-ning for seats on the board.[114] Even as late as 1933, Lawrenson found herself on the outside looking in. That year the Guild celebrated its fiftieth anniversary and there was disagreement about whether to honor Lawrenson by giving her the freedom of the Guild, an honor which had been created specially for Llewelyn Davies in 1921, when she retired as general secretary. Considering Lawrenson's role in the foundation of the organization, debating her entitlement to this award was an outrageous insult.

Lawrenson had hoped to make the Guild an inclusive community of women, but it turned out to be a cliquish sorority. It had no room for the friend of the "owd humpty woman." The leaders of the Guild were unable to get past the legacy left them by the Old Immoral World. As a consequence, they feuded with one another and sometimes refused to listen to the voice of the rank and file. At other times, they were so attentive to it that they only reinforced the prejudices of the ordinary members, thereby allowing the persistence of class consciousness to prevent the unification of "the great band of co-operative womankind." In addition, the cooperative family of mutually supporting men, women, and children that the Guild's early leaders hoped to create would have been stifling of freedom and repressive of differences. As Crane Brinton put it, "there is a strain . . . of benevolent despotism . . . in modern, perhaps all, utopian thinking."[115] The Guild's, indeed the entire Cooperative movement's, visions for the future expressed this. Thus members of cooperation's family would have had to be content with the modes of education and recreation the movement supplied for them, resulting in the indoctrination of children and a suffocating control over the activities of youths. As for women, cooperation would not liberate them from their traditional duties, even in associated homes.

Both female and male cooperative leaders believed that the family, or community, or Commonwealth they envisioned growing from their efforts would be the logical product of the spread of cooperative stores throughout the country and, eventually, the world. They imagined that because their better world had emerged from a grassroots movement it could guarantee both personal freedom and collective well-being. However, the Cooperative movement's leaders—both female and male—functioned in the utopian tradition: the possibilities they offered were limited by the actualities that had generated their dreams. Cooperative leaders constituted an elite group who had overcome their environments and were bent on imposing their notion of utopia on the unenlightened masses.

NOTES

1. "Woman's Corner," *Co-operative News*, January 21, 1888.
2. Ibid.
3. Ibid.
4. Ibid.
5. "Woman's Corner," *Co-operative News*, May 12, 1883.
6. Judy Giles notes in *Women, Identity and Private Life in Britain* that home is not the only private sphere (104–105). Definitions of private space are contingent on such factors as class and, in this case, cooperative ideology.
7. Kent, *Sex and Suffrage*, 92.
8. Gurney, *Co-operative Culture and the Politics of Consumption in England*, 23.
9. Taylor, *Eve and the New Jerusalem*, 223.
10. Gurney, *Co-operative Culture and the Politics of Consumption in England*, 69.
11. "Woman's Corner," *Co-operative News*, May 26, 1883.

12. This analysis is based on the similar thinking of Crane Brinton, "Utopia and Democracy" (50–51), in Manuel (ed.) *Utopias and Utopian Thought*; and Chris Waters, *British Socialism and the Politics of Popular Culture*, 48–49.

13. "Woman's Corner," *Co-operative News*, January 6, 1883.

14. "Woman's Corner," *Co-operative News*, March 3, 1883.

15. "Woman's Corner," *Co-operative News*, March 10 and 17, 1883.

16. Ross, "'Not the Sort that Would Sit on the Doorstep,'" 39–49.

17. Phillips, *Divided Loyalties*, 39.

18. "Woman's Corner," *Co-operative News*, September 15, 1883.

19. "Woman's Corner," *Co-operative News*, March 17, 1883.

20. Ibid.

21. Jane Lewis makes this observation about the middle-class humanitarians who ministered to the working class. Lewis, "The Working-class Wife and Mother and State Intervention, 1870–1918," in Lewis (ed.), *Labour and Love*, 107.

22. "Woman's Corner," *Co-operative News*," March 17, 1883.

23. Ibid.

24. Ibid.

25. "Woman's Corner," *Co-operative News*, January 5, 1884.

26. Ibid.

27. Ibid.

28. Ibid.

29. Ibid.

30. Ibid.

31. Llewelyn Davies, *The Women's Co-operative Guild*, 24.

32. "Woman's Corner," *Co-operative News*, October 25, 1890.

33. Ibid.

34. Ibid.

35. "Woman's Corner," *Co-operative News*, June 2 and 16, 1883.

36. "Woman's Corner," *Co-operative News*, March 8, 1884, and April 12, 1884.

37. "Woman's Corner," *Co-operative News*, July 10, 1886.

38. Seth Koven and Sonya Michel observe that such a point of view was common to relational feminists. "Womanly Duties: Maternalist Politics and the Origins of Welfare States," 1091.

39. Sally Alexander uses these words for describing women who chose the path of relational feminism in "Equal or Different: The Emergence of the Victorian Women's Movement," in Alexander, *Becoming a Woman*, 128.

40. Lewis, *Women in England*, xii.

41. "Woman's Corner," *Co-operative News*, June 20, 1886.

42. "Woman's Corner," *Co-operative News*, January 2, 1886.

43. "Woman's Corner," *Co-operative News*, April 4, 1885.

44. "Woman's Corner," *Co-operative News*, June 29, 1889.

45. Ibid.

46. "Woman's Corner," *Co-operative News*, May 31, 1890.

47. Ibid.

48. Ibid.

49. "Woman's Corner," *Co-operative News*, April 4, 1885.

50. Ibid.

51. Ibid.

52. Ibid.

53. Ibid.

54. Llewelyn Davies, *The Women's Co-operative Guild*, 17.

55. Mary Lawrenson Collection, Cooperative Union Library, Manchester, draft of an 1888 letter to Amy Sharp from Lawrenson.

56. "Woman's Corner," *Co-operative News*, August 21, 1886.

57. Ross, "'Not the Sort that Would Sit on the Doorstep,'" 49–50; and Giles, *Women, Identity and Private Life in Britain*, 50.

58. Gurney, *Co-operative Culture and the Politics of Consumption in England*, 80.

59. Waters, *British Socialism and the Politics of Popular Culture*, 3–4.

60. "Woman's Corner," *Co-operative News*, April 19, 1884.

61. Ibid.

62. Thus the Guild's interest in citizenship issues predates the advent of Margaret Llewelyn Davies as the organization's leader, contrary to the thesis that Gillian Scott presents in *Feminism and the Politics of Working Women*.

63. "Woman's Corner," *Co-operative News*, April 4, 1885.

64. Ellen Ross in *Love and Toil* (23) speaks of gossip as helping to create a working-class culture centered on the neighborhood.

65. "Woman's Corner," *Co-operative News*, January 17, 1885.

66. Ibid.

67. Ibid.

68. Ibid.

69. Ibid.

70. "Woman's Corner," *Co-operative News*, November 1, 1884.

71. Ellen Mappen, *Helping Women at Work: The Women's Industrial Council, 1889–1914* (London: Hutchinson, 1985), 13.

72. Webb, *The Women with the Basket*, 111.

73. Dyhouse, *Feminism and the Family in England*, 59.

74. Phillips, *Divided Loyalties*, 88–89.

75. Ibid.

76. Some examples include the "Notes" column for January 11 and 25, and February 8, 1896.

77. "Woman's Corner," *Co-operative News*, March 13, 1897.

78. Ibid.

79. Ibid.

80. *Co-operative News*, February 27, 1892.

81. Lillian Faderman, *Surpassing the Love of Men: Romantic Friendships and Love between Women from the Renaissance to the Present* (New York: William Morrow and Company, Inc., 1981), 187–188.

82. London School of Economics, coll. misc. 268 m363, vol. I, item 7, folio 11.

83. Dyhouse, *Feminism and the Family in England*, 76, 111–128.

84. Taylor, *Eve and the New Jerusalem*, 38.

85. Ibid., 37, 247. It should be noted that Barbara Taylor observes that not all Owenites wanted to liberate women from their traditional roles.

86. Quoted by Thomson, "'Domestic Drudgery Will Be a Thing of the Past,'" in Yeo (ed.), *New Views of Co-operation*, 108.

87. Ibid., 116–117. Thomson gives this as her rationale.

88. Catherine Webb wrote in detail about Neale's scheme in the "Woman's Corner" of the *Co-operative News* for April 10, 1910.

89. Ibid.

90. Ibid.

91. Ibid.

92. Giles, *Women, Identity and Private Life in Britain*, 68; and Dyhouse, *Feminism and the Family in England*, 186.

93. Giles, *Women, Identity and Private Life in Britain*, 68.

94. Lewis, *Women in England* observes the link between respectability and being house-proud (30–31).

95. Thomson, "'Domestic Drudgery Will Be a Thing of the Past,'" in Yeo (ed.), *New Views of Co-operation*, 109–110.

96. London School of Economics, coll. misc. 268 m363, vol. I, item 7, folio 11.

97. Thomson also comes to this conclusion in "'Domestic Drudgery Will Be a Thing of the Past,'" in Yeo (ed.) *New Views of Co-operation*, 118, 121–122.

98. "Woman's Corner," *Co-operative News*, April 11, 1896.

99. Ibid.

100. Ibid.

101. "Woman's Corner," *Co-operative News*, January 24, 1885.

102. London School of Economics, coll. misc. 268 m363, vol. I, item 48, folio 152.

103. Hull University Library, DCW 1/1, Minute books of the Central Committee, September 30, 1889.

104. "Woman's Corner," *Co-operative News*, October 3, 1891.

105. Ibid.

106. "Woman's Corner," *Co-operative News*, December 12, 1891.

107. "Women's Corner," *Co-operative News*, August 23, 1913, gives an example of her arguments at that time.

108. London School of Economics, coll. misc. 268 m363, vol. I, item 39, folio 102.

109. Pedersen, *Family, Dependence and the Origins of the Welfare State*, 178–179.

110. Ibid., 161–164 summarizes the Guild's arguments.

111. "Woman's Corner," *Co-operative News*, November 21, 1891.

112. "Woman's Corner," *Co-operative News*, December 12, 1891.

113. Hull University Library, DCW 1/2, Minute books of the Central Committee, July 13, 1892.

114. Women's Co-operative Guild, *Twelfth Annual Report of the Women's Co-operative Guild*, 18.

115. Brinton, "Utopia and Democracy," in Manuel (ed.) *Utopias and Utopian Thought*, 53.

Margaret Llewelyn Davies, general secretary of the Women's Cooperative Guild from 1889 to 1921. Reproduced courtesy of the Co-operative Women's Guild.

Chapter 4

Margaret Llewelyn Davies: A Woman with a Mission

In 1901 Catherine Mayo was serving her last year of a six-year stint as branch organizer for the Women's Cooperative Guild. On a hot summer night, she paid a visit to the Guild branch at Kettering. She found the meeting room well filled with Guild members eager to hear her speak. But the atmosphere was stuffy and oppressive. Looking about for a window to open, she observed:

> The hall rejoices in beautiful large windows, but, alas! they are placed so high up that they are very difficult to open. We tugged at the ropes, but could make no impression. One of the guild members said she never remembered seeing them open but once, and that was when Miss Ll. Davies tackled them.[1]

Who was this woman who had managed what no other could in that meeting room at Kettering?

Margaret Llewelyn Davies was general secretary of the Women's Cooperative Guild for thirty-two years, from 1889 until 1921. Official histories of the Guild attribute to her the organization's growth in numbers and influence within and without the Cooperative movement around the turn of the last century. Jean Gaffin and David Thoms in *Caring and Sharing* refer to her election as general secretary as a "turning point" for the Guild and characterize her impact upon the organization as "profound."[2] Catherine Webb, one of Llewelyn Davies's most trusted lieutenants in the business of Guild leadership, considered the general secretary's retirement in 1921 as the appropriate time to commence her history of the Guild, *The Woman with the Basket*, since it seemed to her the end of an era.[3] Indeed, one unpublished history of the Guild, which Llewelyn Davies kept among her private papers, alleged that she should be accorded greater recognition in the pantheon of Guild leaders than the organization's two founders, Alice Acland and Mary Lawrenson.[4] None of these sources investigates her leadership critically and all of them deliberately ignore the dissident voices of those guildswomen who opposed the agenda Llewelyn Davies and her cohorts on the organization's executive, the Central Committee, imposed upon them. Even Guild histories that critically examine other leaders of the organization remain under the spell of the myths that circulate around her. Gillian Scott's thesis in her recent history of the Guild is that every other woman who rose to the position of general secretary was in some way deficient and that those who followed Llewelyn Davies were responsible for the Guild's failure to sustain both the allegiance of the members and the supposed democratic character of the organization in the interwar period.[5] It is hoped here to offer a more critical appraisal of Llewelyn Davies's leadership, complete with an assessment of the manner in which her private life affected her public career. Brian Harrison has remarked that the private lives of feminists illuminate their public careers.[6] So, taking as a maxim the motto of second wave feminism, that "the personal is political," a motto with which Llewelyn Davies herself would have agreed, it will be revealed that the general secretary's class prejudices and possible sexual orientation warped her ability to identify with the married working-class women who constituted the rank-and-file membership of the Guild and, especially, with those who regularly shopped at cooperative stores but chose not to join the organization over which she presided because they were put off by its prioritization of public service over private life.

The Women's Cooperative Guild existed to improve the lot of married working-class women by getting them out of the house for meetings at least one night a week, as well as teaching them how to be activists on behalf of cooperation. As the Guild grew in size, it developed in purpose, undertaking agitations for women's rights within cooperative organizations as well as in the noncooperative public sphere. Catherine Mayo had, as organizer, the job of starting branches of the Guild at cooperative societies that had none and making sure the already established ones held regular meetings. In particular, she ensured that the branches discussed at their meetings the program of work mandated by the Central Committee over which Llewelyn Davies presided. For, as the general secretary asserted, "The policy of the Guild and the direction of its work lie in the hands of the Central Committee."[7] When Llewelyn Davies became general secretary of the Guild in 1889, she lobbied against branches holding either "mothers' meetings" or social nights filled with sewing and relaxed discussions of personal and neighborhood affairs, otherwise known as "gossip."[8] Llewelyn Davies, a single middle-class woman, was confident that that sort of recreation could not benefit married working-class women. So each year, under her direction, the Central Committee chose a topic for the branches to study. These topics included the organization of trade unions for women, protective labor legislation for female workers, women's suffrage, minimum wages for female cooperative employees, national health care for expectant mothers, and the extension of cooperation to the poor. But her attempt to silence the "gossiping" of guildswomen reveals her ignorance of working class life. As Jane Lewis asserts, "gossiping" was for working-class women an important avenue of communication and mutual aid.[9] By stifling it, Llewelyn Davies not only grabbed control of the agendas of Guild meetings, but also the direction of the daily lives of the organization's members.

The histories of the Guild draw for their assessments of Llewelyn Davies's leadership on the testimonials of women who idolized the general secretary. All these women describe how narrow and limited their lives had been until they joined a branch and began the process of self-education under its direction. They attribute their increasing awarenesses of themselves and the wider world to Llewelyn Davies and the direction she gave the Guild. These fans enabled the Central Committee to do a brisk business in sales of the general secretary's picture during her tenure in office. That the committee made these sales under Llewelyn Davies's direction shows she participated in the making and the marketing of her image.[10] Philippa Levine has observed that nineteenth-century feminists preferred not to create among themselves leaders who were "giants," whose "catalytic charisma" was reverenced.[11] They preferred instead leaders with a more communal and collective approach to office. Llewelyn Davies rejected this tradition when she condoned the picture sales. Moreover, in so doing, she subverted any possibility that the Guild could evolve into the sort of democratically run organization that so many believed, and continue to believe, that it was. As Brian Harrison has remarked in connection with the Pankhursts, who encouraged leader worship in their Women's Social and Political Union, fixating the attentions of the rank and file on particular leaders is no preparation for democracy.[12] In sum, Llewelyn Davies's picture sales indicate she probably relished the fact that a member of the Kettering branch of the Guild remembered her as the woman who opened windows few others could. Indeed, the illustration the general secretary helped choose for the Guild's membership card is evidence that that sort of symbolism appealed to her. In 1908 the Central Committee commissioned Muirhead Bone to design a membership card showing a variation on the window motif, and Llewelyn Davies kept among her private papers the official description of the card's meaning.[13]

A copy of the design appears as the first illustration in this book. It shows a woman wearing an apron and holding a market basket under one arm. The woman is standing on a hill in front of a cave-like stone building with an open door, and looking into the sun rising over a factory town. Shielding her eyes with the other arm, she is watching birds as they soar in the sky above the town. And, as was recorded in Llewelyn Davies's papers, "In the golden morning air she experiences strange stirrings within her, which she finds difficult to put into words. . . . She shades her eyes as the light grows stronger, and the sadness in her heart gives place to a sense of power and longing."[14] "Power and longing" because the future is in her hands. Only her market basket can create the utopia of the Cooperative Commonwealth. Once she felt lonely and cramped in the home, but now she has "the feeling of fellowship" because the Guild has put her into contact with other women like herself.[15] Like so many other middle-class reformers, Llewelyn Davies presumed all working-class housewives were "downtrodden, bullied and dependent."[16] She wanted to liberate them from the dark caves within which she thought they dwelt and to teach them how to fly free like birds. It never occurred to her that some of them neither needed nor desired such liberation.

Llewelyn Davies was a talented administrator, but reactive rather than proactive as a leader and dependent upon others for ideas. For instance, she turned the Guild's attention to the causes of divorce law reform and maternity benefits under national health care only after Asquith's Liberal government initiated discussion of these issues. Her notions about what shape these reforms should take were derived from the models offered by Scandinavian legislation and may have also been shaped by the radical and socialist London environment with which she was connected. For instance, the Women's Industrial Council worried about the quality of maternity care, as did the Guild, and Clementina Black, one of Llewelyn Davies's associates, was as interested in the issue of state-sponsored family allowances as the general secretary came to be.[17] In addition, Llewelyn Davies may have committed the Guild to supporting women's trade unions and protective labor legislation because of her friendship with Mary Macarthur and Clementina Black, who were involved in the Women's Trade Union League and the National Federation of Women Workers. However, there is evidence that some Guild members felt the issue of women's trade unionism was irrelevant to their lives. The married working-class women who made up the rank and file of the organization came from the relatively well-off ranks of their class and considered wage labor outside the home to be a temporary condition for females.[18] Marriage had, after all, liberated them from it. So, Llewelyn Davies and her minions had to explain that guildswomen had an obligation to work to promote the welfare of their less fortunate sisters.[19]

Llewelyn Davies also borrowed ideas from the men she counted among her acquaintances. Sidney Webb, Arnold Toynbee, and Seebohm Rowntree are the most obvious examples, as evidenced by the Guild's experiment with the Sunderland Cooperative Society to extend the benefits of cooperation to that segment of the working class too poor to afford to shop at cooperative stores. Sidney Webb's 1891 paper exploring the possibilities for bringing the benefits of cooperation to the working poor stimulated the general secretary's interest in the subject.[20] Then, after many years of pressuring the male leadership of the movement to act, her efforts paid off. In 1902, the Sunderland Cooperative Society expanded its branch store in an impoverished area of the town populated by the underemployed. The store sold goods in small quantities at prices that were uninflated by the expectation of high dividends—because no one thought the outlet would produce the profits of the stores patronized by the better-off workers. Attached to the store was a settlement house, which the middle-class ladies associated with the Guild were invited to staff. Like Toynbee Hall, the Sunderland settlement house aimed at providing "friendship" not "charity."[21] Its workers devoted considerable attention to children, especially young girls, and expectant mothers, as did the workers at Toynbee Hall. Davies lived at the Sunderland house for a time and undertook a survey of the neighborhood on the model of Rowntree's survey of York.

In further illustration of her penchant for imitation, Llewelyn Davies is often credited with rationalizing the Guild's organizational structure so the branches and the Central Committee could communicate more effectively.[22] She divided the country into geographic sections, and the sections into districts, into which the branches were grouped. That design was not invented by her. It was already in use by the Cooperative Union for its own organization. Moreover, Annie Jones, who served as president of the Guild from 1886 until 1892, had argued in favor of adopting the Union's organizational structure even before Llewelyn Davies became general secretary.[23]

As a leader, Llewelyn Davies was criticized by some guildswomen for involving the Guild in too many disparate and diverse activities at once.[24] This tendency caused her to fail to follow through on causes she had adopted for Guild attention. For example, in 1907 when a Middlesbrough County Court judge ruled that married women could not consider as their own the money they had saved from housekeeping expenses because that money had been earned by their husbands, Llewelyn Davies had the Guild drop its plans to discuss opportunities for higher education for women and turn its attention to the defense of "Wives' Savings."[25] The Guild's rank and file eagerly espoused this cause because, as working-class wives, they had always presumed the dividends their purchases accumulated at the cooperative stores were their own, even when the family membership was taken out in their husbands' names. In fact, male store managers had always presumed that, too.[26] The Guild managed to get the issue of "Wives' Savings" put on the agenda of the 1908 Cooperative Congress. It was decided there to refer the matter to the attention of the Union's Parliamentary Committee, which had as its responsibility the drafting of bills sympathetic to the interests of the movement and the finding of sponsors for them in Parliament.[27] But the Parliamentary Committee never took up the matter and Llewelyn Davies never petitioned them to remind them to do so, even though she frequently wrote to them asking them to support women's suffrage.[28] Presumably, like many women's suffragists, she believed that winning the vote would enable women to demand feminist legislation on their own. Hence she gave that cause more priority than agitating, through men, for any particular law to assist women. If that was her rationale, it was a logical one. However, it was one upon which she had no authority to act unilaterally. The rank and file of the Guild, as well as the delegates to congress of the entire Cooperative movement, had spoken; they wanted legislation to protect wives' savings. It was her obligation to remind the Parliamentary Committee of that. This is but one example of the general secretary's penchant for ignoring the wishes of the majority despite her self-proclaimed devotion to the democratic process. Not surprisingly, this penchant was rooted in her class background, which prompted her to feel that she knew better than her lower-class charges what was in their best interests.

The particulars of Llewelyn Davies's life may be found in the first volume of Joyce Bellamy and John Saville's *Dictionary of Labour Biography*.[29] More interesting is what she had to say about herself and her life's work as the unmarried middle-class interpreter of the needs and wants of married working-class women. What little is left of her private papers is housed in the British Library of Political and Economic Science at the London School of Economics. The papers were deposited there after Llewelyn Davies's death, in 1944, by Lilian Harris, the woman with whom Llewelyn Davies had lived and worked for most of her adult life.

In the late twentieth century, it has become fashionable to speculate about the sexual orientation of such life partners as Llewelyn Davies and Harris.[30] As Leila Rupp insists, such speculation can assist in the understanding of the varieties of female networking that women developed to sustain their public activism[31]; it, therefore, is not some sort of titillating and irrelevant exercise. Lillian Faderman examines the functioning of these networks in her work and argues that the bonds that formed between female life partners gave them the strength to pursue careers as activists in a male-dominated world.[32] She says female life partners stimulated in one another the will to achieve when society was either indifferent or opposed to their efforts to sustain careers in the public sphere.[33] While nothing in the Llewelyn Davies papers suggests that Llewelyn Davies and Harris were lovers, the sanitized nature of the materials raises suspicions. For instance, there is nothing of a personal nature in them, and very little pertaining to Llewelyn Davies's activities as general secretary of the Guild—with the exception of the Sunderland experiment.[34] There are no letters from, or drafts of her epistles to, the many notables with whom she corresponded, including Virginia Woolf, L. T. Hobhouse, and Aldous Huxley. Most of the material in the collection covers interests that Llewelyn Davies pursued after she resigned from the Guild's leadership in 1921, although it is true that many of these had grown out of her association with that organization—such as the promotion of schemes for delivering maternity care to the poor and for fostering international peace. Yet there are hints elsewhere that at one time Llewelyn Davies's private papers were richer than they are now. In 1931, when Llewelyn Davies compiled a number of letters she had received from guildswomen into the volume entitled *Life As We Have Known It*, she asked Virginia Woolf to write an introduction to the book. There Woolf recalls the day she visited Llewelyn Davies in 1913, and the general secretary "unlocked a drawer and took out a packet of papers. You did not at once untie the string that fastened them. Sometimes, you said, you got a letter which you could not bring yourself to burn."[35] As Leila Rupp observes, women who loved other women were often reluctant to leave evidence of it and destroyed their private papers.[36] Eleanor Rathbone serves as another case in point. Like Llewelyn Davies, she shared her life with a female companion and became obsessed with ending the domestic subjection of women. Most of her private papers have also vanished.[37]

In what remains today of Llewelyn Davies's papers there are some items in which she describes her hopes for the imminent dawning of the Cooperative Commonwealth; there are also copies of tributes paid to her and Harris by the Guild and the larger Cooperative movement. But the most intriguing materials are several photographs. With these a Freudian could have a field day, and it is therefore surprising that they were not destroyed by either Llewelyn Davies or Harris. Before Freud confirmed the existence of female sexuality, it was assumed that all attachments between women were asexual, even by the women involved in them.[38] When Freud's theories became popularized in the early twentieth century, they took lesbians as much as heterosexuals by surprise. In order to preserve their privacy, women who lived with other women were driven to destroy their papers, whether or not they had ever been sexually active with their partners. Llewelyn Davies and Harris thus bowdlerized their papers, but the pictures they took on their trips abroad on behalf of either the international cooperative movement or the pacifist movement survived. One of the photographs, "Monument der Slachtoffers van 18 April 1902—Stadskerkhof van Leuven," is a shot of a sculpture of a woman with very muscular arms, supporting a fainted man.[39] Another is of a sculpture entitled "Marianne," a *monument funéraire* by von Beveren. This *Pieta*-like piece represents a larger than-life-woman, attired as an Amazon and wearing the expression of a *mater familias*—stern yet capable of love. She is looking down at a small naked man in her lap. The male figure almost appears to be grafted to her belly. He has an exhausted expression and is looking up to her as if in need of her protection and care.[40] In addition to these photographs, there is a pen and ink drawing entitled "Fecondité." This depicts a beautiful, bountiful young earth mother, suckling two infants at once and surrounded by several older children. One of them is an adolescent girl, carrying a basket brimming with ripe fruit.[41]

What conclusions may be drawn from these as to the gender attitudes or sexual orientation of their collectors? Clearly, they show that Llewelyn Davies and Harris considered the female of the human species to be the superior and more important of the two sexes, since men and children depended on the female for strength and sustenance, not to mention the continuation of the race. Does this mean Llewelyn Davies and Harris were lesbians? Neither of them would have used that term in reference to themselves. Yet, as Leila Rupp observes of similar women, they were women "whose primary commitment, in emotional and practical terms, was to other women."[42] She contends that scholars in deciding whether to apply the term lesbian to such women need to focus on "identity, not sexual behavior."[43] She believes the term lesbian appropriate for women-centered women, and argues that "there are lesbians who have never had a sexual relationship with another woman . . . sexual behavior . . . is only one of a number of factors in a relationship."[44]

Neither Llewelyn Davies nor Harris married or appear to have had any wish to do so. Harris's aversion to marriage is understandable. She was one of fourteen children of a wealthy banker who had had two wives, both of whom died as a consequence of their "Fecondité." But Llewelyn Davies's parents were happily married and presided over a loving family of seven children, of whom all but Llewelyn Davies were boys. Both her parents and their families had progressive ideas when it came to social issues having to do with labor and gender. And fortunately, it remains possible to know what Llewelyn Davies thought about her upbringing, or at least how she chose to represent it. Among her private papers is an autobiography she wrote in 1931 when a Norwegian women's magazine, *Norges Kvinder*, requested some information so that it could publish an article about her. There she says she was brought up in an atmosphere of "advanced social and religious thought, and no restraint was put on our religious and political views."[45] Of her mother's side of the family, Llewelyn Davies writes that they were Unitarians and some of her uncles were positivists and supporters of trade union legislation. Unitarians had always been in the forefront of those who espoused "advanced" ideas because of the religious persecution and discrimination they endured for denying Christ's divinity.[46] In addition, several historians have remarked upon the connection between Unitarianism and feminism.[47]

Llewelyn Davies was particularly close to her mother, Mary Crompton Davies. When her mother died in 1895, the general secretary wrote that Mary had been both "mother and sister to me."[48] She described how her mother had supported her in her work for the Guild. Mrs. Davies had paid the salary of the first Guild organizer hired by her daughter and had helped with the organization's paper work.[49] In her autobiography Llewelyn Davies mentions that her father was a friend of F. D. Maurice, T. H. Huxley, Robert Browning, and Thomas Carlyle. In fact, her father's friend, F. D. Maurice, became her godfather. Her father was an Anglican minister who had come under the influence of the Christian Socialists. She then goes on to say about her father's family, "My aunt, Emily Davies, was a pioneer of middle-class women's education, and the originator of Girton College."[50] Llewelyn Davies attended Girton College after beginning her higher education at Queen's College, London. Apparently, her family applied their "advanced" ideas to their own children, as Margaret was treated no differently from her brothers when it came to educational opportunities. However, there was the exception of her given name. Each of her six brothers was christened with the family name, Llewelyn, as his middle name. But she was named Margaret Caroline. She adopted Llewelyn on her own some time prior to the commencement of her public career as an activist for the working class. Perhaps this name change means she wished she had been born a boy, but that is doubtful because of her women-centered life's work and her tendency to bond closely with other women.

Before Lilian Harris entered her life, her closest friend was Rosalind Shore Smith. Shore Smith, under her married name, Nash, later became quite active in the campaign for the endowment of motherhood. However, she held some shockingly conservative opinions with respect to state-sponsored pensions for working-class housewives. She recommended that the government police the behavior of pension recipients.[51] The working-class women in the Guild certainly did not support such intrusive scrutiny, nor did Llewelyn Davies.[52] Nonetheless, the above-described pictures, which the general secretary apparently treasured, suggest that class impeded her ability to appreciate the conditions under which working-class women lived their lives as much as it did Shore Smith's. The drawing, "Fecondité," and the photograph of the monument to Marianne may refer to the 1899 pro-natalist novel by Emile Zola. In Zola's novel, titled *Fecondité*, the main female character is named Marianne. She is a married working-class woman who gives birth to a dozen children. But unlike real-life working-class mothers, she never had any difficulties supporting them financially since her husband's wages miraculously always managed to keep pace with the growth of the family. In her book, *Family, Dependence and the Origins of the Welfare State*, Susan Pedersen characterizes this novel as a conservative text designed to encourage men and women to do their reproductive duty to the state.[53] It was born of turn-of-the-century fears about declining birth rates caused by the advent of the New Woman and the spread, among the middle class at least, of the practice of birth control. Natalists like Zola feared that a decrease in their nation's population would leave it unable to defend itself in the event of war. Llewelyn Davies was a committed pacifist. So she would certainly not have shared Zola's desire to keep people breeding in order to supply the state with soldiers. But it appears she admired his novel and consequently kept the sketch and the photograph named after it and its main character. What may have prompted her admiration was her esteem for working-class mothers, whose lives she regarded as difficult—so difficult that she eventually turned the Guild into an organization primarily devoted to improving the deplorable conditions of working-class maternity. In so doing, she essentialized working-class women as much as Zola had, indicating the potential ideological affiliations between conservatism and the so-called new feminist positions, which came to dominate the English women's movement after World War I and of which the Guild was a harbinger. All working-class women were like the woman on the Guild's membership card for Llewelyn Davies and, ironically, her stereotyping of them in that fashion prevented her from enabling them to imagine other possibilities for their lives, just as much as did the limitations of the women's own desires for themselves. To be sure, a number of guildswomen entered public careers in the service of local government agencies while Llewelyn Davies was general secretary, but they did so to improve the conditions of working-class women as wives and mothers, and like their leader never imagined those women in nontraditional careers. Under Llewelyn Davies's direction, the Guild became no more than a "married woman's trade union," which was a characterization of it devised by Shore Smith and which the general secretary adopted for structuring the organization's work.[54]

Llewelyn Davies befriended Shore Smith at Girton and both their families lived in Marylebone. Llewelyn Davies's father was rector of Christ Church there. Llewelyn Davies and Shore Smith were extraordinarily close, both simultaneously deciding in the mid-1880s to devote their lives to the amelioration of the condition of the working class. Martha Vicinus in *Independent Women* describes how the "passionate positive ideas of celibacy and intellectual dedication," which had shaped their college experiences, made middle-class women eager to reproduce college community life in the world.[55] Llewelyn Davies and Shore Smith typify such women. In Marylebone, they became active in a club designed to provide working-class adults with more wholesome recreation than that offered by public houses and music halls. They played at being what Llewelyn Davies called "amateur sanitary inspector[s]."[56] Finally, in 1886, they encountered the Marylebone Cooperative Society and were taken to a meeting of its newly formed branch of the Women's Cooperative Guild by a mutual friend.[57] It might be claimed that Llewelyn Davies's Christian Socialist father instigated his daughter's interest in cooperation, since back in the 1860s the leaders of that Anglican group had become supporters of the Cooperative movement.[58] However, it is just as likely Llewelyn Davies herself concluded that if she intended to devote her life to advocacy on behalf of the working class, she would have to participate in the movements which that class had generated and in working-class culture. In her autobiography she says she came to realize that trade unionism and cooperation were "woven into the fabric of workers' lives."[59] She adds that joining the Marylebone branch of the Guild "opened up to me a new world, practically unknown to the well-to-do classes."[60] Like the Victorian missionaries to "darkest" Africa, she found she had to get to know the "natives" intimately, and to make their interests her interests, before she could bring them the light. This analogy is a useful one because middle-class reformers like Llewelyn Davies were as guilty of imperializing their charges as were Christian missionaries of imperializing the inhabitants of the colonies. Middle-class reformers thought the working class was in need of "civilizing,"[61] and, as Martha Vicinus observes, often used colonial metaphors to describe their work on behalf of the poor.[62] While missionaries to foreign lands acted out of racist notions of the white man's burden, the reformers were motivated by classist perceptions of the condition of England question. In the last analysis, neither were capable of functioning as interpreters of the needs and wishes of those to whom they ministered.

After joining the Marylebone branch of the Guild, Shore Smith and Llewelyn Davies began to go more separate ways. First distance, then marriage came between them. In 1889, just before Llewelyn Davies assumed her position as general secretary of the Guild, her father was transferred to the parish of Kirkby Lonsdale, in Westmorland. A few years later, Shore Smith fell in love and married. Her husband, Vaughan Nash, was a middle-class propagandist for the Cooperative movement, and after their marriage both husband and wife continued to work for the cause. Shore Smith remained associated with the Guild and for eight years edited the column that organization used in the weekly newspaper of the Cooperative movement. During that period, she and Llewelyn Davies worked closely to use the "Woman's Corner" to represent the Guild's interests. But the nature of their relationship had changed.

Llewelyn Davies met Lilian Harris in Westmorland. Harris lived with her family in the mansion her wealthy father had built in the Lake District. She quickly came to replace Shore Smith in Llewelyn Davies's life. The physical resemblance between Harris and Shore Smith is striking. Photographs show both had dark, wavy hair and wore it similarly. Both had thick-lidded eyes, thin lips, and large noses. It is probable Llewelyn Davies and Harris became fast friends because Harris reminded the Guild leader of Shore Smith.

Harris virtually moved into the room in the vicarage that was used for Guild business and began to function as the general secretary's "girl Friday," even before she was officially appointed the Guild's cashier in 1893. When the Reverend Davies retired in 1908 at the advanced age of eighty-two and the household moved back to London, Harris went with them. Virginia Woolf provides a picture of life in the Davies house in Hampstead from her visit in 1913.

On entering the "very dignified old house," Woolf was greeted by Harriet Kidd, an unwed mother and former factory hand to whom Llewelyn Davies had given a secretarial job.[63] Woolf immediately sensed a class barrier between herself and Kidd, characterizing the receptionist as a "watch-dog to ward off the meddlesome middle-class wasters of time who come prying into other people's business."[64] Woolf seems to be suggesting that because this working-class woman was protecting Llewelyn Davies, the general secretary of the Guild had been accepted as one of the working class to whom she ministered. Again, the missionary analogy proves useful. Whites who had lived for some time in the colonies among the people of color there were sometimes more tolerated by the indigenous population than new arrivals. So too were members of the middle class accepted by the working class to whom they ministered. Yet, class barriers persisted despite familiarity, and both sides may have wanted it that way. While the sentiments of the recipients of middle-class beneficence rarely recorded their perceptions of the relationships they had with their social superiors, the views of middle-class reformers have been preserved. One female middle-class settlement house worker characterized her relationship with her charges as follows:

It means a great deal when our women call us "ladies," and in that word they express their sense of this power given to us by our happier growth. Because of this power they turn to us with a touching faith that we shall never be mean, or ungenerous or fail in knowledge or explanation. Because we live among them they regard us as of special treasure to be guarded and made much of.[65]

Kidd guarded Llewelyn Davies like a "special treasure"; she took Woolf upstairs, where the novelist was met by Lilian Harris, who immediately put the visitor at ease. Harris impressed Woolf as a woman who effortlessly organized events like the Guild's annual congresses.[66] She could answer "questions about figures and put her hand on the right file of letters infallibly."[67] She "sat listening, without saying very much . . . ," and also made the tea.[68] In sum, she was the angel in the house. When Llewelyn Davies was ill or busy caring for her increasingly infirm father, Harris had stewardship of the Guild, having been named assistant secretary in 1901. The general secretary trusted her friend to speak and act for her. The two were married in mind and heart. Finally, Woolf says, Llewelyn Davies, the matriarch of the household, made her entrance, looking "arrowy and decisive"—in a word, masculine.[69] Again, this raises the question of Llewelyn Davies's sexual orientation. Although there is no concrete evidence that Llewelyn Davies's relationship with Harris was a physical one, Virginia Woolf's own predilections would make her likely to recognize a homosexual couple when she saw one. However, it is just as likely that Llewelyn Davies and Harris were celibate humanitarians, devoting their lives to the service of others after the fashion of Roman Catholic nuns.

These two unmarried middle-class women considered themselves spokespersons for married working-class women. During the Guild's agitation for divorce law reform, the limitations their possible sexual orientations and marital status created for their abilities to identify with the wishes of guildswomen surfaced. The publication in 1912 of the royal commission's recommendations for the reform of the divorce laws and the Guild's subsequent agitation to broaden them to include divorce by mutual consent split the Guild. Lancashire women under the leadership of Mrs. Bury, who had served four three-year terms on the Central Committee, was three times president of the Guild, and had emerged as a critic of Llewelyn Davies's leadership, objected to their organization's support for liberalizing the divorce laws. The Lancashire women took their wedding vows seriously. They had promised for better or worse, till death did part them, and they believed that all who entered into such promises should live by them. As women from the relatively well-off ranks of the working class, they knew how trying could be marriage to a man who demanded constant deference because of his ability to provide for the family. Perhaps they were, or at least knew of, women who were battered. They realized that even loving and tender husbands could be a problem because loving meant pregnancy with its attendant physical debilitations and additional caring obligations. Nonetheless, they had committed themselves to living with their husbands for better or worse, no matter how much worse it became. Llewelyn Davies was incapable of understanding the position of these dissident guildswomen.[70] She had never personally experienced a heterosexual relationship or lived intimately with a man. Working-class men from her middle-class perspective would have appeared to be particularly objectionable.[71] Gruff and unwashed as they were, she could not imagine how any woman could endure them, even if they were loving and tender, perhaps especially if they were loving and tender. No wonder she made it her life's work to make working-class wives as independent of their husbands as possible.

Llewelyn Davies occasionally revealed in her own words that she was not innocent of class prejudice. She never objected when her fellow Guild leaders, in the public forum of the *Co-operative News*, blamed the narrow-mindedness of working-class women as much as the sexism of men for the failure of guildswomen to win election to other than educational committees at the cooperative stores.[72] She even made the same accusations herself in the history of the Guild she wrote in 1904.[73] Nor did she have respect for working-class wives who preferred domesticity to public activism, despite the numerical evidence indicating that many more female cooperators wanted quiet private lives than wanted active public ones. Of the millions of women who shopped at cooperative stores, only a few thousand ever bothered to join the Guild.[74] And of those who became members, some left when their branch leaders forced them to discuss topics like women's suffrage or pacifism, which seemed too radical to them.[75] To correct what the general secretary perceived as a misguided preference for domesticity, she used the letters written to her by working-class wives who balanced home duties with other commitments to admonish those who alleged their households kept them too busy for community involvement. In *Life As We Have Known It*, a Mrs. Layton recalls how wrong she was to have assumed that she was too busy to join the Guild when she was first invited[76]; and a "Lancashire Guildswoman" provides a model for scheduling the week's housework around meetings.[77] This second woman was particularly proud of having "never bought a week's baking" during her married life and of her reputation as the woman who always hurried home from out-of-town commitments in order to have a hot dinner ready for her family, proving that working-class women could manage the new double shift of domesticity and public activism.[78] However, this woman did admit she heard the siren song of the private sphere call to her many times in her travels on behalf of her work: "I have trudged through snow and rain with my bag, and I have carried my bag in my hand until my fingers have tingled with the frost, feeling that I should have been better at home."[79] But her "real love for the work" and the receptions she received when she arrived at her destinations helped her resist temptation.[80] Evidence of the atypicality of these women among both Guild members and the larger population of working-class women who participated in the Cooperative movement is provided by the fact that Llewelyn Davies used the same letters in her 1904 Guild history, and for the same purpose—to encourage the domestically oriented to adopted public activism.[81]

Llewelyn Davies also showed class bias when she characterized working-class women according to stereotypes with which the middle-class readers of

Victorian fiction would be familiar. They were either heroines or quaint person-
ages who spoke odd dialects. For instance, the women she chose to represent as
typical guildswomen in *Life As We Have Known It* all overcame monumental
hardships before coming to live happily ever after; these choices illustrate why
one scholar considers this volume a middle-class mediated book in which
working-class women do not actually speak for themselves.[82] One of the women
who appears in this book survived the filth and epidemics of Bethnal Green;
another endured many abusive situations as a domestic servant until finally being employed by a caring couple who taught her to read; another experienced
the lash of the overseer as a child agricultural worker in the Fens; and there was
Harriet Kidd, who was raped and impregnated by the factory owner for whom
she worked.[83] Had the extraordinary survivors in *Life As We Have Known It*
been typical of those who shopped at cooperative stores, or even of guildswomen, there would have occurred the dawn of the Cooperative Commonwealth Llewelyn Davies so eagerly predicted from women wielding their market
baskets like the "revolutionary weapon[s]" she considered them.[84]

In addition to heroines, Llewelyn Davies's publications are populated by
working-class women and men who speak in half-literate, regional dialects like
Dickens characters. In her 1904 history of the Guild, she recounts what one
working-class wife said to her husband when he tried to stop her from going to a
Guild meeting: "Nay, tha's had thy day in leaving me wi' childer, it's my turn
nah, and ah's going."[85] She also reports the conversation she overheard between
two men after a lecture sponsored by a Guild branch:

I say, how don these women manage to get up sich good lecters? They're better nor
moest o' thoose we getten fro' th' Educational Committee, an' th' women hanna so mich
money for to goo at noather, but they beaten us chaps sometimes.[86]

Finally, she displayed her class prejudices by prefacing the testimonials to the
benefits of Guild membership, which she provided in her 1904 history of the
organization, by remarking of working-class women: "Very few have the character and interest to study and think alone, unaided."[87] These prejudices explain
why the general secretary felt compelled to direct the guildswomen's course of
study.

Of her accomplishments as general secretary of the Women's Cooperative
Guild, Llewelyn Davies was most proud of what she had been able to do to
break down what she described as the "isolation" experienced in the home by
working-class wives, and of the improvements her efforts had brought to the
health of mothers and their infants.[88] The positivist bent she had inherited from
her mother's side of the family drove her to measure the former with statistics in
the annual reports of the Guild, which she wrote every year for thirty-two years.
For Llewelyn Davies, proof that a working-class wife had been liberated from
her "isolation" was provided by the number of activities she undertook outside
of the home. Thus the general secretary meticulously cited, in her annual reports, statistics relating to the number of women elected to the educational or
management committees of the cooperative stores, to the various committees of
the Cooperative Union, or to the board of directors of the Cooperative Whole-

sale Society. She listed the numbers of guildswomen who became factory in-spectors, poor-law guardians or justices of the peace.

In her early years as leader of the Guild, Llewelyn Davies had imagined that one day soon such a separate organization for women cooperators as the Guild would no longer be necessary because gender discrimination within the Cooperative movement, at least, would fall before the evidence of women's competency to function in roles that men had hitherto monopolized. Male and female cooperators would then work side by side to advance their cause.[89] But each year the evidence of the numbers indicated to her that gender discrimina-tion was not to be so easily conquered. For every three women elected to educa-tional committees, only one successfully ran for a seat on a management com-mittee.[90] Men were willing to vote for women candidates for educational com-mittees because the instruction of future generations in the principles of coop-eration suited what they considered to be women's natural roles. They continued to think of the reading of balance sheets as men's work, so election to manage-ment committees eluded even those female candidates whom the Guild had trained in accounting.[91] Winning seats on such powerful committees of the Co-operative Union as the Central Board, or election to the CWS's board of direc-tors, was even more difficult. During Llewelyn Davies's tenure as general sec-retary, no more than one or two women ever served at any one time on the Cen-tral Board of the Cooperative Union, and no more than one on the board of di-rectors of the Wholesale Society, as chapter two indicates.[92] Reflecting in her autobiography on this empirical evidence for the persistence of sexism, Llewelyn Davies admitted that she had been too sanguine in her youth about the prospects for the end of gender discrimination. She no longer thought the Guild could one day soon disband. She said: "From my experience I have found that, so long as there is class and sex inequality, it is necessary that working-women should have their own separate and affiliated organisations."[93] She maintained that only within the confines of such bodies would working-class women find the nurturing they needed to prepare them to lead active public lives as coop-erators and citizens. Her many years of reading and editing the correspondence of guildswomen had shown Llewelyn Davies how deficient such women were in basic skills:

the special circumstances of women's lives, and the effects of these circumstances, to-gether with the fact that men are in possession, and not without prejudice as regards women's place and work, make it essential, if men and women are to come together on terms of real equality and comradeship, and if women's point of view is to be properly expressed, that women should for some time yet have special organisations of their own.[94]

She knew working-class women risked ridicule and dismissal from both men and social superiors if they dared enter public arenas untutored and unprepared. As a result, the Guild needed to be there to meet women's special needs. How-ever, this encouraged men to see women as people with special needs and, therefore, as people who were not as good as men were.

It is not surprising that Llewelyn Davies considered what the Guild had achieved for mothers and their infants to be the other great accomplishment of her career. The Guild's fight for the inclusion of maternity benefits in the 1911 Health Insurance Act, and then the payment of those benefits directly to the mother rather than the male head of household, and later for a program of maternity care run by the local government boards, was the one area of agitation in which the Guild had much success.[95] While even this success was limited by the failure of the government to follow all the Guild's recommendations to the letter and by the postwar budget cutbacks, the Guild's other reforming efforts had had even more mixed results.

The Guild's campaign for a minimum wage for the female employees of cooperative stores and manufactories eventually won the support of the CWS, but the Wholesale Society left implementation to the discretion of store and factory managers with the predictable result that many did not enforce the scale. The Guild's support for divorce law reform landed it in a four-year struggle with the Cooperative Union during which the Union cut off its funding of Guild activities. The settlement house established by the Sunderland Cooperative Society was closed after a little more than a year, and the neighborhood store was left to struggle on its own. The international cooperative movement ran afoul of economic depression and the rise of fascism, and Hitler soon made pacifism look foolish. There is no record of what Llewelyn Davies thought about the Second World War. Nor was she in London for the blitz, she and Harris having already left Hampstead for Dorking, where at most they would have heard the war machines rumble by on their way to larger prey than the women's little town.[96]

With respect to the enfranchisement of women, Llewelyn Davies was very proud of what the Guild had been able to do to prove that working-class women wanted and deserved the vote.[97] And even in 1927, after women had had the vote for almost a decade, she still believed that the world was about to be transformed by women's enfranchisement,[98] unlike Virginia Woolf who had already come to the conclusion that a guaranteed income of £500 a year was more useful than the right to vote.[99] Nonetheless, Llewelyn Davies was not about to claim for the Guild the credit for the passing of the 1918 Representation of the People Act, as she did that year's Maternity and Infant Welfare Act.[100]

As for the lack of enthusiasm among guildswomen for agitating for women's trade unionism, it drove the general secretary gradually to abandon efforts to use the Guild to assist in the organization of women's waged labor and to gravitate to the position that the Guild was "a married women's trade union." She then concentrated on using the Guild to promote improvements in the conditions of labor in the home, including the task of reproduction. Such an interest was certainly an understandable one for an organization of married women, most of whom were mothers. They definitely could claim to speak authoritatively about maternity, even if their leader could not. Thus campaigning on behalf of mothers and their infants became the cause for which the Guild and its childless leader received the most recognition from the government and from dignitaries.[101] However, it also meant that women who prioritized occupations other than motherhood could find no home in the Guild, and that men both within and without the Cooperative movement would see guildswomen as people who were not competent to speak on issues unrelated to the family.

Although Llewelyn Davies never bore a child, she appears to have loved children and they seem to have reciprocated her affection. In this she was quite different from her more famous spinster aunt Emily, whom children considered cold and unloving.[102] Among the remnants of the materials from the Sunderland experiment in Llewelyn Davies's private papers are photographs of her with the neighborhood's children and letters to her from girls who wanted to keep in touch with her after she had left the settlement house.[103] One, Frances Jane Davie, was an especially frequent correspondent with the general secretary. She gave Llewelyn Davies her exercise book from a poetry reading at the settlement house,[104] and also sent explanations as to why she could no longer attend the children's league meetings—she had to help her mother at home.[105] She called the general secretary her "Ideal Friend,"[106] and tried to imagine what Llewelyn Davies's home in Westmorland was like, concluding it had to be "like the garden of Eden."[107] Indeed, Margaret Llewelyn Davies must have seemed to the children she encountered at the settlement house like a mythological goddess come to live for a time among them. The photograph of her at the beginning of this chapter fails to do her justice. It was taken when she was already passed 60 years of age. A glimpse of what she looked like in her youth may be had in one of the photographs at the beginning of chapter six. Llewelyn Davies was a tall, graceful woman, with a melodious speaking voice. Her aquiline nose gave her face a classic beauty, especially in profile. More to the point, she was aware of her physical attributes and appears to have used them to seduce the children into becoming cooperators, persuading them to join the store's penny bank and the settlement house's children's league. As one of her fellow missionaries at the house pointed out, "the boys and girls are first-rate propagandists,"[108] effective agents for breaking down resistance to the store among the more reticent adults. This suggests Llewelyn Davies was, in reality, not interested in the children for their own sakes, although the end to which she used them as means was certainly altruistic.

The Guild leader had as her primary objective the mothers of the children, always believing that when you helped the mother, you helped the child. As early as 1889 she had opposed in a Central Committee meeting the notion "that the chief work of the guild was dealing with children rather than women."[109] Her predecessor as general secretary, Mary Lawrenson, a schoolteacher by profession, had tried to make the Guild an organization dedicated to working for the welfare of children. After Llewelyn Davies took over, however, Lawrenson found that she would have to forsake the Guild for involvement with the children's groups sponsored by the Cooperative movement, if she wanted to continue to pursue her interest in the young, because the new general secretary became so successful at redirecting the Guild's emphasis along lines she preferred. Virginia Woolf once described Llewelyn Davies as a person who "could compel a steam roller to waltz"[110]; the less sophisticated working-class women she encountered in the Guild clearly found her a force impossible to resist. Like Mary Lawrenson, most of her working-class opponents opted for retreat from the organization.

However, Llewelyn Davies, a reactive leader who borrowed ideas from others, managed to capture and retain the leadership of the Guild for reasons beyond those of her persuasive personality. A combination of her middle-class advantages and fortuitous developments within the constitution of the Guild also helped her gain and keep her position.

Llewelyn Davies's social background made possible her election as general secretary at the age of twenty-eight, after only three years of involvement with the Cooperative movement. Members of the Central Committee were elected annually. The branches were first circularized for their nominations; nominees were then contacted to be sure they were willing to run; finally, voting papers were sent to the branches and returned by them to the general secretary for tabulation. Llewelyn Davies first ran for a position on the Guild's Central Committee in 1887, after only a year's membership in the Marylebone Cooperative Society. When she tried again the next year, she won, paving the way for her successful bid for the general secretaryship in 1889, when Mary Lawrenson resigned. She was on the ballot for that position with one other candidate, her friend Shore Smith, who posted a notice in the "Woman's Corner" asking that no one vote for her as she considered Llewelyn Davies to be the ideal person for the job.[111] Had Llewelyn Davies been a working-class woman, neither this rapid rise to a position of authority in the Guild nor fixity of tenure in it would have been possible.

A working-class wife would first need a supportive husband to be able to join a Guild branch and work for it. Indeed, most working-class women who rose to positions of national or regional importance in the Guild had husbands who were either employed by the Cooperative movement or were zealous cooperators. Mary Lawrenson and the president of the Guild with whom she had served, Annie Jones, certainly had such husbands. So did the married women in *Life As We Have Known It.*[112]

Next, a working-class wife would need a small family if she hoped to rise within the Guild, because too many pregnancies and childcare obligations would get in the way of her Guild commitments. Again, to use the examples of the only two working-class women on the seven-member Central Committee in 1888, when Llewelyn Davies first gained election to it, Mary Lawrenson had only one child and Annie Jones four children in an era when most working-class families were much larger.

Then, a working-class woman would have to spend years of activism at the branch level of the Guild before running for a national leadership position, since she would need to acquire the basic language and speaking skills, not to mention the self-confidence, that formal education had given Llewelyn Davies. She would also have to have the good fortune to have suffered none of those accidents of fate, such as the death or disability of a husband, which often reduced working-class wives to taking in laundry to support the family. Her husband would have to have a secure, well-paying job too, because there were many incidental expenses that went with Guild work, and she would have to have spending money for them. Beyond the 6d. per annum membership dues owed to her branch,[113] there were additional fees depending on how involved she wanted to become in Guild work. After the Guild was divided into districts and sections in 1890, a working-class woman would have had to become active in those if she hoped to rise in the Guild. The districts held periodic conferences, and if she were chosen as her branch's delegate to one of these, the branch was obligated to pay only half her expenses. If she moved up to sectional work and became a delegate to a sectional conference, the central fund (accumulated from annual contributions from branches at the rate of 2d. per member) paid for half of her expenses. If she became well enough known to become a sectional secretary, an important prerequisite for election to the Central Committee, the central fund would pay her an honorarium annually, but the committee was determined to keep this sum small so that it could not be considered a salary. The policy during the years of Llewelyn Davies's tenure as general secretary was to maintain the principle of voluntarism in leadership positions.[114]

There is evidence that Llewelyn Davies often used her personal wealth and connections on behalf of the Guild. On April 7, 1888, the Central Committee received a special donation from a friend at the Marylebone Guild branch[115]; a gift from Mrs. Davies financed the first Guild organizer; money from a friend, Ada Mocatta, financed the second; and Llewelyn Davies offered her own money for the salary of the third if the Guild agreed to pay the organizer's traveling expenses.[116] When the Cooperative Union tried to stop the Guild from agitating for divorce law reform by cutting off its annual grant of £400, Llewelyn Davies offered to cover any resulting deficits in the Guild's budget from her own pocket, asking only that the Guild pay her back when it could afford to do so.[117] No working-class woman could have afforded such generosity.

When Llewelyn Davies became general secretary of the Guild, it was not yet clear that that particular position on the Central Committee would become the dominant one. Between 1886 and 1892 the president of the Guild wielded great authority. It is true the presidency had been no more than an honorary position in the mid-1880s, when the ailing Alice Acland occupied it and the Guild even considered eliminating the office, but Acland's replacement by Annie Jones in 1886 changed matters.[118] Jones was well connected in the Cooperative movement by virtue of her marriage to Ben Jones, the director of the London branch of the CWS and co-author with Alice Acland's husband of the then definitive textbook on cooperation, *Working Men Co-operators*. She believed passionately in the movement and spoke on platforms on its behalf. She felt women were the ideal propagandists for cooperation because they were the ones who did the grocery shopping. Moreover, she deferred to the male leadership of the movement in a manner both men and traditionalist women found reassuring. At the 1890 Cooperative Congress she told her audience that she would not advise women "to take up co-operative work and neglect household duties . . . [because] they had a duty to their husbands and children, and though they should try to help one another, still they had to remember in the first place home duties."[119] Had Annie Jones been able to remain as president of the Guild as long as Llewelyn Davies served as general secretary, the direction the Guild would have taken would have been different from the one Llewelyn Davies set for it. It would even have attracted a greater proportion of female cooperators as members because a married woman who prioritized the home, like Annie Jones, was more typical of the average woman shopping at a cooperative store than was Llewelyn Davies. But, in 1892, Jones was forced to leave her office because of the new rules governing service on the Central Committee, which the Guild had adopted in 1888, limiting terms of service on it to three years for everyone except the general secretary. After a twelve-month hiatus, Jones again became eligible for election to the committee according to the new rules. So she ran in 1893, and was successful, but she died suddenly the next year at the youthful age of forty-six. Llewelyn Davies had happened upon her position at the right time in the Guild's constitutional history, and the premature death of a leader who might have been able to articulate an alternative vision enhanced Llewelyn Davies's opportunity to shape the direction of the Guild.

Many have claimed that the Women's Cooperative Guild was a democratic organization run by its rank and file and not governed from the top down by the Central Committee or the general secretary. Llewelyn Davies insists on this point in her history of the Guild, and so does Catherine Webb in hers, as do Gaffin and Thoms in their 1983 telling of the Guild's story, and Gillian Scott in her recently published doctoral dissertation.[120] A disputation of this thesis best begins with the following quotation from one of the tributes paid to Llewelyn Davies upon her retirement from office: "whether we like to think it or not, an enormously large degree of the vitality and effectiveness of any association of people, however broadly democratic its government may be, rests upon the personality of its executive official."[121] After thirty-two years under her direction, the Guild and Llewelyn Davies had become synonymous. Comments made about her retirement by guildswomen serve as further illustration: it was impossible for many guildswomen to imagine the organization without her.[122] One woman, A. E. Corrie from the Coventry branch, went so far as to write to the women's column of the *Co-operative News* that there must be some misunderstanding; Llewelyn Davies could not really be resigning.[123] As for those who could bring themselves to believe their leader was leaving them, most pointed out: "It is wonderful, as you say, that the working women should have built up such an organisation, but it would have been impossible without strong personalities [a reference to Llewelyn Davies in combination with Harris] at the head."[124]

"It is wonderful, *as you say*, that the working women should have built up such an organisation." Llewelyn Davies and Guild propagandists tried to use rhetoric to create reality. They wanted the Guild to be democratically run and hoped that if they said often enough that it was, it would become so. The evidence most often used to defend the proposition that the Guild was a democracy is the role played by its annual congress in the organization's governance. Each branch sent delegates to the congress, one delegate for every twenty-five members, but high percentages of the branches never bothered to send delegates.[125] At congress, the delegates would vote on propositions put before them by the Central Committee, support for which the committee had developed over the course of the year. The Central Committee meeting minutes show few suggestions arising from the branches, and moving through the districts and sections, to the Central Committee.[126] Indeed, the traffic in ideas went the other way. The Central Committee would, for instance, select a topic for study at the autumn sectional conferences; the topic would then go on to the district level for discussion; and finally to the branches. The resolutions to support the Central Committee's direction, which invariably arose from these deliberations, would then be voted on at the next summer's congress. On occasions when branches attempted to circumvent this process, the Central Committee ruled them out of order. For instance, in 1918, the Leicester branch of the Guild attempted to introduce a resolution of its own before a sectional conference. (There is no record of what that resolution was.) The sectional council sought the advice of the Central Committee concerning this deviation from protocol. The Central Committee instructed the sectional council to tell the Leicester branch "that in view of the fact that Sectional Conferences are held for the purpose of discussing special subjects agreed on, no resolutions are in order except those moved by the [Sectional] Councils themselves."[127] Gillian Scott believes that the suffocating of democratic branch initiative did not occur until after Llewelyn Davies departed from office.[128] However, authoritarianism was built into the Guild's governing structure and Llewelyn Davies had helped to put it there.

To illustrate the nature of the Guild's governing structure with a specific example, in 1904 the Guild celebrated its twenty-first anniversary and established a Coming of Age Fund. The Central Committee deliberated the purpose to which the fund should be put. These discussions coincided with the decision of the Sunderland Cooperative Society to abandon its support for the settlement house that Llewelyn Davies had made her pet project. She pushed for using the money to support further efforts to extend cooperation to the poor, but suggested the branches be circularized for their opinions first.[129] When the branches proposed a variety of suggestions for using the money, Llewelyn Davies ignored them. The Central Committee brought before the annual congress for a vote only the resolution that the Coming of Age Fund be used to finance schemes for bringing cooperation to the poor.[130] The delegates to the congress, being either unaware of the other proposals or reluctant to speak against such an altruistic motion as the one proposed, unanimously approved it, enabling the Central Committee to appoint a Miss Rushworth to be an organizer at the store the Bristol Cooperative Society had established in a poor neighborhood.[131]

In her retirement, the former general secretary continued to influence the course of the Guild. She had groomed her two immediate successors, Honora Enfield, who had been her personal secretary, and Eleanor Barton, who had stood by her when a number of Guild branches challenged the Central Committee's 1917 and 1918 Guild congress resolutions demanding a negotiated peace to end the war then raging.[132] In 1931, Llewelyn Davies recommended the organization's attentions be focused on the three reforms she considered most urgent for the future. First, she declared the state must be made to give a family allowance to increase the purchasing power of the people as a first step to a more equal distribution of wealth. She also called for a new outlook on marriage, sex, and parental relations—one that would correspond with the growing independence of women and youth. Finally, and most strongly, she called for the abolition of war and fear of war.[133] She did not provide more specific details as to what she meant by a new outlook on marriage, sex, and parental relations; nor did she describe how she thought the state could be persuaded to give a family allowance or abolish war. However, she was certain that the Guild she once led should be in the forefront working to secure these achievements, and that its efforts would make a difference, even if guildswomen represented only a small portion of the women who shopped at cooperative stores. Llewelyn Davies was a great admirer of the communist experiment in which the Bolsheviks of the new Soviet Union were engaged, and indeed, her guildswomen were in a position similar to Lenin's Marxist intelligentsia—few in number when compared to the rest of the population. Yet she was as confident as he had been that, with a few apostles, revolutions could be made. Unfortunately, as the Soviet experiment proved, relying on the leadership of a few neither makes for democracy nor addresses the needs of the majority. That Llewelyn Davies was attracted to such a style for effecting change illustrates biases that were corrosive of democratic participation, and, in particular, it shows that she considered the many too overburdened by the chores associated with everyday life to know what was in their best interests until educated by their leaders. She calls to mind Robert Owen, whom cooperators criticized for not permitting the working class to chart its own course on the road to self-improvement. And ironically, even her one concession to the realities of life for most guildswomen—that they were mothers first and foremost—turned out to have ambivalent consequences. It enabled the Guild to play a significant role in securing better conditions for mothers and infants, but it made guildswomen appear to be qualified to speak only when arguing for the welfare of mothers and infants.

Thus a critical examination of Margaret Llewelyn Davies's background and the circumstances of her private life reveals the extent to which her public career was shaped by them. Her leadership style, the causes she prioritized, and the limits of her ability to identify with others were prescribed and proscribed by her experiences of class and by her lack of personal experience with either marriage or motherhood. Conscious of her own importance to an organization of women without the time, training, and sometimes even the desire for public lives, she kept among her private papers a history of the Guild which accorded her more significance than its founders. She sold pictures of herself to the rank-and-file guildswomen who admired her; she considered herself a breath of fresh air in their lives. In a manner similar to a colonial missionary, she delighted in converting working-class housewives into political activists, showing them that the personal is indeed political, but thereby also imposing on them her own beliefs about what makes for a fulfilling life. Deaf to dissidents in the Guild because either her middle-class background or her possible sexual orientation made her incapable of valuing what they considered important, she made sure the Central Committee usually got its way. She had come to a position of authority within the Guild, not because of her inspired leadership abilities, but because she was a capable administrator who could implement ideas borrowed from others. Her class advantages assisted her in this. Working-class guildswomen had neither the leisure time nor the financial resources that she had. Finally, fortuitous constitutional changes and the untimely death of Annie Jones helped secure for her fixity of tenure on the Central Committee and removed the possibility of competing visions for the Guild's future developing. Margaret Llewelyn Davies was an unmarried middle-class woman with a mission: she wanted to do her part to solve the condition of England question in both its class and its gender manifestations. For her that meant using the Guild to make working-class housewives' views correspond to what she considered were in their best interests.

NOTES

1. "Woman's Corner," *Co-operative News*, July 6, 1901.
2. Gaffin and Thoms, *Caring and Sharing*, 41.
3. Webb, *The Woman with the Basket*, 16.
4. London School of Economics, coll. misc. 268 m363, vol. I, item 48, folio 152.
5. Scott, *Feminism and the Politics of Working Women*, chapters 6–9.
6. Harrison, *Prudent Revolutionaries*, 11.
7. Llewelyn Davies, *The Women's Co-operative Guild*, 57.
8. The Cooperative Union Limited, *The Twenty-first Annual Co-operative Congress* (Manchester: Cooperative Union Ltd., 1889), 106; Women's Cooperative Guild, *Outline of Work with Model Branch Rules* (Manchester: Cooperative Printing Society Ltd., 1891), 7.
9. Lewis, *Women in England*, 54.
10. Hull University Library, DCW 1/5, Minute books of the Central Committee, August 22 and 23, 1912.
11. Levine, *Feminist Lives in Victorian England*, 5.
12. Harrison, *Prudent Revolutionaries*, 41.
13. London School of Economics, coll. misc. 268 m363, vol. I, item 34, folios 77-78.
14. Ibid.
15. Ibid.
16. These are the words of Elizabeth Roberts, who, in *A Woman's Place* (124), asserts that in reality working-class housewives were "respected and highly regarded household manager[s], and the arbiter[s] of familial and indeed neighbourhood standards."
17. Morris, *Women Workers and the Sweated Trades*, 147–149.
18. Roberts, *A Woman's Place*, 137; and Roberts, "Women's Strategies, 1890–1940," in Lewis (ed.), *Labour and Love*, 230. Even in Lancashire, where it was common for married women to work for wages outside the home, working-class women often dreamed of giving up their paying jobs to be full-time housewives and, according to Liddington and Norris in *One Hand Tied Behind Us* (39), this created problems for those who hoped to organize women's trade unions.
19. For instance, Llewelyn Davies and Catherine Webb both argued this point in the "Woman's Corner," *Co-operative News*, September 22, 1894, and September 30, 1893, respectively. Earlier, in 1892, Llewelyn Davies had assigned issues pertaining to women's waged labor outside the home as a topic for branches to study; see "Woman's Corner," *Co-operative News*, October 8, 1892.
20. Sidney Webb, *The Best Method of Bringing Cooperation within the Reach of the Poorest of the Population* (Manchester: Cooperative Union Ltd., n.d.).
21. Vicinus notes that these were the watchwords of Toynbee Hall; see her evaluation of its activities in *Independent Women*, 212–214.
22. Gaffin and Thoms, *Caring and Sharing*, 54–81.
23. "Woman's Corner," *Co-operative News*, June 18, 1887.
24. Mary Lawrenson, Llewelyn Davies's predecessor as general secretary, believed Llewelyn Davies had moved the Guild too far away from cooperative concerns;

see "Woman's Corner," *Co-operative News*, December 17, 1904. Also, in the years before World War I a frequent contributor of letters to the editor of the "Woman's Corner" of the *Co-operative News*, Edith Abbott, was quite critical of Llewelyn Davies's leadership. On April 22, 1911, she voiced the opinion that many of the concerns the Guild had become involved with were "faddist" and asserted that the so-called "minority" who thought as she did was not as small as "some think."

25. This was quickly made the theme for the autumn sectional conferences; see "Woman's Corner," *Co-operative News*, November and December 1907.

26. "Woman's Corner," *Co-operative News*, November 9, 1907.

27. *Co-operative News*, June 6, 1908, gives a verbatim report of the discussion and decision.

28. Cooperative Union Library, Manchester, Minutes of the Parliamentary Committee from 1908, 1909, 1910, 1911.

29. Joyce M. Bellamy and John Saville, *Dictionary of Labour Biography*, vol. 1 (London: Macmillan Press Ltd., 1972), 96–99.

30. Susan Pedersen speculates about Rathbone's sexual orientation in "Eleanor Rathbone, 1872–1946: The Victorian Family Under the Daughter's Eye," in Pedersen and Mandler (eds.), *After the Victorians*, 116–117.

31. Leila J. Rupp, "'Imagine My Surprise': Women's Relationships in Historical Perspective," *Frontiers* vol. 5, no. 3 (1981), 68.

32. Faderman, *Surpassing the Love of Men*, 157.

33. Ibid., 163–164.

34. The library at the University of Hull holds materials having to do with Llewelyn Davies's tenure as general secretary of the Guild, including the minute books she kept of the Central Committee meetings. However, this collection neither contains personal information about her nor focuses entirely on her as a public figure since it is a collection of Guild materials that spans more than the years of her service to that organization.

35. Llewelyn Davies (ed.), *Life As We Have Known It*, xxviii.

36. Rupp, "'Imagine My Surprise,'" 68.

37. Harrison, *Prudent Revolutionaries*, 101; and Pedersen, "Eleanor Rathbone, 1872–1946: The Victorian Family Under the Daughter's Eye," in Pedersen and Mandler (eds.), *After the Victorians*, 106.

38. Faderman, *Surpassing the Love of Men*, 150–152.

39. London School of Economics, coll. misc. 268 m363, vol. VII, item 14, folio 7.

40. London School of Economics, coll. misc. 268 m363, vol. VII, item 15, folio 8.

41. London School of Economics, coll. misc. 268 m363, vol. VII, item 16, folio 9.

42. Rupp, "'Imagine My Surprise,'" 67.

43. Ibid.

44. Ibid.

45. London School of Economics, coll. misc. 268 m363, vol. I, item 39, folio 97.

46. Ursula Henriques, *Religious Toleration in England, 1787–1833* (Toronto: University of Toronto Press, 1961), provides a fine discussion of the contributions of Unitarians to the foundations of political radicalism.

47. Levine, *Feminist Lives in Victorian England*, 33. Also see Kathryn Gleadle, *The Early Feminists: Radical Unitarianism and the Emergence of the Women's Rights Movement* (New York: St. Martin's Press, 1995).

48. "Woman's Corner," *Co-operative News*, March 2, 1895.

49. Ibid.

50. London School of Economics, coll. misc. 268 m363, vol. I, item 39, folio 97.

51. Pedersen, *Family, Dependence and the Origins of the Welfare State*, 174.

52. Land, "Eleanor Rathbone," in Smith (ed.), *British Feminism in the Twentieth Century*, 108.

53. Pedersen, *Family, Dependence and the Origins of the Welfare State*, 26–29.

54. London School of Economics, coll. misc. 268 m363, vol. I, item 41, folio 117.

55. Vicinus, *Independent Women*, 149.

56. London School of Economics, coll. misc. 268 m363, vol. I, item 39, folio 98.

57. Women's Cooperative Guild, *Handbook of the Annual Meeting* (Manchester: Cooperative Printing Society, Ltd., 1894), 34.

58. Bellamy and Saville, *Dictionary of Labour Biography*, 97.

59. London School of Economics, coll. misc. 268 m363, vol. I, item 39, folio 98.

60. Ibid.

61. Rose, *Limited Livelihoods*, 37.

62. Vicinus, *Independent Women*, 219.

63. Llewelyn Davies (ed.), *Life As We Have Known It*, xxiv.

64. Ibid.

65. Quoted in Vicinus, *Independent Women*, 241.

66. Llewelyn Davies (ed.), *Life As We Have Known It*, xxv.

67. Ibid.

68. Ibid.

69. Ibid.

70. See the correspondence between Mrs. Bury and Llewelyn Davies in the "Women's Corner" of the *Co-operative News* between April 19 and May 3, 1913. Also, see the *Co-operative News*'s coverage of the divorce law reform discussion at the 1914 Guild Congress, *Co-operative News*, June 27, 1914.

71. Phillips in *Divided Loyalties* (82) speaks of the middle-class stereotype of the working-class marriage as the union of a brutalized man and a victimized woman.

72. "Woman's Corner," *Co-operative News*, July 22, 1899 and July 14, 1900.

73. Llewelyn Davies, *The Women's Co-operative Guild*, 21.

74. In 1921, there were 1,352 cooperative societies with a total membership of 4,549,000; see Gurney, *Co-operative Culture and the Politics of Consumption in England*, 242. But there were only 905 Guild branches with a total membership of 50,686; see Women's Cooperative Guild, *Thirty-eighth Annual Report of the Women's Co-operative Guild* (Manchester: Cooperative Wholesale Society's Printing Works, 1921), 14.

75. On February 15, 1908 the "Woman's Corner" of the *Co-operative News* printed a letter from a branch secretary who wished to remain anonymous. She reported that her members threatened to resign their memberships when she introduced women's suffrage for discussion. In *Life As We Have Known It*, a Mrs. Scott described how her branch's acceptance of the Central Committee's commitment to a negotiated peace during World War I caused membership to fall "from over 100 to about 20" (99).

76. Llewelyn Davies (ed.), *Life As We Have Known It*, 39.

77. Ibid., 134–135.

78. Ibid.

79. Ibid.

80. Ibid.

81. Llewelyn Davies, *The Women's Co-operative Guild*, 149–153.

82. Giles, *Women, Identity and Private Life in Britain*, 18.

83. Llewelyn Davies (ed.), *Life As We Have Known It*, passim.

84. Webb, *The Woman with the Basket*, 12.

85. Llewelyn Davies, *The Women's Co-operative Guild*, 159–160.

86. Ibid.

87. Ibid., 155.

88. See the introduction Llewelyn Davies wrote to Catherine Webb's *Woman with the Basket* (9–14), evaluating the Guild's accomplishments under her direction.

89. "Woman's Corner," *Co-operative News*, July 7, 1894.

90. In Llewelyn Davies's last year as the Guild's general secretary, for example, 756 women were elected to educational committees and 241 to management committees; see Women's Cooperative Guild, *Thirty-eighth Annual Report of the Women's Co-operative Guild*, 16.

91. In 1891, the Guild began a systematic effort to train women for positions hitherto monopolized by men when it published Catherine Webb's instructional pamphlet on how to read a balance sheet.

92. Seven women served terms on the Central Board of the Cooperative Union during the thirty-two years Llewelyn Davies served as the Guild's general secretary. One of them, Mary Cottrell, also became the first woman CWS director.

93. London School of Economics, coll. misc. 268 m363, vol. I, item 39, folio 100.

94. Margaret Llewelyn Davies, *Women as Organised Consumers* (Manchester: Cooperative Union Ltd., n.d.), 3.

95. The Guild's program is described in the last chapters of the Guild publication *Maternity: Letters from Working-Women* (New York: Garland Publishing, Inc., 1980).

96. The Guild's London headquarters, however, was bombed; see Hull University Library, DCW 8/8, Mrs. Ganley's unpublished history of the Guild, chapter 5, page 6.

97. Webb, *The Woman with the Basket*, 12.

98. Ibid.

99. Woolf, *A Room of One's Own*, 37.

100. Webb, *The Woman with the Basket*, 12.

101. Gaffin and Thoms, *Caring and Sharing*, 68–73.

102. Levine, *Feminist Lives in Victorian England*, 46.

103. London School of Economics, coll. misc. 268 m363, vol. III, item 7, folio 2 and vol. IV, item 21, folios 58–59, item 22, folios 60–61, item 15, folios 44–45, item 16, folios 42–43, item 17, folios 49–50, item 18, folios 51–52, item 12, folios 37–38, item 11, folios 34–35, item 23, folios 62–67, item 29, folios 29–32, item 13, folios 39–41, item 7, folios 13–22.

104. London School of Economics, coll. misc. 268 m363, vol. IV, item 7, folios 13–22.

105. London School of Economics, coll. misc. 268 m363, vol. IV, item 13, folios 39–41.

106. Ibid.

107. London School of Economics, coll. misc. 268 m363, vol. IV, item 29, folios 29–32.

108. London School of Economics, coll. misc. 268 m363, vol. IV, item 48, folio 74.

109. Hull University Library, DCW 1/1, Minute books of the Central Committee, September 30, 1889.

110. Quoted in Liddington and Norris, *One Hand Tied Behind Us*, 140.

111. "Woman's Corner," *Co-operative News*, May 18, 1889.

112. Llewelyn Davies (ed.), *Life As We Have Known It*, passim.

113. By the 1920s, the annual dues had risen to as much as 4s. in some branches; see Catherine Webb, *The Woman with the Basket*, 144.

114. Hull University Library, DCW 1/4, Minute books of the Central Committee.

The January 31, 1908 meeting suggests honorarium scales dependent on section size, ranging from £2 for a section with 20 branches to £12 10s. for a section with 120 branches, and stresses that the sums be kept too small to be considered wages. For further assertions of the Guild's commitment to voluntarism, see Catherine Webb, *The Woman with the Basket*, 47; Women's Cooperative Guild, *Thirty-seventh Annual Report of the Women's Co-operative Guild*, 28; Women's Cooperative Guild, *Thirty-eighth Annual Report of the Women's Co-operative Guild*, 19.

115. Hull University Library, DCW 1/1, Minute books of the Central Committee, April 7, 1888.

116. Hull University Library, DCW 1/2, Minute books of the Central Committee, January 23, 1893; DCW 1/3, Minute books of the Central Committee, April 13, 1898; DCW 1/4, Minute books of the Central Committee, January 8, 1907.

117. Hull University Library, DCW 1/6, Minute books of the Central Committee, October 19 and 20, 1914.

118. "Woman's Corner," *Co-operative News*, April 10, 1886, May 1, 1886, June 5, 1886.

119. The Cooperative Union Limited, *The Twenty-second Annual Co-operative Congress* (Manchester: Cooperative Union Ltd., 1890), 112.

120. This thesis is at the center of the following works: Llewelyn Davies, *The Women's Co-operative Guild*; Webb, *The Woman with the Basket*; Gaffin and Thoms, *Caring and Sharing*; Scott, *Feminism and the Politics of Working Women*.

121. London School of Economics, coll. misc. 268 m363, vol. VIII, item 3, folio 4.

122. London School of Economics, coll. misc. 268 m363, vol. VIII, items 14 to 79.

123. "Our Women's Page," *Co-operative News*, October 15, 1920.

124. London School of Economics, coll. misc. 268 m363, vol. VIII, item 30, folios 44–45.

125. See Table 9 in chapter two for detailed figures.

126. Hull University Library, DCW 1/5, Minute books of the Central Committee. The May 5 and 6, 1910 meeting minutes make no mention of the branches but do concede the sectional councils, at least, some latitude for suggesting topics. However, even they were bound by the final decisions of the Central Committee since "unity of action which is part of the strength of the Guild's work . . . secures discussion of progressive subjects in every section and . . . greatly lessens the expense of printing papers." The comment about printing expenses is further evidence of the point developed in chapter two of this book that the poverty male cooperators imposed on the Guild inhibited the organization's efforts to develop democratically.

127. Hull University Library, DCW 1/7, Minute books of the Central Committee, April 25 and 26, 1918.

128. Scott, *Feminism and the Politics of Working Women*, chapters 6–9.

129. Hull University Library, DCW 1/4, Minute books of the Central Committee, October 14 and 16, 1904.

130. Ibid.

131. Hull University Library, DCW 1/4, Minute books of the Central Committee, July 16, 1905.

132. "Women's Corner," *Co-operative News*, June 23, 1917 and June 22, 1918.

133. London School of Economics, coll. misc. 268 m363, vol. I, item 39, folio 102.

Part III

The Dysfunctional Commonwealth

Miss E. A. TOURNIER,
1892. Sectional Secre-
tary (Southern), 1889.

Mrs. ASHWORTH,
1893 and 1894.

Mrs. ADAMS, 1895.
Sectional Secretary
(Western), 1890.

Miss REDDISH,
1897.

PAST
PRESIDENTS
OF THE
WOMEN'S
CO-OPERATIVE
GUILD.

Mrs. BURY,
1896, 1904, and 1908.

Mrs. CARR,
1898 and 1906.

Mrs. ADAM DEANS,
1899.

Mrs. HODGETT,
1900 and 1907.

Mrs. BOOTHMAN,
1901.

Mrs. GREEN,
1902.

Reproduced courtesy of the Co-operative Women's Guild.

Chapter 5

Rent at the Seams: Sisterhood in the Women's Cooperative Guild

The garment of sisterhood is a fragile construction. When women from different backgrounds come together as activists, they bring with them prejudices and perceptions derived from the cultures that nurtured them as girls. As Judy Giles observes, "Gender identity is not the only form, nor even the most significant form of self-definition" that might prevail among women.[1] Class or race, for example, create divisions in identity among them, which can compromise a feminist agenda. If, as Anne Phillips maintains, feminism is "struggling towards a sisterhood that spans all social divides" in order to unite women as women, the divisions impede that goal.[2] In sum, forces that configure society into oppositional groups or shape the predominantly male world of politics affect feminists.[3] Among the obstacles that confronted the Women's Cooperative Guild in its agitations on behalf of married working-class women in England at the turn of the century were class animosities, regional jealousies, intergenerational suspicions, and a tendency toward the imitation of existing male models for government. All contributed to defeat the Guild leaders' feminist efforts to create an inclusive community of women organized to pursue the special interests of their sex. Guild leaders worked to make possible the dawn of a Cooperative Commonwealth where problems with the distribution of wealth would be solved and gender relations played out in the context of both formal and real equality between women and men. Their efforts to make their dreams reality, however, were defeated by their inability to create an alternative female sociopolitical culture.

Ironically, the garment of sisterhood in the Guild was rent by many of the same divisive forces that defeated male cooperators' attempts to transform the competitive capitalist economy into a democratically controlled system of exchange with human welfare as its primary objective. Like the Guild, the Cooperative movement claimed to operate democratically, but in reality it failed to actualize that aspiration. It produced a class of "professional laymen" to direct

it, just as did the Guild.[4] Similarly, both the leaders of the cooperative movement and the leaders of the Guild strove for the creation of a utopia wherein the
associative ideals of cooperation would govern human relations. However, the
efforts of both groups resulted in the production of a dysfunctional commonwealth. Crane Brinton has observed of utopia builders that the methods by
which they decide policy are elitist, even when a democratic component is in-
corporated as a check on their decisions. He remarks that although
"ratifi[cation] by the majority" is sought in such instances, policy is "planned
and preached by an enlightened minority."[5] Chris Waters has examined this
elitism in operation among socialists. He notes that the socialist goal was to create an inclusive community, but that socialists actually wound up erecting new
barriers, or at least, confirming those already in existence in society, such as the
ones that separated the respectable and the rough, teetotalers and drinkers,
young and old, male and female. He attributes this development of divisions to
the sense of belonging that socialists fostered among themselves and that led to
an awareness of the differences between themselves and outsiders. The result
was the "cultivation of exclusivity" in a movement ostensibly devoted to the
eradication of social distinctions.[6] The research of Peter Gurney confirms that
cooperative culture also tended toward elitism because participants in the
movement endeavored to distance themselves from "the less secure and financially stable strata of the working class," which were viewed by cooperators
with suspicion.[7] In addition, he observes that only 5% of the members of cooperative societies ever attended quarterly meetings and quotes G.D.H. Cole's
concerns that apathy undercut the movement's objective of democratic control.[8]
Interestingly, he attributes, as did Cole, the apathy of the majority to the de-
meanor of "the earnest majority," who invariably dominated meetings and thus
drove away "the less confident and articulate."[9] He closes with the remark that
"the educated working-class minority may have intimidated more people than it
attracted," functioning as "stupefiers rather than energizers."[10] Guided by its
general secretary, Margaret Llewelyn Davies, the Guild produced between the
years 1889 and 1921 an "earnest majority" that silenced "the less confident and
articulate."

Llewelyn Davies dedicated her life to the amelioration of conditions for the
married working-class women who patronized the stores run by the Cooperative
movement, although she was neither working class nor married. She directed the
Guild in its support of legislation that would liberalize the divorce laws and
guarantee that mothers be paid the maternity benefits mandated by the state in
1911. Within the Cooperative movement she urged the Guild to work to win
women positions on the committees that ran cooperative enterprises, and to support open membership so that wives could join the stores in their own names
and thereby become eligible to run for cooperative office. Through all this she
did not wonder much whether it was possible for an unmarried middle-class
woman to function as the interpreter of the needs and wants of married working-
class women; this was for three reasons. First, she believed she and women like
herself could put themselves in the places of women whose life experiences had
been different from their own by living with them, even if only for short periods. Accordingly, in her travels to visit Guild branches and attend their district

and sectional meetings, she stayed in the homes of working-class Guild members, hoping to increase her understanding of their needs. Secondly, she believed that she was not actually speaking for the women she led, but giving them the ability to speak for themselves by training them in the art of public activism in the school of the Guild, even if it was she who established and controlled the curriculum. Finally, she denied the significance of class, regional, or generational barriers to sisterhood, and she confirmed the Guild in this denial, to which it was already prone because of its association with the Cooperative movement. Cooperators were pledged to uniting all people as consumers regardless of their class or religious and political persuasions. Similarly, the Guild sought to unite cooperative women as consumers, homemakers, and mothers.

Cooperators confidently claimed that people of all backgrounds could be bound as consumers into a commonwealth where mutual trading would eradicate the brutal human behaviors engendered by the capitalist economic system. Based as it was on competition, cooperators blamed capitalism for everything from class conflict to war between nations. In keeping with this ideology, Guild leaders believed that every penny women spent at the cooperative stores helped bring the cooperative millennium closer, and this belief motivated them to spread the good news of cooperation. Indeed, when the Guild was founded in 1883, its original name was the Women's League for the Spread of Cooperation. Operating within this tradition, Llewelyn Davies directed the Guild to campaign for the spread of cooperation to socioeconomic groups long ignored by the movement. In 1899, she assigned the topic *Co-operation in Poor Neighbourhoods* to the sectional conferences for discussion.[11]

A number of cooperators had been calling the attention of the movement for a decade before 1899 to the discrepancy between cooperation's ideals and its reality with respect to the inclusion of that section of the working class too poor to afford the entrance fees or purchases of share capital that membership in cooperative societies entailed. They observed that such people could not afford the prices at cooperative stores, inflated as they were by expectations of high dividends, and pointed out that buying in the bulk quantities that the stores sold was out of the question for the poor. They warned that it would be impossible to actualize the Cooperative Commonwealth so long as such large sections of the population were beyond the reach of the movement. Prompted by these concerned cooperators, the Cooperative Union extended to Sidney Webb an invitation to read his paper, *The Best Method of Bringing Co-operation within the Reach of the Poorest of the Population*, at the 1891 Cooperative Congress. Congress then passed a resolution recommending that cooperative societies give "earnest consideration" to schemes for including the poor in their movement.[12] However, cooperative congresses often passed resolutions on which no one intended to act, especially when there were those opposed to them because they considered them impractical, expensive, or at variance with the movement's principles of consumer self-help.[13] In the case of extending the benefits of cooperation to the poor, many cooperators felt the poor had only themselves to blame for their misfortunes.[14] These cooperators argued that habits of thrift and temperance were all that were needed to make the into poor cooperators.[15] The poor thus needed to level up to cooperation; cooperation should not make any accommodations to their special needs. In any case, if cooperators did do anything exceptional for the sake of the poor, the men who led the movement believed it was up to the women to do it, that

if we are to go down to the level of winning those who have not joined our movement, there [is] no agency that would do this better than the Women's Guild. We might have a different system of shopkeeping to meet the wants of these people. In that way the women could help.[16]

The male cooperative leadership clearly recognized the existence of a class barrier separating the working-class participants in the movement and their middle-class associates from the ranks of those who were disparaged as the undeserving poor, and they wanted no serious efforts to eliminate that barrier, believing that it was probably impossible to do so anyway despite the movement's rhetoric about the all-inclusive Cooperative Commonwealth. That they delegated the job of poor relief to women was not due simply to the prevailing conception of gender roles which deemed charitable activity natural for women. The men also knew that women held no positions of authority in the movement and that their Guild was underfunded,[17] so any plans the women devised and implemented could not challenge the status quo. However, even if cooperative women had had the authority and the money to accomplish whatever they wanted, it is doubtful that they would have been any more capable than the men of bridging class divides, since any plans they devised and implemented would have been as tainted by class prejudices as was the larger Cooperative movement. Rank-and-file Guild members were particularly conservative on class issues. Llewelyn Davies believed there was no such thing as the undeserving poor.[18] The working-class women who followed her, however, thought otherwise. When their general secretary insisted that pawnshops be instituted at cooperative stores established in poorer neighborhoods, the rank and file objected.[19] They associated pawning with the rougher sort from whom they had worked hard to dissociate themselves. Participation in cooperation served as "status confirmation" for them,[20] and their general secretary's initiatives would have compromised that by introducing the disrespectable pawning habits of the poor to the movement.

Llewelyn Davies began her campaign to bring cooperation to poor neighborhoods by approaching the Cooperative Union for a monetary grant to study which cooperative trading practices functioned as the greatest deterrents to the poor shopping at the stores. The Union reluctantly gave £50 toward that effort in 1901.[21] The study's findings merely confirmed what every cooperator already knew—the prices and quantities sold, the entrance fees, and the cost of share capital put cooperation beyond the reach of the poor. However, in the course of her investigations Llewelyn Davies was able to publicize the efforts of a few exceptional cooperative societies to found branch stores in poor neighborhoods. Moreover, she was able to show that these efforts did not endanger the high dividends customers at the ordinary stores expected and that it was even possible to turn a profit at stores situated in the slums. The Sunderland Cooperative Society came in for particular praise in the study's final report, which was published in weekly installments in the "Woman's Corner" of the *Co-operative*

News.[22] It had opened three separate branch stores in three different poverty-stricken neighborhoods. In fact, the Sunderland Society was in the process of expanding the one located on Coronation Street, near the docks. The new facilities were designed to have a cooked-meat shop, in addition to the grocery store. But best of all from Llewelyn Davies's point of view, provision was being made for a hall for community activities to seduce the locals away from the public-house culture which predominated in the neighborhood. The hall was to be staffed by resident workers who would plan classes and entertainments in settlement-house style. Since the report concluded that the sort of community resources being provided by the Sunderland Society at its new Coronation Street premises were as essential to confirming the poor in the habit of shopping at the "co-op" as were reasonable prices and pennyworth quantities, the efforts of the Sunderland Society were showered with praise by the report's author. Llewelyn Davies and the director of the Sunderland Cooperative Society, William Archer, ultimately developed such a fine working relationship that Llewelyn Davies was invited to supply guildswomen as the settlement house's first resident workers. The experiences of these women demonstrated how mistaken were the Guild's leaders in their assumptions that class barriers could be easily bridged. In particular, their experiences showed that the resident workers were unable to sustain relationships across class divides. Sadly, neither the resident workers nor the Guild's leaders ever analyzed the meaning of their experiences with the Sunderland settlement, nor what it all meant for their efforts to build a community of women cooperators characterized by interclass sisterhood.

When the new Coronation Street premises opened in the autumn of 1902, Llewelyn Davies became, until January of the next year, one of the resident workers living at the settlement. She wrote detailed reports of her experiences for publication in the "Woman's Corner." In one, she described her accommodations at length.

Our bright sunny little kitchen is over the butcher's shop, and serves as office, sitting-room and kitchen. . . . Much thought was given to the decoration and furnishing of the rooms. . . . And it is delightful to hear the universal admiration for our pale-rose washed walls, the white paint on all the woodwork, doors and cupboards (the women do appreciate our big cupboards, and feel their own houses are so inadequately supplied), and our display of bright leadless glaze crockery. . . . We have ventured to dispense with Venetian or any blinds and with lace curtains, and instead, in front of our two nice large windows we have washing curtains, of white cretonne, with a pink tulip pattern. These we notice look so gay from outside when our electric light is behind them. . . . Two of the five doors of the kitchen open into little slips of bedrooms, where we keep the windows open day and night, in spite of the showers of smuts. The walls are pale grey, the curtains of cream-coloured washable Bolton sheeting, while one room has a thin red patterned cotton bed-cover and a red Japanese mat, and the other a yellow patterned bed-cover and mat.[23]

Llewelyn Davies was in the habit of entertaining the neighborhood women, serving them tea in the kitchen and showing them around the flat.[24] While this probably satisfied their curiosity about the rooms behind the brightly lit, tulip-patterned curtains, it was nonetheless cruel. Such accommodations were beyond their reach, and no habit of shopping at the "co-op" was going to change that. One woman told the general secretary in what she failed to recognize as envy: "It must be fine to live in a new place."[25] Another compared the general secretary's rooms to her own house, which was "bad and damp":

Why, last Tuesday, when I was getting ready to come round and see the magic lantern, the water pipe burst, and there was a mess. 'Twas right over the bed. Miserable, it was! And I had to set to and drag all the things out and get 'em to the fire. The walls was streamin'. It's a wretched old house, that it is, and the landlord won't do anything.[26]

In the unlikely event of a water pipe bursting over Llewelyn Davies's bed, she would not even have had to clean it up. Mrs. Coley, "a kind guildswoman, who lives close by," and who came in each day to light the fire "and help us tidy up for a couple of hours" would have done it.[27]

Llewelyn Davies firmly believed she had formed a bond of sisterhood with the women she had chosen to live amongst at the settlement because she had been in "constant daily contact" with them for several months, "sharing the hourly events, sharing the same shop, smuts, sights, and noise, being within call whenever help were needed."[28] In her estimation, that sharing had enabled "friendship and confidence [to] be most freely established."[29] She was oblivious to the fact that she and her teaparty guests were actually participating in a sort of stylized playacting designed to make the cultural differences generated by class appear less threatening to this middle-class giver of aid. Like all middle-class missionaries to the poor, Llewelyn Davies imagined the recipients of her kindnesses as "deserving, deferential and grateful—stoical victims . . . one dimensional figures, playing out a single role as struggling housewife and mother."[30] She never considered they might feel "envy, resentment or belligerence."[31] Nor did she think that what she interpreted as their efforts to live respectably might be just masks her guests assumed in particular situations, when under the eye of people they knew were their social betters, for instance.[32] Indeed, there is evidence the women on the receiving end of her efforts to bond with them did not feel the tie of "friendship and confidence" that she presumed existed between them and the resident workers at the settlement house. This evidence involves the little girl with whom Llewelyn Davies had become close during her stay at the settlement. Frances Jane Davie, or Jenny, as she was known, continued to frequent the cooperative premises after the general secretary left, and she passed on to the resident workers letters to send to her "Ideal Friend."[33] However, their relationship ended when two of Jenny's brothers were arrested, along with two other boys, after the police had had the store under surveillance for several days. Jenny's mother accused the resident workers "of having set the 'polis' on" her sons, proving that interclass suspicions were much more difficult to eradicate than Llewelyn Davies had estimated.[34]

Setting aside the issue of whether it was *possible* for Llewelyn Davies and her co-workers at the settlement house to construct sisterhood across class lines, it is clear that they *hoped* to do this. However, rank-and-file Guild members, as noted earlier, were less enthusiastic about the prospect. The general secretary consequently encountered the same paradox that the Guild's early leaders had failed to resolve: when she pushed the organization in directions she considered progressive, she alienated ordinary members. And, when she conformed to the rank and file's expectations, she merely confirmed her followers in their prejudices and made no more progress toward constructing an interclass community of women than to the inauguration of the Cooperative Commonwealth. For instance, in 1910 Parliament had before it a bill to amend the 1902 Midwives Act. This act required midwives to summon a doctor in cases where there were complications, but made no provision for the payment of the doctor. The proposed amendment mandated that the board of poor-law guardians was to pay the fee "as parochial relief to the woman and her husband."[35] This proposal insulted the dignity of the working-class guildswomen, who were proud of the boundary that society drew between themselves and paupers and wanted to maintain it. The middle-class leaders of the Guild defended the position of these women in the "Woman's Corner":

This is a grave injustice. . . . The woman and her husband are not paupers—they are not even destitute persons. Through the exercise of thrift they have made the normal provision for child-birth of their class, i.e., a midwife. The Government proposes to make them into compulsory paupers . . . their homes will be visited by the relieving officer with his hated inquiries.[36]

The Guild branches were urged to pass resolutions against the proposed amendment and to send them on to their local MPs with the alternative proposal that the doctors be paid out of municipal funds, as were doctors summoned by the police in cases of emergency.

Guild discussions of provisions for maternity care often revealed the status-conscious impediments that class created in the organization's efforts to unite women as women. In 1911, the Guild's sectional conferences were devoted to considering the Liberal government's National Insurance Bill, which mandated the payment of maternity benefits for some women. There were many guildswomen who supported the government's proposals and, indeed, wanted the state to do even more because they believed only the creation of a welfare state, which would give blanket coverage to all citizens, could eradicate the stigma of charity associated with accepting help in times of need.[37] Middle-class guildswomen who spoke from this position did so because they had become converts to socialism, while guildswomen from the respectable working class spoke from their personal experiences of the difficulty of having to provide for confinement even though their husbands made good wages.[38] There were, however, opponents to any state provision for maternity. These women argued that "a man had no right to take a wife unless he could see his way to make provision for such times."[39] They resented giving help to "the thriftless, who 'trusted in providence,' and made no attempt to help themselves."[40] These women certainly had no intention of accepting the poor as their sisters and would even go so far as to deny them the opportunity for motherhood.

Nor was it only the poor who might be excluded. By the end of the period under this book's consideration, middle-class women were often no more welcome as associates by some guildswomen. This was undoubtedly due to the increasing *class* consciousness developing among working-class women at the close of the First World War, which historians have noticed as stifling *feminist* consciousness in women of that class.[41] In 1917, the Guild sent a deputation of working-class women to Lord Rhondda to make a case for the organization's scheme for nationally organized maternity care. These were women whom the Guild had trained to speak for themselves so that they would not have to accept middle-class interpreters of their wants.[42] The deputation pointedly told Lord Rhondda that middle-class women would not be welcomed as appointees on the boards overseeing the maternity provisions the Guild envisioned. They insisted that women representatives be "elected by the working women's organisations" (bodies like the Women's Cooperative Guild), thereby increasing the chance that they would be women like themselves.[43]

In addition to divisions created by class, regionalism further complicated the Guild's efforts to construct a community of women dedicated to social reform. For example, the issue of half time divided guildswomen. The half-time system, whereby children as young as ten or eleven would be released from school for part of the day so they could engage in waged labor, predominated in Lancashire with its textile mill-based economy. In 1895, the Guild's governing body, the Central Committee, circulated a survey among its sixty northern branches in an effort to ascertain whether Lancashire guildswomen would be amenable to seeing the age limit raised for participation in the half-time system. Only seventeen branches even bothered to respond and of those seven were opposed.[44] If it is true that among women silence does not mean consent, but rather opposition,[45] it is clear that a large number of northern Guild members expected their children to work for wages as soon as they could and were against the Central Committee's plans to support changes in the half-time system. Nonetheless, the Central Committee pressed ahead. At the 1895 Congress the possibility of eliminating the system, or at least, raising the age for participants in it, was discussed. The Central Committee selected a working-class mother from Lancashire to prepare and read a paper on possible reforms of the half-time system, undoubtedly hoping that her example would shame women like her into supporting reform. She opened her remarks by pointing out that she had spent "a large portion of her life in the factory."[46] She claimed to have witnessed how factory labor more than any other type of waged labor hurt the health and morals of children, and she characterized mothers who permitted their children to work as selfish. But the Lancashire origins of the speaker failed to convince her sisters from that county. In the discussion that followed the presentation of the paper, the delegates from Guild branches in Lancashire voiced the objection of members to any changes in the half-time system. One delegate reported the members of her branch believed children became idle when they did not start work by the age of ten.[47] Another argued, in her branch, that "some said that the big strong lads of twelve had better be earning money [to help buy food] to build up their bodies, even if they got less schooling, for the body came before the mind, and, if well nourished, they could better stand the wear and tear of the world."[48]

Some Lancashire delegates, like Sarah Reddish, who had herself been a half-timer, were personally opposed to the system, but felt obligated to state that most of the members of their branches objected to any alterations in the half-time system.[49] Finally, there were Lancashire delegates who objected to the insinuation in the paper that mothers who sent their children to work were selfish and that factory labor was more morally corrupting than any other form of wage earning. Mrs. Bury, from the Guild's Darwen branch, whose mother had had to send her to work, argued that a woman who depended on her child's labor was not necessarily a bad mother. After all, she was using the money to feed her family. Mrs. Bury also stressed that vice is everywhere, not just in factories, and although personally in favor of raising the age for participation in half-time work, she could see no reason to agitate for it by exaggerating the dangers of factory work.[50] In her history of the Guild, Catherine Webb acknowledges that opposition to changes in the half-time system existed among Lancashire guildswomen. She says such women "needed to be converted to the idea that child labour could be done away with entirely."[51] It seems unlikely, however, that this conversion took place suddenly at the 1895 Guild Congress as both her history and Llewelyn Davies's suggest.[52] Although a resolution to support reforms in the half-time system was passed with only "five dissentients,"[53] it must be borne in mind that the congress that year was in London. It was therefore possible for many more southern than northern delegates to attend. Also, since London already had a higher school-leaving age than anywhere else in England,[54] it provided the perfect setting for the discussion of reforms that would raise the age of half-timers. This atmosphere would have contributed to silencing opposition as much as women's tendency to vote no by absention.

In 1895, when Mrs. Bury delivered her remarks on the half-time system at the Guild congress, she was just beginning her career as one of the national leaders of the organization. Ultimately, she was to be elected to four three-year terms on the Central Committee. Three times she would serve as the Guild's president, once as its vice-president, and four times as its treasurer. Had it not been for the rule imposed in 1888 that all people elected to the seven-member committee, with the exception of the general secretary, must take a year's sabbatical after three years of service, she might have been able to challenge Llewelyn Davies's leadership. Mrs. Bury did not agree with Llewelyn Davies's management style, and on several issues, including women's suffrage and divorce law reform, she believed the general secretary was imposing her own perspectives instead of voicing those of the married working-class women she claimed to represent.

Mrs. Bury had spent her childhood in poverty on the slope where it was possible for members of the lower middle class to slide down into the working class. She was the daughter of a day school headmaster who died when she was only two years old, leaving her mother with three little children.[55] She was put to work in a factory at age eleven. She attended night classes after work during her factory years. She loved reading Dickens and claimed his novels were what attracted her to working for social reform. She married in 1882. There is no record of her husband's occupation, but he must have earned a good wage or salary because by the time she became involved with the Guild, she had a comfortable home and one of her two sons was planning to study to become a medical doctor.[56] Her personal experiences made her more attuned to the needs of rank-and-file working-class guildswomen, especially those in Lancashire, than the London-raised and middle-class Llewelyn Davies could be.

Mrs. Bury's conflicts with the general secretary help to highlight the regional rifts in the Guild's sisterhood, as well as the divides created by class. Moreover, they indicate two additional areas of difficulty for the Guild. First, since Mrs. Bury was about ten years older than the general secretary, their relationship illustrates how attitudinal differences born of age colored guildswomen's perspectives. Secondly, because Mrs. Bury objected to the way Llewelyn Davies imposed her will on the Central Committee, which in turn contrived to create sufficient branch backing to have its way at congress, their relationship shows the extent to which the Guild had adopted a model of government that would undermine its efforts to make it inclusive of all the women associated with the Cooperative movement.

The Central Committee was like the cabinet of a parliamentary government, with a prime minister—the general secretary—who was ostensibly the first among equals. At meetings of parliament—the annual Guild congresses—the equivalent of party whips worked the branch delegates when the resolutions the Central Committee sponsored came up for vote. Those who spoke occupied what might be characterized as the Guild's front benches, having served as Central Committee members, or sectional and district secretaries. Ordinary delegates, who might be dubbed back benchers, seldom said anything, and when they did, could often not be adequately heard because they sat in the galleries.[57] Their names were rarely recorded; the references to them in the proceedings appear as "a delegate" because nobody knew them.[58] Worse, they were sometimes laughed at for what delegates associated with the Central Committee considered their unprogressive views. It was natural for the Guild to have adopted this style of government, since it was the one with which its members were most familiar as Englishwomen. Moreover, it was certainly a more representative form of government than most of the other models available in the world. But it definitely did not contribute to the creation of a responsive, grassroots democracy as the Guild leaders claimed it did.[59] It tended to impose a top-down traffic in ideas that silenced divergent opinions, which among women is easy to do, since they are not socialized to be assertive. More is the pity for that, since the Guild claimed it was in the business of teaching women how to speak up. The result was that only a few thousand of the almost two million women who held shares in cooperative societies or shopped at the stores bothered to join the Guild, and of those who did, only a few ever made the effort to attain leadership positions either at the branch or national levels.

Mrs. Bury did not start her career as a Guild leader in opposition to the dictates of the organization's general secretary or the Central Committee because in temperament she was a pragmatist and a team player. At the 1907 Congress, 1907 being a year in which she served on the Central Committee as the Guild's treasurer, she displayed these traits on two occasions, first, during the assembly's discussion of its campaign to win a minimum wage for female employees of cooperative establishments, and second, during a misunderstanding of some remarks made by Rosalind Nash, one of Llewelyn Davies's closest friends.

The Central Committee had set before the delegates a resolution urging the Cooperative Wholesale Society to adopt a minimum wage for its female employees. The Wholesale Society had recently adopted a minimum wage scale for its male workers, so the Guild's leaders devised one for women workers, but their wage scale stipulated that women should be paid less than men even if they did the same work. The Central Committee knew there was resistance among the male directors of the Wholesale Society to paying even a living wage to females, and that if forced to pay women as much as men, men would be hired in preference. So it chose the more realistic path of suggesting a lower minimum wage for women rather than push for equal pay for equal work. However, the representatives of the Toxteth branch wanted congress to declare for equal pay for equal work. Interestingly, this was one case where some members of the rank and file were more progressive than the Guild's leadership because the Toxteth delegates were women who worked for wages outside the home, unlike the majority of guildswomen or their leaders. As was reported in the *Cooperative News*:

The supporters of the Toxteth amendment relied upon personal knowledge. . . . They . . . disregarded the laws of supply and demand, commercial standards of women's worth, and all other considerations brought forward by speakers for the resolution, and pressed for the condemnation of a standard which they felt to be inadequate and unworthy of guild traditions. . . . Miss Whitelaw . . . a delegate from the Employes' [*sic*] Union, gave a few forcible figures to prove that in some districts disgraceful wages are common. . . . These things are unfortunately true, but probably had less weight with the Congress than Mrs. Bury's argument, that in improving industrial conditions it is good policy to accept instalments. [60]

On the next day of the congress, Rosalind Nash delivered a paper entitled *The Position of Married Women*. Nash, a middle-class woman with scant personal experience of doing housework, compared the position of a working-class man's wife to that of a domestic servant. Three delegates voiced strenuous objections to the comparison.[61] One said she thought it "was a slur, particularly on women co-operators."[62] Another argued that she and other wives of working-class men "took their positions voluntarily, and they did their work, which they could do just when they liked," unlike a domestic servant.[63] Without question these women were annoyed by Nash's comparison because they believed their positions superior to servitude. While they might be economically dependent on their husbands, they considered that they had what Elizabeth Roberts characterizes as moral force authority due to their managerial control over the household finances.[64] As Roberts observes, had they not had this, they would have been the equivalents of domestic servants as the middle-class Nash wrongly suggested they were.[65] Nash presumed, like many middle-class feminists, that all working-class men were despots.[66] Working-class wives did not share that perspective. They saw their marriages as partnerships in which they permitted men to reign as the senior partners. In fact, the last woman who spoke articulated this position when she asserted, "Married women made their own positions, and good men looked after their wives."[67] Mrs. Bury's intervention, however, saved Nash and her paper from further criticism. The treasurer said that she felt Nash's paper had been misunderstood. She added, "that those present had got good husbands; hence they had not grasped the spirit of the paper."[68] What Mrs. Bury and other working-class wives understood as a "good" husband has been revealed by the research of Ellen Ross. Such a husband was a man who would surrender most of his pay, seldom be violent, often be helpful, and make few sexual demands.[69] Mrs. Bury's remarks cooled the assembled women and enabled Nash to explain that she had only been comparing conditions of labor, not status.

Mrs. Bury was at first willing to play the game of Guild politics according to the Central Committee's rules. However, even early in her career as a Guild leader she was wary of what she called the growing tendency to "over-organisation" in the Guild.[70] In addition, during her 1909 presidential address at the opening of congress, she called attention to the exclusivity of the Guild, which then had only 26,000 members although there were a million and a quarter women shareholders in cooperative societies.[71] Ironically, at that congress she would discover in debate over the issue of votes for women the cause of this tremendous apathy on the part of women cooperators—the failure of the Central Committee and, in particular, of Llewelyn Davies to attend to the voice of the majority.

The merits of women's versus adult suffrage was a subject of intense debate among suffragists in the early years of the twentieth century. Women's suffragists sought to break the sex barrier on the franchise by backing any bill that would enfranchise women, even if it might exclude poor women by failing to remove property qualifications for the vote. Adult suffragists supported only bills that would remove all property qualifications, as well as gender ones, and thereby hoped to enfranchise any working-class men who remained excluded from the body politic as well as all women. Hostility often developed between the proponents of the two views.[72] Today the issue continues to divide, as historians can come to no agreement as to which strategy was more "progressive" or "revolutionary." Brian Harrison, for example, endorses adult suffrage as the only "right" strategy and supports his judgment by claiming that it could unite "progressives" and feminists.[73] Susan Kingsley Kent, on the other hand, argues that it is a mistake to consider the advocates of women's suffrage more conservative than adult suffragists, because women's suffragists had a "revolutionary" agenda that aimed at collapsing the separate spheres into which women and men were segregated. Choosing between women's and adult suffrage was particularly problematic for working-class women. They had allegiances both to their class and to their sex.[74] These conflicting allegiances drove some notable working-class suffragists, like Helen Silcock and Ada Nield Chew, to change sides on the question at least once during their public careers as activists.[75] Two guildswomen who advocated the women's suffrage position were Sarah Reddish and Selina Cooper. They were convinced that even without the removal of the property qualification, a bill that eliminated the gender qualification would enfranchise a number of working-class women.[76] Both Reddish and Cooper were from Lancashire and had worked in the mills. Cooper never rose to national prominence in the Guild, unlike Reddish. However, both were quite active in trade unionism and painfully aware that the Trades Union Congress (TUC) was hostile to the enfranchisement of women. The TUC eventually chose to commit itself to adult suffrage in the hope that a bill would be passed that would eliminate the property qualification for the vote, but not the gender qualification, and after that the trade unionists anticipated the agitation for the enfranchisement of women would be unable to sustain itself.[77]

In 1904, during another of Mrs. Bury's terms as president, the Central Committee had declared for the Guild what its policy on the contentious issue of votes for women would be: "the Guild is in favour of Adult Suffrage, but would be willing to accept a Limited Bill as a step [toward the enfranchisement of women]."[78] This policy directive was then announced in the "Woman's Corner" of the Co-operative News on December 31.[79] But at the 1909 Congress, the Central Committee put before the delegates a resolution to change this policy to one that would accept nothing less than adult suffrage, on the grounds that "adult suffrage [is] the method most consistent with the democratic principles of this Parliament, and the form of enfranchisement by which equality is established between men and women, married and single, rich and poor."[80] Several delegates objected. They felt that the removal of the gender qualification was more likely to be legislated than the removal of all property qualifications. Moreover, they argued that the Guild was abandoning fellow women who were working for the removal of the gender disability even if it did not enfranchise all women immediately. However, the debate did not really take off until a member of the "front bench" spoke in opposition to the resolution, thereby giving dissidents the courage to speak. Sarah Reddish rose to say she was a believer in adult suffrage, but she and the other working-class women she knew demanded women's suffrage because "women at present were not 'adults' . . . in electoral law . . . they were not regarded as 'persons.'"[81] Therefore, she was "strongly of the opinion that they should help women to secure women's suffrage; they ought not to be too much concerned at present as to whether the vote was limited or not; the limited Bill would remove sex disability and marriage disability."[82] This brought Rosalind Nash to her feet in defense of the resolution and also Llewelyn Davies. The general secretary argued:

The abolition of the sex disqualification would take place in an Adult Suffrage Bill much more so than in a limited Bill. It was as human beings that women wished to press forward their case for the vote. . . . If they were to have votes on the same terms as men, they must be prepared with a great force of opinion in the country to demand it on democratic lines; women must be brought in manhood suffrage on the same terms as men. . . . The time had come for a new agitation—for working women to unite and demand the vote for women without any class distinction at all.[83]

The middle-class Llewelyn Davies was telling the working-class delegates that they should prioritize class over gender and make common cause with disfranchised working-class men to obtain the vote for all "human beings" instead of just for their sex. It was at this juncture that Mrs. Bury vacated the presidential chair to address congress on the subject. She wanted the delegates to realize that by passing the resolution they would be changing the suffrage policy of the Guild. The Guild would no longer be able to support bills that would enfranchise only a portion of the female population. She advised against such a move because, while she supported adult suffrage, this was not the way to get it. Instead,

they must band themselves together and get the sex disability removed. England had never given anything only in piecemeal, and the leopard could not change its spots in a minute. Let them stand together as women . . . and if enfranchisement was not wide enough in a limited measure, they could proceed to have it extended.[84]

In their book on the radical suffragists of Lancashire, Jill Liddington and Jill Norris quote a 1904 manifesto from the Lancashire and Cheshire Women Textile and Other Workers' Representation Committee, of which Sarah Reddish was treasurer. Mrs. Bury's remarks in 1909 paraphrased portions of this document: "in England it is idle to expect revolutions . . . the most we can hope for at first is an instalment of justice."[85] In 1904, the Guild had agreed. Llewelyn Davies and Mrs. Bury had then written together to Robert Blatchford's influential *Clarion* to declare that while adult suffrage was their organization's goal, the Guild would support "any measure which would be a step in the direction of this goal."[86] Mrs. Bury considered that the general secretary was making a mistake by abandoning the 1904 policy. Her personal experiences of factory work and life in Lancashire enabled her to understand why some working-class suffragists were willing temporarily to settle for less than adult suffrage. All their lives they had had to make do with less than they wanted; there was no way they could imagine it should be any different with the suffrage. Let there be a limited bill passed; eventually it would be broadened. They could wait; life had taught them how to delay personal gratification. Middle-class adult suffragists, on the other hand, may have thought they had the best interests of the working class at heart, but their perspectives had been affected by the world of plenty and possibility in which they lived. They needed only to ask and there was a good chance they would receive. As Lilian Harris, the daughter of a wealthy banker, said during the course of the debate: "The more they [supporters of franchise reform] asked for the more they were likely to get."[87]

In the voting on the resolution before the 1909 Congress there was confusion and demands for a recount, but it was eventually decided to accept the original tally, which gave victory to the Central Committee by six votes, 238 to 232.[88] Later that year, Llewelyn Davies would regret not having agreed to a recount, because Mrs. Bury was able to use what had happened at congress to reveal in the pages of the "Woman's Corner" the extent to which the general secretary manipulated what was ostensibly a democratic process to have things her own way.

Mrs. Bury had not meant to wait till later in the year to act on what she felt had been a miscarriage of democracy at congress, but the evening after the debate she was taken ill. The health problems that would force her to curtail her work for the Guild had begun, although she was only in her late fifties. By the autumn, however, she was well enough to object to Llewelyn Davies's unilateral decision to affiliate the Guild with the newly formed People's Suffrage Federation.

The People's Suffrage Federation was a London-based organization, formed in 1909, which counted both men and women as its members. It believed that

persons, not property, should be represented. Men and women should vote, not because they live in lodgings of a certain value, under certain conditions, or because they are tenants of houses, but because they are human beings, whose wishes ought to be represented.[89]

Llewelyn Davies wanted to affiliate with the federation because many of the other London-based, middle-class-led organizations that agitated for working-class women and with whose leaders she was friendly, such as the Women's Trade Union League and the Women's Industrial Council, had already done so. She also believed that focusing on suffrage for unfranchised men, not just on votes for women, would mollify the opposition to discussing the suffrage issue that had erupted among Guild branches. Many rank-and-file guildswomen associated the entire question of votes for women with the radical suffragettes and the militant tactics of the Women's Social and Political Union. They had therefore become opponents of giving women the vote.[90] Finally, Llewelyn Davies rationalized her affiliation of the Guild with the People's Suffrage Federation by claiming she was only implementing the democratically passed congress resolution to support adult suffrage.[91] Mrs. Bury could accept neither the affiliation nor the rationale. She said she felt obligated to "draw attention to the methods adopted by the C.C. [Central Committee] during my service there."[92] She said the Central Committee in the past had been approached by several suffrage societies and it had never promised to affiliate with any of them. Moreover, she felt it was disingenuous to use the congress vote as evidence for a popular mandate for affiliation to an adult suffrage society. She pointed out that there had been 763 voting delegates at congress, but only 470 of them had voted on the adult suffrage resolution, which had only passed by 6 votes. She concluded, "I think you presume too much to infer such an unsatisfactory vote from every standpoint gives a mandate."[93]

Mrs. Bury's protest in the "Woman's Corner" prompted other guildswomen to write to the column to complain about the impertinence of the Central Committee and the general secretary. More significantly, Mrs. Bury received letters urging her "to lead an opposition fight."[94] Unfortunately, she said, her health did not permit it and, in any case, she "never wanted to do anything to injure the Guild," even though she did "not want peace at any price."[95] Mrs. Bury hoped that now that she had revealed the problems in the Guild's governmental processes another woman, preferably a working-class woman, perhaps from the north, would take up the fight against the London-based, middle-class "autocracy" which dominated the Guild.[96] But no such leader emerged, and the Central Committee continued on its course until it again compelled Mrs. Bury to rise from her sickbed to protest the committee's stand, this time on divorce law reform.

In the autumn of 1912, the royal commission Asquith had appointed in 1909 to study the possibility of divorce law reform issued its recommendations. The Guild was very interested in its findings because it had been asked to provide testimony before the royal commission as to any difficulties working-class women might have experienced with the current law. The commission's majority report recommended that the law be made equal for men and women, and that the cost of divorce proceedings be lowered. It also suggested that the grounds for divorce be extended to include desertion after three years' separation, cruelty, insanity, drunkenness, and imprisonment in the case of commuted death sentences. The Guild's leaders applauded the recommendations but were displeased that mutual consent had not been added as a ground for divorce.[97]

The Central Committee assigned the topic of divorce law reform for discussion at the spring 1913 sectional conferences of the Guild's branches in preparation for the annual congress, where it hoped to secure the passage of a resolution in support of starting a campaign to get mutual consent added to any divorce law reform bill that might arise from the commission's recommendations.[98] Ordinarily when sectional conferences discussed topics, they voted at the end of the meeting on the resolution that the Central Committee would ultimately propose at congress. However, Llewelyn Davies had learned from her earlier attempts to create support for liberalization of the grounds for divorce that the Guild's rank and file were divided about the matter.[99] So, she appointed the most persuasive speaker she knew to represent the Central Committee at the sectional conferences; this was Margaret Bondfield, who had become associated with the Guild during its agitation to amend the 1911 National Insurance Act so that maternity benefits would be paid directly to the mother instead of the male head of household. Bondfield was from a respectable, lower-middle-class, evangelical background. She had worked as a shop girl in her youth and had become involved with women's trade unionism, working with Mary Macarthur to organize women workers. She eventually went on to have a political career that, some historians have concluded, led her to prioritize labor's interests over women's to such an extent that she cannot be considered a feminist.[100] In 1913, Bondfield undertook the job of whipping the Guild's sections into conformance with the wishes of the Central Committee with respect to divorce law reform. Llewelyn Davies attempted to smooth the path for her associate's efforts by decreeing that no resolutions were to be moved and voted on at the conferences, contrary to precedent. In the April 26, 1913 edition of the "Women's Corner,"[101] Llewelyn Davies explained the reason for the deviation from standard practice was to educate guildswomen about the need for divorce law reform so that "they will realise the responsibility that is laid upon the Guild, as an organisation of married women, to take the lead in a campaign which is concerned with the dignity and self-respect of married women, the welfare of children, with a more spiritual view of marriage and its greater happiness and stability."[102]

Bondfield's experiences at the sectional conferences proved that the general secretary had been wise to step carefully; they revealed that the issue of divorce law reform could split the Guild along class, regional, and generational lines. There was much objection to the whole concept of divorce, as unsuited to women of their class. Many delegates expressed the view that "workers lived the cleanest lives, and it was among the idle rich and the low-down poor where they met uncleanliness."[103] Others protested they could not consider the possibility of making divorce easier until they knew how the poor, divorced, working-class woman and her children were to be supported once the breadwinner had won his freedom in the divorce court.[104] These delegates felt it was better to remain in loveless marriages that guaranteed them economic security than to have laws that would make it easier for their husbands to abandon them. When, at a North-West sectional conference, Bondfield characterized affectionless marriages where a wife exchanged her labor for economic support as no better than prostitution,[105] Mrs. Bury contained herself no longer.

Mrs. Bury said she supported providing equal access to divorce for men and women, and she also approved cheapening divorce proceedings. However, neither insanity nor mutual consent should be grounds for divorce in her opinion. In the case of the former, she believed, "a highly principled man would never turn against the woman he had loved because some misfortune had deprived him of her companionship. Nor would a good woman be content to live with another man while the father of her children was in an asylum."[106] As for mutual consent, Mrs. Bury asked, "where did the wedding come in?"[107] She took seriously the wording of the vows that two people make before God in the wedding service. She was a devout Congregationalist. In fact, she had begun her public career in the service of her chapel at Hollin's Grove, where she conducted classes for women.[108] In her conviction regarding the promise to stay together for better or worse until death, she spoke for many other women of her generation, as well as for the significant population of Catholic women who lived in Lancashire. She acknowledged that such a conviction, which required virtues like "self-control and self-sacrifice," was "getting old-fashioned and out of date, like myself."[109] But she was certain it made for "morality" and contributed to "the sacredness and stability of marriage" to a greater degree than the sort of reforms the Central Committee proposed to support, which tended toward "nothing short of free love."[110]

Students of late nineteenth- and early twentieth-century attitudes toward marriage have discovered that middle-class feminists tended to consider loveless marriages prostitution because of a wife's economic dependence on her husband.[111] Margaret Bondfield's comments at the above-mentioned sectional meeting indicate she was in agreement with that perspective. Working-class women, however, thought it better to put up with a bad husband than to divorce him and be thrown on the poor law.[112] They were more interested in legislation that would force bad husbands to maintain them than in reforms that would make it easier to obtain separations or divorces.[113] In addition, from the nature of Mrs. Bury's comments it is clear that more than economic concerns informed the more conservative attitudes of working-class women toward divorce. Religious belief was also a factor. Women like Mrs. Bury took their faith seriously because religion could reinforce sexual behaviors that helped to sustain a working-class woman's respectability. Carol Dyhouse notes that middle-class feminists who hoped to reconstitute the institution of marriage on more egalitarian lines envisioned a period of experiment before the emergence of a "new monogamy."[114] Mrs. Bury was revolted by the prospect of such a period because she thought it created possibilities for "free love." She considered marriage a Christian institution wherein both partners promised before God to fulfill the duties to one another that the ceremony specified. She firmly believed that it was in the best interests of working-class women to uphold the sanctity of marriage rather than to open the institution up to a period of experimentation that might result in working-class wives losing their respectability in addition to their main means of support.

Mrs. Bury was planning to attend the annual Guild congress in June, despite her poor health, because she felt the women whose views were misrepresented by the Central Committee's support of liberalizing the grounds for divorce to include mutual consent needed a champion. As a woman whose advantageous marriage had freed her from waged labor outside the home and had given her the leisure time to devote to the service of others, she said of the women whom she had offered to lead that she often felt she was "not fit to lace their shoes," given the lives of self-sacrifice they led when compared to her own.[115] Unfortunately, on May 31, 1913, she was found dead on the landing leading to the bathroom in her home.[116] The congress went on without her, of course. And a new champion did finally emerge, in 1914. However, it was a champion of the Central Committee, Eleanor Barton.

During the 1913 Congress, the late Mrs. Bury's Darwen branch teamed up with the Bristol branch to propose an amendment to the Central Committee's resolution that would delete the words, "That mutual consent after two years' separation should be included as a ground for divorce."[117] The amendment was defeated by 199 votes to 182, and the Central Committee's resolution to endorse the recommendations of the royal commission, but to urge the inclusion of mutual consent as a ground for divorce, was passed without a division.[118] However, the reticence of the delegates to commit themselves on the issue of divorce may be measured by their refusal to participate in the voting on the issue. There were 617 voting delegates at congress and only 381 bothered to declare themselves on the matter of mutual consent, while the Central Committee did not even dare to take a precise count of delegate preferences with respect to their own resolution.[119]

At the time of the 1913 Congress, Eleanor Barton was on the Central Committee as the Guild's treasurer. She did not speak to the resolution at congress; perhaps she was too busy whipping the delegates into place on the issue of mutual consent. When Llewelyn Davies first met Barton, she immediately recognized in her a loyal lieutenant. Barton therefore became one of the two women the general secretary groomed to succeed her.[120] Barton was from Yorkshire, and joined the Guild's Hillsbury branch in 1901. For seventeen years she served as that branch's secretary, and she was elected to the Central Committee in 1912.[121] She is reported to have had a rather authoritarian leadership style, the kind that got things done and tolerated no opposition.[122]

At the 1914 Congress, Barton spoke in introduction of another Central Committee resolution, calling on the government to prepare a divorce law reform bill that would include mutual consent as a ground for divorce. She marshaled her resources so effectively on that occasion that no dissenting delegates even dared to speak up during the discussion, until the Guild's president asked, amid cries that the resolution should be brought to a vote before dissidents were permitted to speak, whether anyone present had divergent opinions. Despite the uproar, a woman poorly practiced at public speaking amazingly mustered the courage to say something. She feared that liberalized divorce would act as a cover for male libertinism. Her remarks are interesting given Anna Clark's thesis that concepts of respectability among the working class developed in the early nineteenth century as a result of a battle against male libertinism.[123]

[The delegate] thought it her duty to come forward to oppose the resolution, because she had two daughters about whose safety she was anxious, and for whom she desired good husbands. (Disturbance and cries of "Oh, oh.") "Well, you desire good husbands for your daughters, don't you?" . . . She was afraid divorced men would be going about as unmarried men. (Laughter.)[124]

The laughter recorded in the proceedings must have been of the derisive variety because it shocked one perennial member of the Central Committee into remembering that the Guild's business was to support women's efforts to make their voices heard, not to ridicule them. Edith Eddie admonished the meeting in disgust: "How dare you laugh? How dare you laugh?"[125] Eddie was a midwife by profession and, because of the atrocities she had witnessed in her intimate contact with married couples, thoroughly supported the Central Committee's position on divorce law reform.[126] However, she was not about to tolerate behavior so corrosive of the community of women the Guild was trying to build as that encouraged by the atmosphere at congress that Barton had created. Edith Eddie's reprimand made three other opponents brave enough to speak up. Two of them reminded the assembled women of the promise "for better or worse."[127] Unfortunately, the third introduced the issue of child welfare—a topic often used to sway votes among mothers. Barton pounced on this opportunity to turn the debate back in the Central Committee's favor, in the process making a speech that attempted to allay working-class women's fears of pauperization in the event of divorce.

The third woman speaker was an unknown back bencher making her maiden speech, since the minute taker only managed to catch her name but not her branch. She said that

they wanted to go back and think of the class of people who always liked liberties and changes. She agreed with the lady who wanted to protect her daughters, and thought of those men who would be willing to put one girl aside if they could marry another. Women would rather put up with things than allow the children to suffer.[128]

In reply to this Barton asked: "Are children to-day cared for?"[129] She immediately answered her own question: "To-day, the children of deserted parents [are] sent to the Poor Law."[130] She asserted it would therefore be better to permit divorce and to have the state pass legislation for the endowment of motherhood, so that divorced women with children need not fear pauperization.

Guildswomen were by no means all in favor of legislation to "socialize private life," as one of them characterized plans for the endowment of motherhood.[131] As Peter Gurney points out, many cooperators distrusted the state and opposed the institution of welfare schemes under state direction.[132] Also, it would have been surprising if all of the women present at the Guild congress had been reassured by Barton's promise that the state would take care of them in the event of divorce, because they would have considered the prospect little different from relying on the poor law. As for those women at the congress who were supportive of socialism, some of them may have wanted to see the legislation on the books before they would trust to it. However, when the resolution was put to a vote it was "carried, with fifty-four dissentients."[133] There is no record of how many voted for it out of the delegates present at the congress and therefore it may be presumed that opposition was registered by silence as it had been on past occasions.

Perhaps it was envy of political behaviors in which they had no right to participate that made the Guild's leaders structure the government of their own organization after parliamentary models. It is certainly natural for the excluded to think that when the dominant party refuses entry to them, it is trying to monopolize something of value. This psychology would explain what prompted the Guild's leaders to imitate what they were denied. However, these same women, like other feminists, often proclaimed the limitations of the male-dominated system. In the words of Philippa Levine, "Parliament, male behaviour, the campaign trail were means and not ends within the feminist philosophy."[134] Feminists were therefore able to assert that when women won the vote, things would change. Governments would be more responsive to the people; wars would not occur; the welfare of the poor would be considered. In sum, the divisions which create conflict and oppression would disappear. Why, then, were the Guild's leaders driven to copying exclusionary, top-down modes of government when creating and running their own parliament? It was because too many of them were either unwilling to imagine a world without class, regional, and generational divisions just like the women they led, or, like Llewelyn Davies, overconfident that such a world could be easily created. Thus they never stopped to consider the implications of the political behaviors in which they engaged or the modes of government they adopted. They governed themselves as men had governed, and the consequences were the same: an exclusionary atmosphere was created. The majority of women who held shares in cooperative societies and shopped at the stores thus elected to forego participation in the Guild because the Guild was run by its leaders for its leaders, not by or for the majority. The burdens and poverty of working-class women's lives were only partial explanations for their apathy.

NOTES

1. Giles, *Women, Identity and Private Life in Britain* (12), is here paraphrasing the findings of Alice Kessler-Harris.
2. Phillips, *Divided Loyalties*, 80.
3. Ibid., 106. It is Phillips's thesis that "Feminism operates within the confines of a class society and has not escaped its pressures."
4. G.D.H. Cole, quoted by Gurney, *Co-operative Culture and the Politics of Consumption in England*, 236.
5. Brinton, "Utopia and Democracy," in Manuel (ed.), *Utopias and Utopian Thought*, 56.
6. Waters, *British Socialism and the Politics of Popular Culture*, 157–158.

7. Gurney, *Co-operative Culture and the Politics of Consumption in England*, 76.

8. Ibid., 236.

9. Ibid., 49.

10. Ibid.

11. Margaret Llewelyn Davies, *Co-operation in Poor Neighbourhoods* (Nottingham: Cooperative Printing Society Ltd., n.d.) was initially a paper written for sectional conferences of the Guild.

12. To the January 5, 1901 issue of the *Co-operative News* Llewelyn Davies contributed an article giving the history of the movement's lip service to bringing opportunities for cooperative shopping within reach of the poor. In it she quoted the resolution of the 1891 Congress.

13. Resolutions in support of profit-sharing with the employees of cooperative stores and workshops were regularly passed, but large sections of the movement opposed such schemes and the resolutions came to nothing, as is shown in Backstrom's *Christian Socialism and Co-operation in Victorian England*.

14. Gurney, *Co-operative Culture and the Politics of Consumption in England*, 78.

15. Llewelyn Davies frequently encountered such objections from the men with whom she spoke regarding her plans to extend cooperation to the poor. A report on one such occasion may be found in the coverage given to a conference on the subject at Blackpool in the "Woman's Corner" of the *Co-operative News* on March 22, 1902.

16. *Co-operative News*, January 5, 1901.

17. The annual reports of the Women's Cooperative Guild provide statistics indicating the difficulty women had getting elected either to the management committees of cooperative societies or to leadership positions on the national level. The reports also show that Guild branches typically received grants of less than £10 per annum, if they received anything at all, from their cooperative societies' educational committees, whose budgets were usually in the thousands of pounds.

18. Llewelyn Davies, *The Women's Co-operative Guild*, 95.

19. Ibid., 78.

20. This is Waters's phrase. *British Socialism and the Politics of Popular Culture*, 164–165.

21. Hull University Library, DCW 1/3, Minute books of the Central Committee, October 9, 1901.

22. "Woman's Corner," *Co-operative News*, April 5, 1902 to May 3, 1902.

23. "Woman's Corner," *Co-operative News*, November 29, 1902.

24. "Woman's Corner," *Co-operative News*, January 17, 1903.

25. Ibid.

26. Ibid.

27. "Woman's Corner," *Co-operative News*, November 29, 1902.

28. "Woman's Corner," *Co-operative News*, November 19, 1904.

29. Ibid.

30. Giles, *Women, Identity and Private Life in Britain*, 111–112.

31. Ibid., 112.

32. Ross, "'Not the Sort that Would Sit on the Doorstep,'" 41.

33. London School of Economics, coll. misc. 268 m363, vol. IV, item 13, folios 39–41.

34. London School of Economics, coll. misc. 268 m363, vol. V, item 21, folio 6.

35. "Woman's Corner," *Co-operative News*, April 16, 1910.

36. Ibid.

37. "Woman's Corner," *Co-operative News*, April 15, 1911.

38. "Woman's Corner," *Co-operative News*, May 20, 1911.

39. "Woman's Corner," *Co-operative News*, April 15, 1911.

40. "Woman's Corner," *Co-operative News*, May 20, 1911.

41. "Labourism," as it is sometimes called, in particular caused women and organizations associated with the Labour Party to prioritize class issues over those of gender. See, for example, the examination Harrison makes of the careers of Margaret Bondfield, Susan Lawrenson, and Ellen Wilkinson in chapter 5 of *Prudent Revolutionaries* and compare it to the career of Eleanor Rathbone (examined in Harrison's chapter 4), who remained politically independent.

42. Land, "Eleanor Rathbone," in Smith (ed.), *British Feminism in the Twentieth Century* (110), notes that the Guild was especially interested in getting working-class women involved in the administration of public welfare. Thane, "Visions of Gender in the Making of the British Welfare State," in Bock and Thane (eds.), *Maternity and Gender Policies* (106), observes that like guildswomen, Labour Party women insisted only working-class women could speak for working-class women and consequently demanded working-class women be on the maternity committees created by the 1918 Maternity and Infant Welfare Act.

43. "Women's Corner," *Co-operative News*, May 19, 1917.

44. Llewelyn Davies, *The Women's Co-operative Guild*, 128.

45. Thomson, "'Domestic Drudgery Will Be a Thing of the Past,'" in Yeo (ed.), *New Views of Co-operation* (109), suggests this happens among women and argues that rank-and-file Guild members used silence to vote against their leaders' schemes for cooperative homes.

46. Hull University Library, DCW 2/2, Report of the Fourth Annual Meeting, 18.

47. Ibid., 20.

48. Ibid., 26.

49. Ibid., 24.

50. Ibid., 25.

51. Webb, *The Woman with the Basket*, 112.

52. Ibid., 113; and Llewelyn Davies, *The Women's Co-operative Guild*, 139.

53. Catherine Webb makes no mention of the number of ayes or of absentions in *The Woman with the Basket* (113).

54. Ross, *Love and Toil*, 25.

55. *Co-operative News*, June 18, 1904.

56. *Co-operative News*, June 14, 1913.

57. Edith Abbott, a middle-class woman and former member of the Central Committee, became, like Mrs. Bury, a critic of the Guild's governmental structure. In the July 18, 1914 issue of the "Women's Corner" in the *Co-operative News*, she pointed out the deficiency in the number of working-class women who spoke at congresses and blamed it on the stranglehold of the Central Committee over congress proceedings.

58. The characterization, "a delegate," even appears in the proceedings of sectional conferences, which were smaller and presumably more intimate, but apparently not small enough to allow those without reputations to be identified; see, for example, the report on the North-West's sectional conference in the "Woman's Corner" of the *Co-operative News* of April 15, 1911.

59. Llewelyn Davies, *The Women's Co-operative Guild*, 35–62.

60. *Co-operative News*, June 29, 1907.

61. Scott, *Feminism and the Politics of Working Women* (82), claims this paper was "the most significant landmark in the Guild's perspective on the domestic sphere." Obviously, Scott is unaware of the strenuous objections working-class guildswomen made on the occasion of its presentation. However, since she does not acknowledge the presence of a rift between the general secretary and her Central Committee on the one

hand, and ordinary Guild members on the other, it is not surprising that she did not see the class prejudices in the Nash paper.

62. *Co-operative News*, June 29, 1907.

63. Ibid.

64. Roberts, *A Woman's Place*, 117.

65. Ibid.

66. Pedersen, *Family, Dependence and the Origins of the Welfare State*, 166.

67. *Co-operative News*, June 29, 1907.

68. Ibid.

69. Ross, *Love and Toil*, 73–74.

70. "Woman's Corner," *Co-operative News*, March 28, 1896.

71. *Co-operative News*, June 28, 1909.

72. Liddington and Norris, *One Hand Tied Behind Us*, 179, 232.

73. Harrison, *Prudent Revolutionaries*, 34, 213.

74. Phillips, *Divided Loyalties*, 91.

75. Liddington and Norris, *One Hand Tied Behind Us*, 235. Silcock was a supporter of women's suffrage but became an adult suffragist; Chew moved in the other direction.

76. Ibid., 180–181.

77. Ibid., 150.

78. Hull University Library, DCW 1/4, Minute books of the Central Committee, November 14, 1904.

79. "Woman's Corner," *Co-operative News*, December 31, 1904.

80. *Co-operative News*, June 26, 1909.

81. Ibid.

82. Ibid.

83. Ibid.

84. Ibid.

85. Quoted in Liddington and Norris, *One Hand Tied Behind Us*, 182.

86. Ibid., 183.

87. *Co-operative News*, June 26, 1909.

88. Ibid.

89. "Woman's Corner," *Co-operative News*, October 23, 1909.

90. Women's Cooperative Guild, *Twenty-seventh Annual Report of the Women's Co-operative Guild* (Manchester: Cooperative Wholesale Society's Printing Works, 1910), 11.

91. "Woman's Corner," *Co-operative News*, November 20, 1909.

92. "Woman's Corner," *Co-operative News*, November 13, 1909.

93. Ibid.

94. "Woman's Corner," *Co-operative News*, November 27, 1909.

95. Ibid.

96. Ibid.

97. "Woman's Corner," *Co-operative News*, November 23, 1912.

98. Hull University Library, DCW 1/5, Minute books of the Central Committee, January 30 and 31, 1913.

99. "Woman's Corner," *Co-operative News*, April 16 and 23, 1910.

100. Harrison suggests in *Prudent Revolutionaries* (9, 145–146), that Bondfield was not a feminist; and Pugh in "Domesticity and the Decline of Feminism" (156–157), in Smith (ed.), *British Feminism in the Twentieth Century*, observes that she put loyalty to the Labour Party before loyalty to her sex.

101. It will be remembered that the reason for the variation in the title of the column is that, in January 1913, its editor changed its name from "Woman's" to "Women's Corner."

102. "Women's Corner," *Co-operative News*, April 26, 1913.

103. "Women's Corner," *Co-operative News*, April 19, 1913.

104. "Women's Corner," *Co-operative News*, June 7, 1913.

105. "Women's Corner," *Co-operative News*, May 3, 1913.

106. "Women's Corner." *Co-operative News*, April 19, 1913.

107. Ibid.

108. *Co-operative News*, June 14, 1913.

109. "Women's Corner," *Co-operative News*, May 3, 1913.

110. Ibid.

111. Dyhouse, *Feminism and the Family in England*, 155; Pedersen, *Family, Dependence and the Origins of the Welfare State*, 41; Kent, *Sex and Suffrage*, 85.

112. Lewis, *Women in England*, 47.

113. Ross, *Love and Toil*, 74.

114. Dyhouse, *Feminism and the Family in England*, 157.

115. "Women's Corner," *Co-operative News*, May 3, 1913.

116. "Women's Corner," *Co-operative News*, June 7, 1913.

117. *Co-operative News*, June 21, 1913.

118. Ibid.

119. Women's Cooperative Guild, *Thirty-first Annual Report of the Women's Co-operative Guild*, 42.

120. Eleanor Barton became the assistant to the general secretary, Honora Enfield, when Llewelyn Davies retired in 1921. Upon the resignation of Enfield, in 1925, Barton became general secretary.

121. Gaffin and Thoms, *Caring and Sharing*, 264.

122. Ibid., 91–92. Also, see Gurney, *Co-operative Culture and the Politics of Consumption in England* (232), where Barton is characterized as a leader who strengthened the central governing structure of the Guild; and, of course, Scott, *Feminism and the Politics of Working Women*, chapters 6, 7 and 8, which argue that Barton was responsible for turning the Guild away from nonaligned socialism to right-wing labourism.

123. Clark, *The Struggle for the Breeches*, 170.

124. *Co-operative News*, June 27, 1914.

125. Ibid.

126. "Women's Corner," *Co-operative News*, May 10, 1913.

127. *Co-operative News*, June 27, 1914.

128. Ibid.

129. Ibid.

130. Ibid.

131. "Women's Corner," *Co-operative News*, June 23, 1917. Mrs. Penny became quite a spokesperson for the more conservative view in the years during and after the First World War. Lewis, "The Working-class Wife and Mother and State Intervention, 1870–1918," in Lewis (ed.), *Women's Experience of Home and Family* (114) confirms that she was not alone among guildswomen.

132. Gurney, *Co-operative Culture and the Politics of Consumption in England*, 187.

133. *Co-operative News*, June 27, 1914.

134. Levine, *Feminist Lives in Victorian England*, 41.

Chapter 6

The Battle between the Sexes in the Cooperative Movement

The gender war over the question of votes for women ended in England when hostilities broke out among the nations in August 1914.[1] Both Millicent Fawcett's suffragists and the suffragettes of the Pankhursts' Women's Social and Political Union suspended their agitations to win the enfrancisement of women.[2] Fawcett and Emmeline and Christabel Pankhurst supported their country's involvement in the conflict, as did many of their followers.[3] However, there was one women's organization whose gender war with the men who controlled its funding had only just begun in the summer of 1914, and neither it nor its male opponents were prepared to conclude an armistice until they needed to make common cause against a mutual enemy. Between 1914 and 1918, the Women's Cooperative Guild was at war with the body that represented the educational and legal interests of cooperators, the Cooperative Union. Hostilities began in the spring of 1914, when the Union threatened to withdraw its annual grant-in-aid from the Guild because of the Guild's support for divorce law reform. The Union ultimately attached a contingency to the grant, which made the Guild unable to accept the money without relinquishing what Guild leaders characterized as their organization's "independence."[4]

In 1916, the conflict escalated when two new fronts opened. The Guild became involved in a dispute with the Cooperative Union's Central Education Committee over courses for which the Guild supplied the teachers, but the Education Committee provided the funding, and the Guild's general secretary initiated a conflict with the national leadership of the movement over the forthcoming recommendations of the Survey Committee. The second of these two new issues of contention produced what might be characterized as the most casualties, since it had negative ramifications for the entire Cooperative movement. The Survey Committee had been appointed in 1914 to study the workings of the movement as a whole, including the constitution of the Cooperative Union, to which it was ready to make suggestions for reform by 1916. Llewelyn Davies

Coronation Street Store.

Little customers
at the Store.

THE GUILD'S
SUNDERLAND
EFFORT AMONG
THE POOR.

Miss Ll. Davies, Miss Partridge (standing),
and little customers at Sunderland Settlement.

Reproduced courtesy of the Co-operative Women's Guild.

perceived some of the reform recommendations as threatening to the Guild's independence and launched against the Survey Committee a preemptive strike; this backfired because she violated the confidence to which she, as a member of the committee, had been bound. She consequently alienated some of the men who had supported the Guild in its struggles with the Cooperative Union as well as many guildswomen. Moreover, since her arguments against the Survey Committee's suggestions played to the anti-centralization sentiments that were general among cooperators, she bears some of the responsibility for the failure of the Cooperative movement to make the structural changes required for success in the post–World War I economy.[5]

What eventually drove the Guild and the Union into negotiations to settle their differences was the realization that the Cooperative movement was under attack by Lloyd George's coalition government. The government desired to treat cooperative earnings and dividends as profits and to tax them. It also consistently failed to include cooperators as representatives on wartime food committees, even though 10% of the nation's sales of food and household goods was in the hands of the Cooperative movement.[6]

The relations between men and women in the Cooperative movement had been adversarial, but politely so, before the actual onset of open warfare. Guild leaders believed their organization represented the entire population of women who shopped at cooperative stores, despite their failure to enroll most of those women as Guild members. For the good of the female cooperators it believed it represented, the Guild pushed to win women access to the inner sanctums of power within the movement. The men, of course, resisted. However, the Guild's general secretary was always tactful in her handling of male opposition, unlike her predecessor, Mary Lawrenson. In a Fabian-like fashion she endeavored to use the system to change the system, and was willing to wait for results. For instance, in the 1890s Guild leaders had fought with the editor of the *Cooperative News* over how much space should be given to women's activities and concerns in that publication.[7] In 1910, it looked as though that dispute was about to recur, despite the presence of the sympathetic William Bamford as the paper's editor.[8] The Guild's Central Committee was then demanding more space than even he was willing to give. So as not to embitter relations with him, the Guild's leadership switched from pressuring the editor to a campaign, which eventually bore fruit in 1920, to get a woman elected to the board of the Cooperative Newspaper Society.[9] The Central Committee reasoned that a woman representative on the board would be able to make a case as an insider for expanding the women's column in the *News*.

By 1914, the Guild and its general secretary had weathered many disputes with the male leadership of the movement, and had done so diplomatically despite there being sufficient cause for more acrimonious behavior on the part of both rank-and-file guildswomen and their leaders. There had been, for example, conflicts between guildswomen and the male-dominated committees that ran the cooperative societies. Management committees were in the habit of failing to provide Guild branches with meeting rooms, or charging fees for their use, or withdrawing the promised facilities at the last minute.[10] Meanwhile, educational committees were parsimonious with their funding of the classes and lectures the

Guild branches sponsored.[11] One guildswoman complained that the educational committee at her store had an annual budget of £2000, but would not give "one farthing" to her branch of the Guild.[12] The Cooperative Union, too, begrudged the Guild funding, often denying requests for increases in the annual grant, although it was always ready to pay the women in compliments for all that they did on behalf of cooperation.[13]

Guildswomen also encountered male resistance when they ran for offices at either the local or the national level. It proved especially difficult for them to secure places on committees that oversaw the business side of the movement. In 1911, Florence Toon wrote an irate letter to the *Co-operative News* describing what had happened to her when she was nominated to run for the management committee at her store by two male supporters, "but, of course, was not elected":

The absurd reasons for opposing me . . . are unworthy [of] the word "argument.". . . It was stated as improper for a woman to be elected as the merits of horses could not be discussed before her. . . . Then a great outcry was made against the store being ruled by a woman. How one woman was to do this against so many men I hardly know. The influence we are credited with is truly wonderful.[14]

She reported that when her defeat was announced in the local issue of the Cooperative Wholesale Society's publication, the *Wheatsheaf*, the correspondent editorialized, "We beg of our co-operative women not to make their husbands unhappy by the thought that they may some day be rival candidates for office."[15] Toon concluded, "We know it will need repeated efforts . . . before the bitter prejudice against women having any direct representation in things co-operative will be subdued."[16] However, even when women managed to overcome "the bitter prejudice" and win election to management committees, their male colleagues tried to exclude them at every opportunity. An example of such behavior was reported in the March 15, 1913 issue of the "Women's Corner" of the *Co-operative News*. The director of the Barrow Cooperative Society and the male members of its management committee refused to permit their female colleague to accompany them on a buying expedition.[17] Finally, because the "truly wonderful" influence of women was so feared, few guildswomen could hope to find themselves elected to the Central Board of the Cooperative Union or to the board of directors of the Cooperative Wholesale Society; male-dominated management committees determined who the movement's national officers would be. Nor was it only men in leadership positions within the Cooperative movement who discriminated against women. The perennial underdogs of the movement, the employees of cooperative establishments, made little effort to get women co-workers to join the Amalgamated Union of Cooperative Employees (AUCE) and ignored the Guild's campaign to win women a minimum wage.[18] This was despite the support the Guild always gave the AUCE in its efforts to secure decent working conditions from cooperative employers, whose attention to cost cutting often prompted them to forget cooperative ideals.

The history of women's efforts to win themselves formal equality within the Cooperative movement might be characterized as a struggle against male amnesia with respect to the ideals that informed the cooperative motto emblazoned on the front page of the *News*: "In things essential, unity. In things doubt-ful, liberty. In all things, charity." The men seemed to have particular difficulty remembering the charity portion of the motto. The Cooperative Union had, after all, no enthusiasm for extending the benefits of Cooperation to that segment of the working class too poor to afford the high prices and entrance fees associated with the stores. It had initially refused Llewelyn Davies's request for £50 to fund a study of cooperative business practices that excluded the poor before finally giving in, in 1901.[19] Store management committees were particularly hostile to schemes to extend cooperation to the poor.[20] In fact, it had been the Sunderland Cooperative Society's management committee that had scuttled Llewelyn Davies's settlement house at the Coronation Street store. William Archer, the director of the Sunderland Cooperative Society, had invited the gen-eral secretary to staff the settlement house with guildswomen, but no sooner then had Archer left this position than the society's management committee voted to close the settlement, contending that the salaries offered the resident workers impinged too much on profits.[21]

With respect to other equity issues, the Guild's campaign to secure female cooperative employees a minimum wage was not well received by the Coopera-tive Wholesale Society. Its directors offered the usual excuses that the market would not bear paying women decent wages, forgetting that cooperators were supposed to have a commitment to higher principles if they ever hoped to create an economy that was more moral than the capitalist-based one.[22] Then, in 1912, when the Wholesale Society finally agreed to adopt the wage scale for which the Guild had been agitating for roughly five years, it left its implementation to the discretion of each cooperative concern. The result was the Guild found itself undertaking many little local agitations at branch level to convince cooperative managers and foremen to pay their women workers the minimum wage.[23]

Men also had difficulty applying the liberty portion of the cooperative motto, when it came to wives, as the Guild's efforts to convince cooperative societies to adopt open membership illustrated. Many societies prohibited mem-bership by more than one person in a household; so even though the shopping was done by the wife, the membership was in the husband's name. This practice effectively excluded married women from participating in the government of cooperative societies. As nonmembers, they were usually ineligible to attend quarterly meetings or to stand for election to either educational or management committees. There was fierce resistance to open membership by management committees and directors of societies in Lancashire and Yorkshire in particular. The director of the Oldham Cooperative Society wrote to the Guild that the wives he knew had no desire to become members, and even if they did, it would be unfair to extend membership to them because "it would be unjust for a man and wife, without children, to have two votes, whilst a widower, with five or six children could only have one vote."[24] Furthermore, he argued, it would only increase the working expenses of societies to have to keep track of more than one membership per household. Other men reckoned that open membership would cause the feminization of the Cooperative movement, "weaken[ing] the interest of men in the movement."[25] That would be bad because "if ever the trade and commerce of the country is to be carried on for the equitable benefit of capital and labour, working men will have to take a much deeper and more earnest interest in the movement."[26]

Cooperative men feared giving their wives any sort of economic independence. In the 1880s and 1890s the "Woman's Corner" had been forbidden to carry discussions about wives' entitlements to their husbands' wages for household expenses after Thomas Hughes, a prominent spokesperson for the movement, had protested against one such discussion in 1885.[27] Also, the Union's Parliamentary Committee never acted on the decision of the 1908 Cooperative Congress that the committee should draft a bill to be brought before Parliament to guarantee a wife's right to the money she managed to save from the wages her husband had given her to spend.[28] Then, when the Guild began to agitate for the payment of the maternity benefit stipulated in the 1911 National Insurance Act directly to the mother instead of the male head of household, male cooperators objected that since they were legally responsible for any debts their wives contracted, they should be guaranteed any benefits to which their wives were entitled.[29]

Given this history of male neglect of the cooperative commitment to charity and liberty, the Guild's general secretary might be forgiven her decision to flout the portion of the motto that called for unity, since that is what Llewelyn Davies did when she decided to make public, in April 1914 in the pages of the *Cooperative News*, all the bitter details of her organization's conflict with the Cooperative Union over divorce law reform. Such behavior was uncharacteristic of the general secretary. She had always believed that since the Cooperative Commonwealth to come was going to be a mixed-sex world, cooperative women had to work with the men in the movement. In many respects, she was like the Labour Party women Pat Thane has studied.[30] Like them, Llewelyn Davies believed in the possibility of mutual cooperation and partnership between the sexes. She was also similar to the Guild's early leaders who had thought it was up to the women in the movement to bring the attention of cooperators to issues having to do with the home, which men might neglect, and to lend their expertise as mothers and homemakers to questions that came under discussion in the public sphere, since men could not speak from those perspectives. Once the Cooperative Commonwealth arrived, however, the general secretary believed there would be no more purely women's issues or separate spheres because there would be both formal and real equality between the sexes. Under those circumstances, she thought a separate organization for women, like the Guild, would no longer be necessary.[31] Llewelyn Davies was a utopian and that was why working with the Cooperative movement had attracted her. Utopianism, derived in particular from Owenism, infused cooperation. Like their Owenite forebears, cooperators believed that opposition to their enlightened positions came from ignorance[32]; a little education would eradicate it.[33] The general secretary subscribed to that position and had hoped to convert the men in the movement, not to confront them. However, the 1914 imbroglio with the Cooperative Union was in her estimation the last straw in a series of male affronts to the movement's ideals and to the Guild's feminist agenda. She thereupon judged the male leaders of the Cooperative movement uneducable, and this pacifist (when it came to international politics) was ready to fight. This was a radical departure from her earlier policy of conciliating male opponents and courting sympathetic men. She now considered that a state of war, not mutual cooperation, existed between the sexes.[34]

It is true that the published proceedings of the annual cooperative congress and the Central Board meeting that preceded it would have eventually revealed to cooperators all they could ever want to know about the dispute between the Guild and the Union. However, the general secretary's pre-congress exposure of it guaranteed that an atmosphere of conflict would prevail when cooperators finally assembled for congress, battle lines already having been drawn, people already having chosen sides, even before the formal meetings had begun. Indeed, the pre–congress exposure of the dispute caused one male Guild sympathizer to write to the *Co-operative News* to caution the organization about declaring war over what could be construed as a religious issue just when the Co-operative movement was about to hold its first annual congress ever in Ireland.[35]

In October 1913, the Central Committee of the Guild had received from the Salford Catholic Federation a letter protesting the Guild's association of the Cooperative movement with the cause of divorce law reform.[36] The Federation argued that Catholic cooperators considered divorce a religious issue and since cooperators had always made it their policy never to discuss topics that might disrupt the unity of the movement, the Guild might want to reconsider its commitment to divorce law reform. The Central Committee obviously did not think the letter very important because it decided to postpone its discussion until the next formal committee meeting, in January 1914.[37] At the January meeting, the letter was not foremost on the agenda; it was the ninth and last item of discussion, and the committee "agreed that a short reply to the effect that we should continue to deal with the subject [of divorce law reform] should be sent."[38] The men of the Salford Catholic Federation did not appreciate the way the Guild's leaders had dismissed them, and they immediately referred their complaint to the United Board of the Cooperative Union. The United Board was a smaller, fourteen-person working committee of the seventy-plus-member Central Board; the United Board governed the Union, controlled its funds, and encouraged the enforcement of congress resolutions. In March, the United Board sent the Central Committee a letter objecting to the Guild's support of divorce law reform as divisive of the movement, but the Guild's leadership "unanimously agreed to continue action" on behalf of liberalizing the divorce laws.[39] It was at this juncture that Llewelyn Davies unilaterally decided to make the dispute public.

The editor of the *Co-operative News*, William Bamford, was a supporter of divorce law reform. When the royal commission examining the divorce laws had issued its majority report in 1912 calling for the extension of the grounds for divorce, the cheapening of divorce proceedings, and equal accessibility to divorce for men and women, he endorsed their recommendations in an editorial.[40] He also refused to publish in his paper letters from opponents of the majority report.[41] Llewelyn Davies was consequently confident that Bamford would defend the Central Committee in its decision to continue its support for divorce law reform. On April 18, 1914, Bamford published for her in the *News* the letter from the United Board asking the Guild to cease its propaganda on behalf of divorce law reform as well as the reply of the Central Committee to that letter.[42]

Although the Central Committee's reply was signed by both the Guild's president and its general secretary, it was almost certainly written by Llewelyn Davies alone. In it she argued that the Guild had no desire to impose its views on divorce on anyone; that the Guild had been agitating for divorce law reform for four years without complaints; that it had never associated the cause with cooperation; and that it was inappropriate for a non-cooperative body like the Salford Catholic Federation to dictate its preferences either to the Guild or the United Board of the Cooperative Union.[43] But these arguments failed to convince the United Board. The Guild's leaders were consequently informed that the larger Central Board of the Cooperative Union would meet the morning before the opening of the annual cooperative congress, on May 30, in Dublin, to act on a resolution that would renew the yearly grant of £400 to the Guild only on condition that it cease its agitation on behalf of divorce law reform and that, in the future, it would undertake no work disapproved by the United Board of the Cooperative Union.[44]

The leaders of the Guild considered the proposed resolution a serious threat to the Guild's independence of action.[45] For many in the organization's rank and file it stirred memories of the "Wives' Savings" crisis of 1907.[46] In 1907, a Middlesbrough county court judge had declared that a wife could not consider as her own any money she had saved out of the housekeeping expenses because that money had been earned by her husband in the form of wages.[47] Since working-class housewives usually stinted themselves to accumulate those savings, they considered themselves to have earned them no less than their husbands had earned their wages. They consequently argued for control over them. To the leaders of the Cooperative movement the Guild made the case that wives' jurisdiction over the savings was good for cooperation because it would ensure women's loyalty to the stores if they knew the dividends they were accumulating were legally their own.[48] It was because it agreed with that reasoning that the 1908 Cooperative Congress had recommended to the Union's Parliamentary Committee that a bill to override the court decision be drafted, and it was surely the men's reluctance to make wives' control over the household savings *de jure* that prompted the Parliamentary Committee to ignore the congress decision. In the resolution to make the Union's grant to the Guild contingent on its approval for the way the Guild spent it, guildswomen saw patriarchy at work. It was now attempting to control their organization's expenditure of funds, just as it had once tried to deny them their savings. There is no doubt that many rank-and-file Guild members who opposed liberalizing divorce were now driven to join with the Central Committee to fight for the Guild's right to exercise its own judgment over the disposition of the funding it was given. They saw a similarity between the Central Committee's position vis-à-vis the Union and their own position as economically dependent homemakers.

The Guild had many male supporters in its dispute with the Union. These men did not impose the feminist analysis on the conflict that guildswomen did, however. Instead, their motivations derived from cooperative culture, which valued independence and resented any form of coercion by the center of the periphery.[49] As a consequence, even some men who were not enthusiastic about the Guild's position on divorce law reform were able to argue for its right to independence of action.[50]

The Central Board of the Cooperative Union met on May 30, 1914. There was only one woman on that body of more than seventy men, and she spoke eloquently on behalf of the position that divorce law reform was a humanitarian issue not a religious one. But the men on the board did not see it that way. They considered the Guild to have violated the cooperative ban on discussing either religious or political topics, the discussion of which was judged by cooperators as potentially disruptive of the movement's unity.[51] They also said they feared the loss of custom to the movement of Catholic cooperators who might elect to boycott the stores in protest.[52] So, the resolution to make the Guild's grant contingent upon approval of its work passed. One male member succinctly summed up the Board's position: "If the Board had to pay the piper, they should be able to call the tune."[53]

The Guild was thus faced with the prospect of doing without its annual grant, unless it was willing to accept the condition imposed, which the Central Committee refused to do. This put the Guild's central fund in difficult straits because the £400 it got from the Cooperative Union constituted the better part of the fund.[54] So the Guild's leaders tried to persuade the Central Board to delay its withdrawal of the grant until cooperators had had an opportunity to meet again in congress, in 1915, to vote on whether to endorse the board's action.[55] The Central Board made the counter proposal that the Guild should abandon its agitation on behalf of divorce law reform for a year, and then take a referendum among its branches as to whether it should be continued after that.[56] The Guild's leaders may have been eager to protect their right to select the issues on which they chose to campaign for reform, but they were reluctant to give their own rank and file similar freedom of choice by turning the decision about the continuation of divorce law reform agitation over to them in a referendum. Ultimately, neither side was willing to accept the other's offer, and the Central Committee issued what amounted to a declaration of independence, which Bamford published in the *News* on June 20, 1914.

The manifesto asserted that the Cooperative Union's attempt to control the causes for which the Guild agitated put "the independence of the Guild at stake."[57] It argued that the Union had no right to decide how the Guild should spend the grant because the Union's budget was contingent upon women's custom at the cooperative stores.[58] The Guild was thus as entitled to jurisdiction over its portion of the Union's funds as a wife was to the control over her savings out of the household budget. The declaration then launched into a litany of humanitarian causes that the Guild had supported but male cooperators had opposed, causes that kept the movement true to its ideals, like the extension of cooperation to the poor and a minimum wage for female employees.[59] It asked whether those sorts of campaigns would have been possible if the Union had had control over the Guild's use of its funds. Finally, the Central Committee appealed to all Guild members, and especially to the delegates coming to the annual Guild congress, to support the Guild in its fight to maintain its independence.[60]

At the Guild congress the delegates considered the following "emergency resolution" prepared for them by the Central Committee:

Seeing that the position of the Guild has been attained through its power to act independently and to develop on its own lines, this Congress declares that it cannot accept the conditions laid down by the Central Co-operative Board as regards its grant to the Guild, believing that the future progress of the Guild and of the co-operative movement depends on the Guild being democratically controlled as in the past by the members themselves.[61]

After an animated discussion in which several delegates suggested that women should boycott cooperative stores to prove how much the movement depended on them, the delegates were requested to show their voting tickets: "there was a great sea of red cards, and loud and prolonged cheering when the resolution was declared carried."[62]

The Central Committee then launched a special "Independence Fund" to be collected from the branches in order to make up some of the deficit resulting from the loss of the Union's grant.[63] It is interesting to note that the committee eventually decided to rename this fund the "Self Government Fund."[64] The reason given was that the word independence suggested the idea that the Guild wanted no controls on it, whereas self-government suggested "control and restraint."[65] The committee was hoping that a more judicious wording of its public utterances would help it build up enough support so that when the annual cooperative congress met in May 1915, it might be able to defeat the resolution the Central Board planned to bring before it seeking endorsement of its action with respect to the Guild's grant. The Guild's leaders reasoned that congress delegates, whose opinions on gender issues tended toward the conservative, might be more willing to support the Guild's position if it did not appear as though women were declaring their "independence" from men. An appeal to "self-government," however, could play to generally accepted democratic principles in cooperative culture, and might consequently attract sympathy. The Central Committee was especially worried about a resolution that the Eccles Provident and the Longridge Industrial Societies planned to bring before congress. The resolution bluntly condemned the Guild for becoming involved in the divorce law reform question, because it was a religious issue. The Guild's leaders had always asserted that divorce law reform was a legal issue, not a religious one. They therefore decided to approach the Central Board with a compromise, hoping that if the board agreed to it, the Eccles resolution, as it was called, would not be placed on the agenda of the upcoming congress. The compromise suggested:

(a.) that the Central Board Grant should not be spent on work for the Reform of the Divorce Laws, (b.) that the Grant should only be spent on subjects approved by the Board after a joint Conference between the Guild and Board had been held, (c.) that a joint Conference should be held yearly.[66]

Llewelyn Davies and the Guild's president, Eleanor Barton, met with the Central Board during its pre-congress meeting to present the compromise. The board, however, refused their attempt to negotiate. Many of the board members believed the compromise would not sufficiently dissociate the name of cooperation from support for divorce law reform because it permitted the Guild to continue in the agitation, only prohibiting it from spending Union funds on the effort.[67] Others wanted more; they wanted the Guild to promise to abide by the decisions of cooperative congresses.[68] Llewelyn Davies refused to pledge the Guild to that because her organization had no official representation at congress and, in any case, had a congress of its own, according to whose resolutions the Central Committee claimed to direct Guild policy.[69]

When the cooperative congress convened, the discussion over the resolutions brought before it having to do with the dispute with the Guild was heated to the point of descending to name-calling on the part of the men who were attempting to portray the Guild's obstinacy as beyond the pale of respectable behavior.[70] The Central Board member who moved the board's resolution referred to the Guild's allegations that its freedom was threatened as "a great deal of wild cat talk."[71] His remark reminded the delegates of women's association with the disorderly and irrational, and therefore of the obligation men had to control them.[72] His characterization made the women's refusal to conform to what had been deemed in the best interests of the movement by a democratically chosen body appear as a violation of cooperative principles. The man who seconded the resolution built on the theme of democracy. He delivered a long, condescending lecture on the necessity of even democratic organizations enforcing discipline. He had made a similar argument the year before in a pamphlet he had written, *The Central Board and the Grant to the Women's Co-operative Guild*.[73] One woman delegate found the tone of his speech offensive. She said he had "talked to them as though they were pet rabbits."[74] But the moderator of the discussion ignored the acrimonious tenor of the proceedings. He was determined that all should have their say before any vote was taken, but what was said embittered further the relations between the sexes in the movement.[75]

During the course of the debate, a guildswoman who was present at congress as a delegate of the Bristol Cooperative Society moved the Guild's resolution that would endorse the principle of self-government for the Guild and guarantee its annual grant, leaving the Central Board without jurisdiction over how it would be spent, thereby putting the board into a position similar to that of husbands who turned over to their wives their weekly pay packets without asking for an accounting of expenditures.[76] Then, the Eccles resolution was moved. The representative who introduced it criticized the Guild for its failure to remember the cooperative principle of unity. He found the whole concept of divorce antagonistic to unity because "it was tearing asunder—disruption in the home life of the individual," and admonished "if they, as co-operators, were out for unity, why should an important branch of the movement be allowed to preach disruption and disunity?"[77] As it turned out, the Eccles resolution censuring the Guild was too radical for most of the delegates, who wanted only to assert the Central Board's position that "he who pays the piper calls the tune," and it was declared defeated after "a show of hands was taken."[78] The Guild's resolution "was put against the Central Board's," and a formal vote showed 796 for the former as against 1,430 for the latter, a two to one defeat for the Guild.[79]

In 1916, the Guild's dispute with the Union escalated, affecting its relationship with the Central Education Committee (CEC) on which guildswomen had had for years a guaranteed representative and with which it usually worked well. The CEC funded courses for the Guild in which women trained other women how to teach subjects having to do with cooperation. These Guides' Courses, as they were called, were quite popular among guildswomen, not only because the topics they covered were geared to women as citizen-homemakers, but because they necessitated no long absences from home. They usually required two days of attendance at a site not far from the student's home, since the Guild arranged to hold courses in each of the seven sections into which it had divided the country. Hence they were convenient for working-class housewives who had neither the time nor the money to spend traveling about for the sake of self-education. But the Central Committee was informed by the CEC that it was refused sanction for one of the subjects on its suggested syllabus, and that the CEC planned to reduce the number of sites at which classes were offered. The CEC argued that this stricter control over the contents of syllabi and greater centralization would improve the academic quality of the classes.[80]

Llewelyn Davies insisted that "academics" was not what the Guild was after; it wanted to gear its instruction to education for life.[81] For example, the CEC had cut from the Guild's suggested syllabus coverage of "international relations, carefully prepared," the general secretary argued, "to show how nations should live together."[82] The carnage on the Western Front had turned her and several of the Guild's leaders into pacifists who favored a negotiated peace. Many rank-and-file guildswomen considered their leaders' opinions on the war unpatriotic and resisted the direction of the Central Committee on the matter.[83] Apparently the CEC felt similarly and struck the subject from the suggested syllabus, insisting that the committee "had a perfect right to control the classes, as they financed them."[84] The Central Committee then retaliated by instructing guildswomen to refuse to participate in CEC classes as either teachers or students. Guildswomen, however, declined to support their leaders in this boycott[85]; half the teachers reported for work and more women than ever attended the classes.[86] Moreover, guildswomen were growing tired of the war their leaders were waging with the men in control of the movement. One reminded the Central Committee:

Self-government is all right if we have the wherewithal to uphold it, but when we objected to the suggested alterations, and at the same time asked for the grant to be renewed, I fail to see where self-government or co-operation comes in. "Unity is Strength."[87]

This woman was not unusual in her concerns. By 1916, cooperators of both sexes were becoming aware of the extent to which they were going to need unity in the future. When the cooperative congress met that year, it was preoccupied by the plans Lloyd George's coalition government had for financing the war by taxing cooperation's earnings as well as by levying taxes on store dividends for shareholders whose annual incomes qualified them to pay income taxes.[88] The realization of the seriousness of the situation that the movement faced drove even the editor of the "Women's Corner," herself active in the

Guild, to advise in an editorial that it was time "to consider most carefully whether we can use our powers better."[89] She argued that a showdown between cooperation and capitalism was coming and suggested the government was directed by capitalists inimical to the democratic control of industry and trade. She urged the Guild to direct its attention to the recruitment to its ranks of as many female cooperators as possible, even if that necessitated abandoning "other interesting and valuable pieces of work."[90] It may be presumed she had in mind agitation for divorce law reform and a negotiated peace, topics on which the ordinary housewives who shopped at the cooperative stores did not hold progressive views.

The Guild's disputes with the Union involved the issue of control. It is therefore not surprising that its general secretary objected to the recommendations the Survey Committee planned to make at the 1916 Cooperative Congress regarding the constitution of the Cooperative Union. When the Survey Committee had been created at the 1914 Congress, the Guild was given representation on it. Llewelyn Davies was appointed a member. By 1916, the committee was ready to announce some preliminary recommendations, and since these suggested increasing the power of the Union to control the movement's auxiliary bodies, Llewelyn Davies could not accept them. The Guild was an auxiliary body, and she thought the Union already had too much power over it because the Union controlled the money that financed so many Guild activities. The Survey Committee's recommendations would extend the Union's control because they would give the Union final say over the constitutions of auxiliary bodies, put Union representatives on the executives of those bodies, and bind auxiliaries to accept all congress decisions. Moreover, the committee recommended the appointment of a paid executive to replace the Union's Central Board. Llewelyn Davies found this objectionable because she knew women would have even less of a chance of winning an appointment to that executive than they had had of getting elected to the existing board. Since the Survey Committee would not permit her to release her own minority report, Llewelyn Davies resigned and then went public with the committee's recommendations before they were ready to be announced.

She and Lilian Harris wrote a pamphlet entitled *The Platform and the Floor* for discussion at spring sectional conferences of the Guild and had it published in the "Women's Corner" of the *Co-operative News* without claiming authorship.[91] The pamphlet's anonymity suggested to some of the Guild's male opponents that its authors were ashamed of its perspective and did not have the courage to stand by their opinions in public debate. It was weeks before the general secretary admitted that she and Harris had written the pamphlet, and when she did she claimed the only reason a title page showing authorship had been omitted was to save paper due to wartime shortages.[92] In the pamphlet the Guild's dispute with the CEC was used as an example of an abuse of power by central authorities in the movement, an occurrence which the authors alleged would become more frequent should the Survey Committee's recommendations be adopted. The CEC was as infuriated by the paper, as was the Survey Committee. One of the CEC's members wrote a series of irate letters to the *Co-operative News* about the pamphlet.[93] Ironically, the letter writer also used the cloak of anonymity. He complained that the revelations in the pamphlet regarding the Survey Committee's recommendations had prejudiced them before the committee had been ready to make its case in public. Interestingly, guildswomen weary of fighting with the Union agreed.[94] Many guildswomen were angry with their leaders for the boycott they had tried to impose on the classes the CEC sponsored, and they were feeling the pinch of the extra levy that had been placed upon them to make up the deficit in the central fund from the loss of the Union's grant.[95] They were also aware of the threats Lloyd George's government had made to their "divi" and believed it important to join forces with the men in the movement to make common cause against them.[96]

The crisis caused by *The Platform and the Floor* highlighted a division in perspective that existed among guildswomen, born from two contrasting notions about how women should make their way in a man's world. Llewelyn Davies had always said that once sex prejudice had been banished from the Cooperative movement, there would be no need for separate organizations for women and the Guild would be able to disband.[97] However, until that day arrived she argued that such organizations were needed because the conditions of working-class women's lives made them incapable of competing as equals with men.[98] She felt a separate organization for women and special treatment for women were necessary if working-class women were going to make any inroads at all into the monopoly men had on power in the public sphere. In fact, in a counter proposal to the recommendations made by the Survey Committee she suggested that women be considered a special interest group always entitled to elect their own representatives to every committee and board of the Cooperative Union. She argued:

The principle of providing for the representation of different interests is already accepted in the Co-operative Union by the provision for *sectional representation*. There is exactly the same reason for securing representation for women as there is for securing by rule representation, say, for the Southern and Western Sections.[99]

Cooperators had divided the country into sections that each elected representatives to the Union's Central Board. Had they not done so, the northwestern parts of the country would have dominated the movement because that was where cooperative societies were most numerous. Llewelyn Davies was suggesting that women constituted a group deserving of representation analogous to a geographic section of the country because, like the so-called "cooperative deserts" in the south and west, their interests were liable to be ignored.

Other guildswomen did not agree with the general secretary's approach to providing women with access to opportunities or for defending their interests within the Cooperative movement. Edith Abbott, a middle-class woman, former member of the Central Committee, and vocal opponent of Llewelyn Davies, opposed treating women as a special category since it would guarantee that they would never be considered equal to men by men. She asserted: "The Union and the Central Education Committee, with their executives elected to administer the affairs of the movement, ought not to give preferential treatment to any party."[100] The working-class Mrs. Penny was more blunt. At one of the sectional conferences where *The Platform and the Floor* was discussed she said, "I fight my way as a man. . . . I do not want preferential treatment."[101] She believed women were more likely to be accepted by men if they were not treated as a special category; Llewelyn Davies thought that unlikely.

The storm which broke over *The Platform and the Floor* jeopardized the Guild's male support in its fight with the Union and showed that Abbott and Penny had a better understanding of the psychology of cooperative men than Llewelyn Davies was showing at that moment. Those men who sympathized with the Guild presumed the women they supported would play the game of cooperative politics by men's rules and, if they did, they would be welcomed as colleagues. For example, the anonymous CEC member who had written to the *Co-operative News* claimed to be a supporter of the Guild and its activities. However, he could not condone the pamphlet's premature revelations of the Survey Committee's findings. He understood cooperative culture and the extent to which it opposed centralization. He knew that would require the Survey Committee to prepare its audience for the release of its centripetal recommendations in order to ensure a fair hearing of them. He also realized that an increase in the control of the periphery by the center would be necessary if cooperation were to survive assaults from corporate trusts and the government, so he did not want the Survey Committee's work scuttled by preemptive attacks. Thus he condemned the pamphlet for seeking "insidiously to prejudice the minds of co-operators in advance" regarding the recommendations coming before congress.[102] He asserted: "Such conduct is not democratic; it is not playing the game."[103] Llewelyn Davies's refusal to play the game also led William Bamford to question his support for the Guild. He pointed out that the Guild had decreased in membership in 1916 and attributed it to the organization's excessive radicalism.[104] But despite this restlessness among her troops, both female and male, the general secretary continued to pursue the Guild's war with the Union, opening another front in 1918 involving the movement's new Parliamentary Representation Committee.

The creation of the Parliamentary Representation Committee was welcomed by guildswomen. Disfranchised because of their sex, they appreciated better than the men in the movement the extent to which ordinary people were at the mercy of the laws passed by Parliament and, consequently, how vital it was to take political action even if that meant plumping for one party over another. Although the Union long had a Parliamentary Committee, the movement had always refused to become involved in party politics because it considered them divisive. It was argued that if the movement ever decided that the Liberal Party, for example, did the best job of representing cooperative interests, Conservative and Labourite cooperators would be alienated. But the attacks of Lloyd George's coalition government on cooperative interests made the male leaders of the movement feel as helpless as disfranchised women; so at the 1917 Congress it was decided to form a Parliamentary Representation Committee.[105] By 1919, this committee had evolved into the movement's very own political party—the Cooperative Party—which often teamed up with Labour to fight electoral contests. The Cooperative movement had thus been driven to violate its precedent of political neutrality by the government's wartime actions, which had appeared to cooperators as attacks upon them.[106]

The Guild's leaders were delighted by the movement's historic decision to abandon nonpartisan politics and they looked forward to votes for women more than ever now because it would double the force of cooperation's strength at the polls.[107] They accordingly devised a scheme to train newly enfranchised women as "speakers and workers for co-operative politics," and the Parliamentary Representation Committee approved it, but the Union refused to fund it.[108] It already had its own scheme, one it could direct, whereas the Guild's plans had presumed Guild control over the program.

While rank-and-file guildswomen may have blamed their leaders for the battle with the Union over *The Platform and the Floor*, they felt the men were responsible for the torpedoing of the Guild's program for the political education of women. One guildswoman therefore reminded the Union that

Women are about to enter the political arena, and . . . it must be remembered that women's votes will largely decide the issue. Then do not refuse help to the Guild for educating the women. The Guild cannot afford the expense involved in this work, which is really the cause of the whole movement.[109]

This woman had inadvertently summed up what had been the crux of the Guild's argument throughout all its disputes with the Union and its bodies: the Guild was doing the work of the movement and deserved to be paid for it. Even divorce law reform agitation, it might be argued, had been undertaken for the movement. Though the Guild had been politic enough not to associate its efforts on behalf of liberalized divorce with cooperation, cooperation did have as its objective the creation of a more just world.[110] Fairer divorce laws would be consonant with that objective. Besides, the Guild made the case that in asking for the Union's financial support for their activities, guildswomen were only requesting their own money since their shopping had put the funds into cooperative coffers in the first place. Hence no one but they had the right to control how the money was disbursed. For married working-class women, the issue of "Wives and Money," which Samuel Bamford had tried to push from the pages of the *Co-operative News* in the 1880s and 1890s, was a most vital one. It was the reason that some guildswomen had begun to hope that one day the nation would recognize the work housewives did in the home as labor. When the Liberal Party began to lay the foundations of the welfare state in the years before the First World War, some of them began to argue that the state should provide some sort of entitlement to housewives so that they would not have to be dependent on their husbands' incomes.[111] Only when they had their own money would they be free from patriarchal control. Of course, this reasoning presumed the state was no patriarchy, but once women won the vote, feminists thought, it would no longer be. The dependent situation in which housewives found themselves was the same as the Guild's in its disputes with the Union. Llewelyn Davies once asked, "If the Co-operative Union is to have control of Guild work because it makes a grant, why should not the C.W.S. make a similar claim? And all local Educational Committees and quarterly meetings which make grants might claim control of local branch work."[112] She was very aware that "He who pays the piper calls the tune."

By 1918, the men on the Central Board were divided. They had come to recognize the importance of the Guild to the Cooperative movement. Support for cooperation by newly enfranchised women at the polls would help the movement fight the government's designs on its profits; women's shopping at the stores would help combat the competition the movement faced from chain stores and trusts; the idealistic vision of the Guild's leaders for the coming Co-operative Commonwealth could inspire future generations. As one member of the Central Board put it: "It is all very well to talk about the control of the Women's Co-operative Guild; what we forget is that the women are in the ad-vance of the movement."[113] On the other hand, the political-economic environ-ment created by the alliance between capitalism and the state had required that cooperators look for ways to control the centrifugal forces in their movement. Unity was essential if they hoped to survive. As another board member said: "If we allow everyone to do as they want, God help discipline. While I am a mem-ber of the Board I shall endeavour to see that the tail shall not wag the dog."[114] In the end, the gender prejudices that Llewelyn Davies had hoped to eradicate worked to the advantage of the Guild because they provided the men with a pretext for compromise without losing face. The Central Board declared:

If we are the stronger and the wiser of the two sexes, then . . . we should take the nobler stand. It is not strength and wisdom that we should stand apart. We should invite the women to discuss the situation, and, if we find the women in the right, we can admit it.[115]

It was therefore decided at the 1918 pre-congress Central Board meeting to hold a conference with the Guild's leaders for the purposes of restoring the grant to the Guild.

By 1918, the Guild had already come to terms with the CEC. The year be-fore, the CEC had agreed to pay for the institution of special "Two-Day Schools" over whose course syllabi the Guild would have control.[116] Moreover, the Guild was also given the power to make the final decision regarding the sites that would sponsor these schools. This way the CEC could have its academic courses at locations inconvenient for working-class housewives, and the Guild could have courses that suited the special needs of its women.[117] In other words, the Guild had established its right to control the syllabi and locations of courses, but at a price. It came to be understood by both the Guild and the CEC that the academic courses were for men, and such courses were supposed to contain more rigorous material than that covered at the Two-Day Schools.[118] A system of educational apartheid had been inadvertently created where separate was not equal, proving that Mrs. Penny may have been right to have tried to "fight [her] way as a man," refusing preferential treatment.

In the summer of 1918 the talks that the Central Board had authorized were held with Guild leaders in order to discuss the restoration of the grant. At these it was "unanimously" agreed and "in a most harmonious spirit" to renew the grant.[119] No mention was made of attempting to control its use, except for the caveat that the Union would have to give its reasons for withholding the grant if it ever decided to do so again. It was also decided that the Guild's Central Committee and the Union's United Board should "meet together at least once each year to discuss the possibility of co-operating in work in which both organisations are interested," work like the political representation of cooperation's interests.[120] These meetings began in November, and as a result of them, the Guild was given for the first time the right to send a voting delegate of its own to the annual cooperative congresses. Peace had been restored, and the men were apparently disposed to be most generous to the sex with less strength and wisdom, although what one Guild delegate among more than a thousand others could do for her organization's interests at congress may be questioned.

There remained, however, one problem—the recommendations of the Survey Committee. For a time in 1919 it looked as though these would destroy the working relationship the Guild was building with the Union. The 1919 Cooperative Congress had voted to accept the Survey Committee's recommendations despite the efforts of the Guild's delegate to muster support for an amending resolution designed to guarantee the independence of auxiliary bodies.[121] But the Union assured the Guild that it had no plans to claim oversight of the Guild's constitution, or demand the right to place representatives on the Guild's Central Committee, or even to control the Guild's expenditures. As proof of its sincerity the Union increased its annual grant to the Guild to £500.

The Union had, in fact, no plans to implement any of the recommendations of the Survey Committee,[122] and the 1919 Congress decision to accept them would become one of the many congress actions in the history of the movement on which no one ever bothered to act. The centrifugal culture of cooperation had triumphed, which was fortunate for the independence of auxiliary bodies like the Guild, but it left the movement less able to meet the competition presented by large international capitalist concerns with their seductive advertising techniques. Three years after the restoration of peace between the sexes in the Cooperative movement, Margaret Llewelyn Davies resigned her position as general secretary of the Women's Cooperative Guild. Ironically, she left behind her an auxiliary organization of women that was much more centrally directed than the Cooperative movement could ever hope to be, and equipped with a new generation of leaders eager to impose the Central Committee's wishes on the larger body of its members.[123]

NOTES

1. Kent, "Gender Reconstruction after the First World War," in Smith (ed.), *British Feminism in the Twentieth Century* (75–76) speaks of the widespread understanding of feminism as gender war.

2. Kent, *Sex and Suffrage*, 220.

3. Liddington and Norris, *One Hand Tied Behind Us*, 253.

4. *Co-operative News*, June 20, 1914.

5. Gurney, *Co-operative Culture and the Politics of Consumption in England* (232), mentions how centralization could have assisted cooperation's adjustment to economic realities. The Survey Committee and the issue of centralization are also covered in Sidney and Beatrice Webb, *The Consumers' Co-operative Movement*, 146–150; and G.D.H. Cole, *A Century of Co-operation*, 293–297.

6. Gurney, *Co-operative Culture and the Politics of Consumption in England*, 209.

7. Women's Cooperative Guild, *Thirteenth Annual Report of the Women's Co-operative Guild*, 26–27; and Women's Cooperative Guild, *Fourteenth Annual Report of the Women's Co-operative Guild*, 10.

8. "Woman's Corner," *Co-operative News*, August 6 to September 10, 1910.

9. Eleanor Barton became the first woman elected to the board governing cooperative publications.

10. "Woman's Corner," *Co-operative News*, December 11, 1897, May 11, 1901, March 5, 1910.

11. Each year the annual reports of the Guild recorded that few branches received more than £10 annually in grants from the educational committees of the cooperative societies to which they were affiliated.

12. "Woman's Corner," *Co-operative News*, March 23, 1912.

13. *Co-operative News*, September 28, 1912.

14. *Co-operative News*, June 17, 1911.

15. Ibid.

16. Ibid.

17. "Women's Corner," *Co-operative News*, March 15, 1913.

18. "Woman's Corner," *Co-operative News*, October 7, 1911.

19. *Co-operative News*, January 5, 1901.

20. "Woman's Corner," *Co-operative News*, November 29, 1902.

21. "Woman's Corner," *Co-operative News*, November 19, 1904.

22. "Woman's Corner," *Co-operative News*, May 20 and June 10, 1911.

23. Gurney, *Co-operative Culture and the Politics of Consumption in England* (173) mentions the resistance of local societies to implementing the Cooperative Wholesale Society's directive on wages.

24. "Woman's Corner," *Co-operative News*, May 30, 1903.

25. Ibid.

26. Ibid.

27. "Woman's Corner," *Co-operative News*, September 5, 1885.

28. Cooperative Union Library, Manchester, Minutes of the Parliamentary Committee from 1908.

29. "Women's Corner," *Co-operative News*, August 30, 1913.

30. Thane, "The Women of the British Labour Party," in Smith (ed.), *British Feminism in the Twentieth Century*, 134–135.

31. "Woman's Corner," *Co-operative News*, June 29, 1907 contains a good summation of Llewelyn Davies's philosophy as a cooperator and feminist.

32. Adam Ulam, "Socialism and Utopia," in Manuel (ed.), *Utopias and Utopian Thought* (128), discusses utopians' belief in harmony and their notion that opposition to utopian ideas comes from ignorance.

33. Gurney, *Co-operative Culture and the Politics of Consumption in England* (25), describes cooperators as being overoptimistic about "the power of knowledge and peaceful persuasion." This was certainly true of Llewelyn Davies before her encounter with the Union over the divorce issue.

34. This is Susan Kingsley Kent's definition of sex war in her *Sex and Suffrage*, 157.

35. *Co-operative News*, May 2, 1914.

36. Hull University Library, DCW 1/6, Minute books of the Central Committee, October 23, 1913.

37. Ibid.

38. Ibid., January 13 and 14, 1914.

39. Ibid., March 26, 1914.

40. *Co-operative News*, November 16, 1912.

41. The Reverend T. S. Hudson, whose letter had been refused, complained about the editor's policy during the debate over the Guild's support for divorce law reform held at the annual Cooperative Congress in 1915. See Cooperative Union Limited, *The Forty-seventh Annual Co-operative Congress*, 523.

42. *Co-operative News*, April 18, 1914.

43. Ibid.

44. The Cooperative Union Limited, *The Forty-sixth Annual Co-operative Congress*, 16.

45. *Co-operative News*, June 20, 1914.

46. Ibid.

47. "Woman's Corner," *Co-operative News*, August 21, 1907.

48. *Co-operative News*, June 6, 1908.

49. Gurney, *Co-operative Culture and the Politics of Consumption in England*, chapters 2, 7, 8, 9.

50. *Co-operative News*, June 14, 1914.

51. The Cooperative Union Limited, *The Forty-sixth Annual Co-operative Congress*, 14–15.

52. Ibid.

53. Ibid., 14.

54. Women's Cooperative Guild, *Thirty-first Annual Report of the Women's Co-operative Guild*, 46. It also received a grant of £75 from the Cooperative Wholesale Society, and the rest of the money came from branch contributions at the rate of 2d. per member, which in 1913–14, amounted to £230 9s. 4d.

55. Hull University Library, DCW 1/6, Minute books of the Central Committee, June 15, 1914.

56. Ibid.

57. *Co-operative News*, June 20, 1914.

58. Ibid.

59. Ibid.

60. Ibid.

61. Ibid.

62. Ibid.

63. Hull University Library, DCW 1/6, Minute books of the Central Committee, October 19 and 20, 1914.

64. Ibid., January 4 and 5, 1915.

65. "Women's Corner," *Co-operative News*, March 15, 1915.

66. Hull University Library, DCW 1/6, Minute books of the Central Committee, May 9 and 10, 1915.

67. The Cooperative Union Limited, *The Forty-seventh Annual Co-operative Congress*, 25.

68. Ibid.

69. Ibid.

70. Taylor, *Eve and the New Jerusalem* (151), observes that name-calling is an attempt at control and is particularly useful against women who wish to be seen as respectable, such as working-class women, who might fear being considered "rough" more than would middle-class women, because name-calling calls into question their respectability.

71. The Cooperative Union Limited, *The Forty-seventh Annual Co-operative Congress*, 515.

72. Clark, *The Struggle for the Breeches* (151) sees this theme operating in gender relations even in an earlier period.

73. G. Goodenough, *The Central Board and the Grant to the Women's Co-operative Guild* (Manchester: Co-operative Newspaper Society Ltd., 1914), 6.

74. The Cooperative Union Limited, *The Forty-seventh Annual Co-operative Congress*, 523.

75. Ibid., 525.

76. Ibid., 517.

77. Ibid., 518.

78. Ibid., 528.

79. Ibid.

80. "Women's Corner," *Co-operative News*, April 8, 1916.

81. Ibid.

82. "Women's Corner," *Co-operative News*, May 6, 1916.

83. "Women's Corner," *Co-operative News*, June 23, 1917, and June 22, 1918.

84. "Women's Corner," *Co-operative News*, February 5, 1916.

85. "Women's Corner," *Co-operative News*, April 22 and 29, 1916.

86. "Women's Corner," *Co-operative News*, April 29, 1916.

87. Ibid.

88. The Cooperative Union Limited, *The Forty-eighth Annual Co-operative Congress* (Manchester: Cooperative Union Ltd., 1916), passim.

89. "Women's Corner," *Co-operative News*, July 22, 1916.

90. Ibid.

91. "Women's Corner," *Co-operative News*, April 8, 1916.

92. Llewelyn Davies finally admitted the authorship at a Guild sectional conference: "Women's Corner," *Co-operative News*, May 6, 1916. But later she qualified her admission, claiming that the whole Central Committee had checked the pamphlet's proofs and had approved them: *Co-operative News*, June 17, 1916.

93. *Co-operative News*, April 15, May 20, June 10, 1916.

94. "Women's Corner," *Co-operative News*, April 29, 1916.

95. "Women's Corner," *Co-operative News*, April 22, April 29, May 6, May 13, May 20, 1916, and June 15, 1918.

96. "Women's Corner," *Co-operative News*, July 29, 1916.

97. "Woman's Corner," *Co-operative News*, July 7, 1894.

98. Llewelyn Davies, *Women as Organised Consumers*, 3.

99. Women's Cooperative Guild, *Thirty-fourth Annual Report of the Women's Co-operative Guild* (Manchester: Cooperative Wholesale Society's Printing Works, 1917), 4.

100. "Women's Corner," *Co-operative News*, May 13, 1916.

101. "Women's Corner," *Co-operative News*, April 22, 1916.

102. *Co-operative News*, April 15, 1916.

103. Ibid.

104. *Co-operative News*, June 24, 1916.

105. The Cooperative Union Limited, *The Forty-ninth Annual Co-operative Congress* (Manchester: Cooperative Union Ltd., 1917), 623.

106. Gurney notes in *Co-operative Culture and the Politics of Consumption in England* (211), that this has been the thesis explaining cooperation's entry into politics since the work of G.D.H. Cole. But even before Cole, the Webbs used the state's attacks on the movement during the First World War to explain cooperation's abandonment of nonpartisan politics: Sidney and Beatrice Webb, *The Consumers' Co-operative Movement*, 244–266.

107. "Women's Corner," *Co-operative News*, January 26, 1918.

108. Hull University Library, DCW 1/7, Minute books of the Central Committee, January 24, 1918.

109. "Women's Corner," *Co-operative News*, March 16, 1918.

110. "Women's Corner," *Co-operative News*, August 8 and 15, 1914.

111. "Women's Corner," *Co-operative News*, March 18, 1911, and December 13, 1913.

112. Women's Cooperative Guild, *Thirty-fifth Annual Report of the Women's Co-operative Guild*, 5.

113. The Cooperative Union Limited, *The Fiftieth Annual Co-operative Congress*, 45.

114. Ibid.

115. Ibid., 46.

116. Women's Cooperative Guild, *Thirty-fourth Annual Report of the Women's Co-operative Guild*, 2–3.

117. "Women's Corner," *Co-operative News*, June 2, 1917.

118. As early as the spring of 1916 Llewelyn Davies had begun to characterize the courses proposed by the Central Education Committee as "dry and difficult" and therefore not suited to guildswomen; see "Women's Corner," *Co-operative News*, May 6, 1916.

119. Women's Cooperative Guild, *Thirty-sixth Annual Report of the Women's Co-operative Guild* (Manchester: Cooperative Wholesale Society's Printing Works, 1919), 4.

120. Ibid.

121. Women's Cooperative Guild, *Thirty-seventh Annual Report of the Women's Co-operative Guild*, 9.

122. Flanagan, *A Centenary Story of the Co-operative Union*, 61.

123. Gillian Scott's *Feminism and the Politics of Working Women* deals at length with the post–Llewelyn Davies era but does not acknowledge that the former general secretary established the trends toward centralization and Labourism that led to the Guild's decline in the interwar years.

Conclusion: Contradictions and Conflicts

While the First World War raged on the Continent and gender war divided the Guild from the Cooperative Union, the male custodians of the cooperative press were entertaining the notion of creating a separate magazine for women cooperators. When the leaders of the Guild and the editor of the "Women's Corner" learned about this, they became agitated. They objected to the creation of such a periodical because it might compete with the *Co-operative News* and undermine the sales of the movement's official paper. More importantly, the matriarchs of the movement feared that the new women's magazine would be used as an excuse for excluding women's voices from the *News*.[1] Giving women their own space separate from men's, they argued, would contribute to a division between the interests of men and women in the movement. Under such conditions it would be impossible for both sexes to work together for the realization of the Cooperative Commonwealth. Accordingly, at the 1917 Guild Congress the Central Committee moved the following resolution:

That this Congress considers that it is vital to the welfare of the Movement to maintain an independent journal, and urges that every co-operator should buy and read the *Co-operative News*; it condemns the proposal that a separate women's paper should be started, but instead asks that a Women's Supplement should be published quarterly as part of the *News*, in order that there may be no severance of the activities and interests of men and women in the Movement.[2]

There had been several times in the past when a separate women's periodical had been considered by the Cooperative Newspaper Society. They usually coincided with occasions when the leaders of the Guild were demanding that the "Woman's Corner" be enlarged. For example, after the Guild's contretemps with William Bradford in the late summer of 1910 concerning the size of the "Corner,"[3] there was discussion about creating a women's newspaper. William's sister, Annie Bamford Tomlinson, spoke out in opposition to the proposed paper in the "Corner" she edited. Her objections anticipated those of the 1917 Guild Congress resolution:

we do not wish to see the interests of men and women divided in the movement, as they would tend to become if we women had a paper of our own. . . . Ideally, of course, there should not be a "Woman's Corner," but then there is always the woman's point of view on any question, and it is convenient to voice this opinion in a part of the paper devoted to the interests of women. . . . There are so many reforms to be won for women yet . . . though we may have yet to fight to get all-round equality . . . we are all working for one object—the realisation of the Co-operative Commonwealth.[4]

The matriarchs of the Cooperative movement all agreed. Women and men had complementary roles and by working together they could achieve the creation of a Cooperative Commonwealth wherein gender and class distinctions would no longer contribute to hierarchical divisions that privilege some and disadvantage others. All citizens of the Commonwealth would have both formal and real equality with one another, even though some might be women who had chosen to remain in roles traditionally assigned to women and some might continue to have incomes larger than those of others. Like Bamford Tomlinson, the leaders of the Women's Cooperative Guild from Mary Lawrenson to Margaret Llewelyn Davies believed each sex had its own "point of view," which complemented that of the other, and they therefore stressed the importance of erecting no divisions that would decrease opportunities for women and men to collaborate for the purpose of achieving the common goal of a cooperative utopia. Unfortunately, the matriarchs of the movement incorrectly presumed that their vision of the future cooperative utopia was the same as that of the men who led the movement. Both male and female cooperative leaders agreed that in the Commonwealth to come women would continue to perform their traditional roles and that they would have opportunities to apply in the public sphere their knowledge as homemakers and mothers. However, while the matriarchs presumed women's entry to the public sphere would destroy the boundaries between private and public and achieve the elimination of gender-based social and cultural hierarchies,[5] the patriarchs of the movement looked forward to keeping women confined to ghettos within the public sphere where they would be empowered to speak on women's issues but nothing else. And, of course, women's concerns would not be prioritized as highly as men's.

To think that each sex has its own "point of view," as did the matriarchs of the Cooperative movement, and that it is convenient for women to voice their opinion "in a part of the paper devoted to the interests of women," both essentializes women and contributes to the ghettoization of their concerns. Herein lies a difficulty with which relational feminists especially have had to wrestle because they hope at once to maintain gender differences and promote equality between the sexes. To paraphrase Judy Giles, in concentrating on gender differences as two sets of dichotomized attributes, relational feminists limit women's potential roles to those traditionally associated with women and find themselves affirming "quasi-essentialist" forms of gender difference.[6] The leaders of the Guild thought that the advent of the Cooperative Commonwealth would magically eradicate the paradox inherent in seeking equality in difference. That thinking was what supported Llewelyn Davies's assertion that once gender discrimination in the Cooperative movement was eliminated, separate organizations for women like the one she led would no longer be necessary. But till then, she argued, they were needed because working-class women in particular required training for public activism before they could compete with men.[7] She felt it more likely that such women would be discriminated against should they dare to enter the arena of public work without adequate skills than if they admitted that the circumstances of their lives required that they receive preparation that men did not need in order to embark on careers as activists.[8] It seems to have crossed Bamford Tomlinson's mind, however, that separate spaces designed to assist the disadvantaged guarantee nothing and can actually contribute to women's marginalization. "Ideally, of course, there should not be a 'Woman's Corner,'" she said. But as a relational feminist she believed that women have a point of view peculiar to them and the only way to make it heard given the gender inequities that prevailed in both the Cooperative movement and society as a whole was in a separate space, but not too separate a space. She had stumbled on yet another difficulty peculiar to relational feminism: how is it possible to distinguish between gender segregations that serve to promote equality and those that actually contribute to the maintenance of inequality? Why, for example, did the matriarchs of the movement believe that a separate column in or supplement to the official newspaper of the Cooperative movement would not marginalize women's viewpoint, but a separate magazine or paper would? More importantly, how could they imagine that a separate auxiliary body functioning independently of the Cooperative Union—the Guild—would not disrupt opportunities for women and men to work together, but would actually promote them?

Mrs. Bury had been vexed by the paradox of seeking equal opportunities for women while maintaining the separation of the sexes. In 1895, after she was elected to the poor-law board of guardians, she contributed articles to the "Woman's Corner" about her experiences. In her first submission, she expressed a very conservative definition of "true womanhood" (one with which Annie Jones would have agreed) in her effort to explain why she had run for a position on the board of guardians.[9] She said that while she always believed a woman must put her responsibilities to her home first, a "true woman" also needed outside interests, and those interests should be directed toward helping others.[10] Service to others was for Mrs. Bury an expression of "the maternal instinct," which "in a true woman" is always "strong."[11] She condemned the "New Woman" and categorized Mrs. Sidney Webb as a radical feminist,[12] which is surprising because Mrs. Bury became a convert to women's suffrage long before the former Beatrice Potter did. Clearly, Mrs. Bury did not consider women's suffrage to be a radical issue. What she considered radical and despised about both the "New Woman" and Mrs. Webb was that they had "essay[ed] to do something for which [they were] not fitted and therefore deserved to "fail, and rightly so."[13] Obviously, Mrs. Bury believed there were certain tasks in the public sphere unsuited to women, and both the "New Woman" and Mrs. Webb had dared to undertake them. (It is a pity she did not specify what those tasks were, since more detailed remarks would have permitted a fuller analysis of her opinions.) As a poor-law guardian, Mrs. Bury shouldered work that was separated by gender. She and other women guardians ministered to female venereal disease victims, while male guardians were assigned cases involving diseased men.[14] However, when separate meetings were held for female and male guardians, she objected because "it seemed to me to be building up a wall of separation with one hand while trying to pull it down with the other."[15] Now that women had managed to win seats on the board of guardians, she believed female and male poor-law officials should meet together. She saw no way for women to make clear to men their sex's point of view without joint meetings.

There is a difficulty with the presumption that the genders each have their own peculiar points of view; it assumes that all women have one perspective, which they share simply because they are women, while all men have a different perspective, which they share simply because they are men. Notice that Bamford Tomlinson did not speak in the plural when she referred to "woman's point of view." Undoubtedly, the presumption of a uniform feminine perspective on the part of Guild leaders like Llewelyn Davies and Eleanor Barton was what made it difficult for them to negotiate the divisions they encountered among women who participated in the Cooperative movement. When Guild leaders tried to fashion solidarity around gender, they encountered class, regional, and generational obstacles. For instance, when they assumed that women who occupied traditional roles would all speak from the same perspective, class intruded and undermined sisterhood as evidenced by working-class guildswomen's objections to Rosalind Nash's characterization of them as domestic servants and Llewelyn Davies's inability to see that the women at the Coronation Street settlement envied her new flat and its tulip-patterned curtains. It particularly perplexed Guild leaders when they heard a multiplicity of viewpoints expressed by women of the same class, as occurred over the issue of reforming the half-time system. Lancashire women objected to proposals that would change that system because their children's wages helped them feed their families. Guild leaders therefore bound themselves to educate Guild members to the "correct" point of view, the Central Committee's.

The successful education of the rank and file to positions on issues that most of them considered radical required that ordinary members be given the impression that their participation in the organization affected policy. Every Guild member was therefore given a vote. However, voting only ensures that the members of an organization develop a sense of involvement with it; it does not necessarily guarantee that their votes will determine the policy decisions of leaders.[16] In fact, while it is impossible to have democracy without voting, it is perfectly possible to have voting without democracy, as the government of the Women's Cooperative Guild indicates. The constitution of the Guild enabled the individual who occupied its general secretaryship to serve for long, uninterrupted periods of time, unlike any other member of the Central Committee. The Central Committee determined the agendas of sectional conferences and prescribed activities for branch meetings. Since the circumstances of working-class women's lives made it impossible for most of them to seek national or regional offices in the organization, the Guild culled its leaders from a very small population. Indeed, for many working-class women even joining the Guild was out of the question. The poverty in which men kept the organization also compromised the Guild's democratic pretensions, reducing branch participation rates at national congresses. The Guild was therefore easily captured by a clique of women with views ordinary cooperators considered advanced and, once these women were ensconced in power, it was unlikely that challengers from a disaffected rank and file would rise to unseat them since most working-class women were too busy with housework to bother or too poor to have the wherewithal. In the end, the leadership's persistent pursuit of radical policies undermined the Guild's membership base because it confirmed the majority of women who shopped at the cooperative stores in their suspicions that the organization had nothing to offer them. The movement's matriarchs never solved the problem of how to lead the rank and file without imposing their own opinions. They knew that when they tolerated the prejudices of ordinary cooperators, no progress was made toward the utopia they envisioned. However, they failed to consider that their urge to acquaint their followers with perspectives they deemed more enlightened derived as much from their own failure to renounce hierarchical management styles as from their desire for reform. The irony of the situation was that the Guild's leaders claimed their organization was in the business of teaching working-class housewives to speak for themselves. Unfortunately, those who dared to speak contrary to the dictates of the Central Committee were ostracized, and often very cruelly so, as was the unfortunate delegate to the 1914 Congress who wanted to protect her daughters from male libertinism and therefore objected to divorce law reform.[17]

The treatment of that delegate raises the issue of the Guild's supposed "caring and sharing" values, to use Jean Gaffin and David Thoms's characterization.[18] Mrs. Bury believed it was important for a woman's children to see her in the public sphere doing service for others because her good example would ensure that her children would be inculcated with a predisposition to behave charitably toward their fellow human beings.[19] As cooperators and feminists, Guild leaders emphasized the cultivation of associative values and believed that a person's environment determined adult personality. In the Cooperative Commonwealth to come it was presumed that associative values would prevail, replacing the old capitalist ethos of competition and self-interest. The matriarchs of the movement thought that women were by nature predisposed to selflessness and sacrifice for others. They therefore argued that women could do more than men to prepare the way for the Commonwealth's advent. However, as Joan Scott has cautioned, it is a mistake to think "femininity predisposes women to certain (nurturing) jobs or (collaborative) styles of work."[20] The parliamentary procedures by which the Guild leaders ran their congresses certainly proved neither nurturing nor collaborative. Moreover, Llewelyn Davies's preemptive strike against the Survey Committee's recommendations shows that she, in particular, understood the often brutal rules involved in the game of politics. That her male opponent complained she was not "playing the game" because she had violated confidentiality actually showed that she did know how to play at games men had once monopolized, and was willing to "play for broke."[21] Her opponent had been taken aback by that sort of behavior coming from a woman, especially from one who had dealt diplomatically with male opposition, until 1914, and the challenge to the Guild offered by the Cooperative Union over divorce law reform. Yet, the irony underlying these circumstances is that the matriarchs of the movement refused to encourage guildswomen like Mrs. Penny, who wanted to "fight [her] way as a man,"[22] and leaders like Mary Lawrenson, who lectured male cooperators as though they were schoolboys. Granted, women with attitudes like Mrs. Penny's allow men to set the standards for behavior, but the equality-in-difference orientation of leaders like Llewelyn Davies was no more effective in undermining that male prerogative. It merely led male cooperators to conclude that their female colleagues were deficient because of their difference. And, in the end, Guild leaders like Llewelyn Davies and Eleanor Barton wound up resorting to "male" behaviors, themselves rejecting nurturing and collaborative styles in their interactions with their cooperative colleagues, both male and female.

What accounts for the contradictions and conflicts exemplified by the female leaders of the Cooperative movement is their environment. Robert Owen was right; nurture determines nature. The women who emerged as leaders of their cooperative sisters may have been an elite group who dared to imagine the transformation of socioeconomic conditions, but they were actually as much the products of their untransformed environment as the "unenlightened" masses that they led were of theirs.[23] Their failure to relinquish class as a category for interpreting interactions among women is the most obvious example of the extent to which these utopians were unable to shake the dust of the Old Immoral World from their shoes. For example, when it appeared as though reforms in the 1902 Midwives Act would require working-class women to resort to dependency on the poor-law authorities for the payment of doctors, the leaders of the Guild helped their followers maintain the line that separated the respectable from the rough.[24] Interestingly, only in instances when the rank and file insisted that class divisions be maintained did the matriarchs attend to their voices. The prejudices and paradoxical behaviors exhibited by the Cooperative movement's female leaders had their roots in the socioeconomic realities of the larger culture in which they lived. Since cooperation shared those roots, the movement expressed similar contradictions and conflicts, which it reinforced in the behaviors of those who participated in it. Peter Gurney's recent study of cooperative culture summarizes the janus-faced qualities of the movement.[25] Cooperative culture was a "culture of control," but cooperators valued democracy and independence, refusing to tolerate an increase in control from the center even when the economic survival of their movement was at stake.[26] They believed environment determined human behavior, but asserted anyone could become a cooperator with the application of a little self-help. Participation in the movement served as status confirmation for cooperators who wanted to demarcate themselves from the disrespectable, rougher elements in society. Yet, cooperators looked forward to a utopia without poverty. When a caste of "professional laymen" grabbed control of what was supposed to be a democratically run movement, the rank and file surrendered to them without a fight.[27] The Cooperative movement as a whole was a product of the environment it was attempting to refashion and consequently was incapable of refashioning it. The matriarchs of the movement encountered the same contradictions and conflicts in the pursuit of their goals and likewise failed to resolve them.

The operation of the cooperative matriarchy was also determined by the gender politics that the female leaders had to play with the men who controlled the movement. Male cooperators set the boundaries in which the women were forced to operate. The men feared the feminization of cooperation because they understood that it, more than any of the other movements the efforts of nineteenth-century working men had generated, had the capacity to conflate the public and private spheres; its success depended on the custom of women provisioning their homes. Male cooperators consequently controlled how much space women were permitted in the cooperative press and what could be said in it. They decided which elected offices in the movement suited women's natures and made sure women's ambitions to influence cooperation were restricted by providing them with insufficient funds and inconvenient meeting places. Only when men saw some advantage in it for them did they encourage women's participation. "Cooperative deserts," for instance, welcomed women on management committees, and advocates of profit-sharing supported Mary Lawrenson's bid for national office because she shared their views. In fact, the Women's Cooperative Guild owed its very existence to Ben Jones and Arthur Acland's idea of using cooperative women as missionaries to their sisters to combat female "divi-mindedness." The female leaders who fared best in this male-controlled environment were those who either accepted it, like Annie Jones, or learned to work with it, like Margaret Llewelyn Davies.

Annie Jones rejected Alice Acland's prohibition on public speaking and wanted to see women elected to the management committees of cooperative societies, but she told the men that she agreed that women's first duties were to their homes and that women gossiped too much. Llewelyn Davies involved the Guild with feminist causes external to the Cooperative movement, but she showed the men that like them she was interested in the proverbial bottom line. She rejected costly profit-sharing schemes and assembled data to prove that efforts to extend cooperation to the poor could pay off. She thanked the male directors of the CWS for finally adopting a minimum wage for female employees by enlisting guildswomen in a "push the sales of CWS products" campaign. The men at the CWS appreciated her efforts and refused to join the Cooperative Union in withholding funds from the Guild during its agitation in support of divorce law reform because "women could, and did, help the Wholesale very materially."[28] With the exception of the years between 1914 and 1918, the general secretary had been careful, when she lifted up her "banner with 'Women's Rights' inscribed on it in large red letters," that she did not then "proceed to make war upon co-operative mankind."[29] The matriarchs of the movement operated from a relational feminist position which accommodated the patriarchs' determination to maintain separate spheres. Unfortunately, it also reinforced those spheres, providing the men who controlled the movement with opportunities to maintain their monopoly of management committees and national offices. If the men conceded women a minority voice on these committees, it was merely to help wives and mothers in the performance of their traditional task of provisioning the home. Any suggestion that women had as much right as men to these positions would have been rejected. However, cooperation's female leaders had no alternative but to adopt a difference-based feminism due to the en-

trenched male opposition they encountered. That they worked primarily on behalf of working-class women, for whom formal equality would have accomplished little, deepened their commitment to the relational feminist position.

Though Mary Lawrenson had railed against her male opponents, early female cooperative leaders like her had not felt embattled by them. They were
wives, some of them working-class wives, and accustomed to permitting men
the exercise of their patriarchal prerogatives. However, the single women who
came to dominate the Guild's second generation of leaders were less comfortable working with men, even though they believed the advent of the Cooperative Commonwealth depended on the collaboration of the sexes. Llewelyn Davies, in particular, was disgusted by the deference that husbands demanded from
their wives and recommended that Guild members insist on "an equal give-and-
take-companionship" from their spouses.[30] She was dismayed by guildswomen
who were "loth to deprive their husbands of rights, however much they may
desire to exercise their own."[31] Underlying the diplomacy she and other second
generation Guild leaders like Catherine Webb used in handling their male colleagues was a guardedness that came from their being ill at ease around men,
especially working-class men who were seen as brutes by such middle-class
women.[32] Under the direction of such single middle-class women, the Guild's
Central Committee imposed its will on the organization's federated structure in
an effort to create as unified a body of women as possible—one that could with-
stand male challenges to its independence, such as the one that occurred in
1914. Male cooperators were well aware of the potential threat this body posed.
As one of them remarked in 1895: "A body of 8,000 women united in aim is not
a force to be ignored."[33] The men therefore became even more determined to
marginalize it. Had married working-class women been able to dominate the
Guild's leadership positions during the organization's formative years, they
might not have been able to prevent male efforts to marginalize cooperative
women, but they certainly would not have been driven by fears of men's power
to make the Guild's Central Committee an authoritarian body. They would have
accorded more autonomy to the branches than did the Guild's second generation
of leaders. Both Annie Jones and Mrs. Bury, for example, showed themselves to
be more tolerant of the differences in opinions that existed among cooperative
women and of their preference for private over public life. Had either of them
been able to lead the Guild for thirty-two consecutive years the organization
might have attracted more members from among the women who shopped at the
stores. The careers of both Jones and Bury indicate that they could have negotiated the class, regional, and generational differences that separated cooperative
women in a less authoritarian way, giving latitude to those who refused to take
advanced positions on the issues of the day, and accepting those who simply
wanted to use branch meetings as opportunities to gather and talk with other
women from their neighborhoods. Albeit, this might not have advanced the advent of the Cooperative Commonwealth, but neither did the policies of matriarchs like Margaret Llewelyn Davies.

NOTES

1. The new magazine, *Woman's Outlook*, was started in 1919 but cooperative women also retained the space they had in the official newspaper of the movement. The "Women's Corner" of the *Co-operative News* was at that time retitled "Our Women's Page," and its editor, Annie Bamford Tomlinson, was assigned the job of editing the *Woman's Outlook* as well.

2. Women's Cooperative Guild, *The Thirty-fifth Annual Report of the Women's Co-operative Guild*, 20.

3. "Woman's Corner," *Co-operative News*, August 6 to September 10, 1910.

4. "Woman's Corner," *Co-operative News*, February 4, 1911.

5. In this wish to conflate the public and private spheres they resembled other first wave feminists; see Levine, *Feminist Lives in Victorian England*, 3.

6. Giles, *Women, Identity and Private Life in Britain*, 11.

7. "Woman's Corner," *Co-operative News*, April 13, 1901. Here she was defending the Guild holding its own annual congresses against men who argued that if women wanted to be equal, they should not hold separate meetings but participate more in the movement's annual gatherings.

8. Ulla Wikander, "Some 'Kept the Flag of Feminist Demands Waving': Debates at International Congresses on Protecting Women Workers," in Wikander et al. (eds.), *Protecting Women* (30), describes further the rationale behind the strategy of training women in separate women's-only spaces in order to decrease the likelihood that more politically experienced men would dismiss them and their causes.

9. "Woman's Corner," *Co-operative News*, February 9, 1895.

10. Ibid.

11. Ibid.

12. Ibid.

13. Ibid.

14. "Woman's Corner," *Co-operative News*, May 4, 1895.

15. "Woman's Corner," *Co-operative News*, October 26, 1895.

16. Maren Lockwood, "Experimental Utopia in America," in Manuel (ed.) *Utopias and Utopian Thought*, 188.

17. *Co-operative News*, June 27, 1914.

18. Gaffin and Thoms entitled the book they wrote in 1983, in honor of the Guild's centenary, *Caring and Sharing*.

19. "Woman's Corner," *Co-operative News*, February 9, 1895.

20. Scott, "Deconstructing Equality-versus-Difference," 47.

21. "Women's Corner," *Co-operative News*, April 22, 1916.

22. *Co-operative News*, April 15, 1916.

23. Brinton, "Utopia and Democracy," in Manuel (ed.), *Utopias and Utopian Thought*, 53.

24. "Woman's Corner," *Co-operative News*, April 16, 1910.

25. Gurney, *Cooperative Culture and the Politics of Consumption in England*, chapters 6 and 7.

26. Ibid., 80.

27. Ibid., 236.

28. *Co-operative News*, June 21, 1913.

29. "Woman's Corner," *Co-operative News*, July 10, 1886.

30. Llewelyn Davies, *The Women's Co-operative Guild*, 22.

31. Ibid., 99.

32. Phillips, *Divided Loyalties*, 82.

33. *Co-operative News*, July 6, 1895.

Bibliography

PRIMARY SOURCES

Annual Cooperative Congress Reports, 1883–1922.
Annual Reports of the Women's Cooperative Guild, 1893–1922 (published format).
Co-operative News, 1871 and 1882–1921.
London School of Economics, coll. misc. 268 m363, Margaret Llewelyn Davies and Lilian Harris Papers.
Mary Lawrenson Papers, Cooperative Union Library, Manchester.
Minutes of the Parliamentary Committee, 1908–1911, Cooperative Union Library, Manchester.
University of Hull Women's Cooperative Guild Manuscript Collection, DCW 1–8.

BOOKS AND PAMPHLETS BY COOPERATORS AND SYMPATHIZERS

Acland, Arthur H., and Benjamin Jones. *Working Men Co-operators*. Manchester: Cooperative Union Ltd., 1914 (1884).
Barton, Eleanor. *Women as Co-operators*. Chicago: The National Women's Trade Union League of America, 1919.
Black, Clementina. *A Natural Alliance*. London: Cooperative Printing Society Ltd., n.d.
Bondfield, Margaret. *Women and the Labor World*. Chicago: The National Women's Trade Union League of America, 1919.
Bonner, Arnold. *British Co-operation*. Manchester: Cooperative Union Ltd., 1970 (1961).
Cole, G.D.H. *The British Co-operative Movement in a Socialist Society*. London: George Allen & Unwin, Ltd., 1951.
———. *The Case for Industrial Partnerships*. London: Macmillan & Company Ltd., 1957.
———. *A Century of Co-operation*. London: George Allen & Unwin Ltd., 1944.
Flanagan, Desmond. *A Centenary Story of the Co-operative Union*. Manchester: Cooperative Union Ltd., 1969.

Goodenough, G. *The Central Board and the Grant to the Women's Co-operative Guild.* Manchester: Cooperative Newspaper Society Ltd., 1914.

Grey, J. C. *The System of Credit as Practised by Co-operative Societies.* Manchester: Cooperative Printing Society Ltd., 1908.

Hall, Fred. *The History of the Co-operative Printing Society, 1869–1919.* Manchester: Cooperative Printing Society, 1919.

Holyoake, George Jacob. *The History of Co-operation in England*, vols. 1 and 2. New York: AMS Press, 1971 (1875 and 1879).

———. *Self-Help by the People.* London: Holyoake & Co., 1858.

Llewelyn Davies, Margaret. *Co-operation in Poor Neighbourhoods.* Nottingham: Cooperative Printing Society Ltd., n.d.

———. "The Co-operative Store Abroad." Paper prepared for the annual congress, 1906.

———. *The Extension of Co-operation to the Poor.* Manchester: Cooperative Newspaper Society Ltd., 1902.

———. *Life as We Have Known It.* New York: W. W. Norton & Company, Inc., 1975 (1931).

———. *The Vote at Last! More Power to Co-operation.* London: Cooperative Printing Society Ltd., 1918.

———. *Women as Organised Consumers.* Manchester: Cooperative Union Ltd., n.d.

———. *The Women's Co-operative Guild, 1883–1904.* Kirkby Lonsdale, Westmorland: Women's Cooperative Guild, 1904.

Llewelyn Davies, Margaret, and Lilian Harris. *After the War: The Work of Co-operation.* Issued by the Central Committee of the Guild, 1916.

Macarthur, Mary. *Women Workers of England.* Chicago: The National Women's Trade Union League of America, 1919.

Potter, Beatrice. *The Co-operative Movement in Great Britain.* London: Swan Sonnenschein & Company, 1895.

Reddish, Sarah. *Women's Guilds, with Special Reference to Their Claims on the Attention and Support of Educational Committees.* Boston: Henry Smith, 1890.

Redfern, Percy. *The Story of the C.W.S.* Manchester: Cooperative Wholesale Society Ltd., 1913.

Rules of the Co-operative Educational Committees' Association Limited. Manchester: Cooperative Wholesale Society's Printing Works, 1912.

Sharp, Evelyn. *Buyers and Builders: The Jubliee Sketch of the Women's Co-operative Guild, 1883–1933.* London: Women's Cooperative Guild, 1933.

Webb, Catherine. *Industrial Co-operation: The Story of a Peaceful Revolution.* Manchester: Cooperative Union Ltd., 1929.

———. *Lives of Great Men and Women: Short Biographies of Some Heroes and Friends of Co-operation.* Manchester: Cooperative Union Ltd., 1920.

———. *The Woman with the Basket.* Manchester: Cooperative Wholesale Society's Printing Works, 1927.

Webb, Sidney. *The Best Method of Bringing Co-operation within the Reach of the Poorest of the Population.* Manchester: Cooperative Union Ltd., n.d.

Webb, Sidney and Beatrice. *The Consumers' Co-operative Movement.* London: Longmans, Green Company, 1921.

Women's Cooperative Guild. *The ABC of the Women's Co-operative Guild.* Manchester: Cooperative Wholesale Society Printing Works, n.d.

———. *Co-operation's Great Opportunity.* London: Women's Cooperative Guild, n.d.

———. *Festival at Manchester.* Issued by the Central Committee of the Guild, n.d.

———. *Handbook of the Annual Meeting.* Manchester: Cooperative Printing Society, Ltd., 1894 and 1895.

———. *Maternity: Letters from Working Women*. New York: Garland Publishing, Inc., 1980 (1915).

———. *The Meaning of Co-operation*. Manchester: Cooperative Wholesale Society's Printing Works, 1916.

———. *Outline of Work with Model Branch Rules*. Manchester: Cooperative Printing Society Ltd., 1891.

———. *Women's Co-operative Guild Handbook*. Issued for the annual congress, 1916.

———. *Working Women and Divorce*. New York: Garland Publishing, Inc., 1980 (1911).

Woolf, Virginia. *A Room of One's Own*. London: Granada, 1981 (1929).

SECONDARY SOURCES

Alexander, Sally. *Becoming a Woman and Other Essays in 19th and 20th Century Feminist History*. New York: New York University Press, 1995.

Alexander, Sally, Anna Davin, and Eve Hostettler. "Labouring Women: A Reply to Eric Hobsbawm." *History Workshop* vol. 8 (1979), 174–182.

Anderson, Michael. *Family Structure in Nineteenth Century Lancashire*. London: Cambridge University Press, 1971.

Backstrom, Philip N. *Christian Socialism and Co-operation in Victorian England: Edward Vansittart Neale and the Co-operative Movement*. London: Croom Helm, 1974.

Banks, Olive. *The Biographical Dictionary of British Feminists*. Brighton: Wheatsheaf Books Ltd., 1985.

———. *Faces of Feminism. A Study of Feminism as a Social Movement*. New York: St. Martin's Press, 1981.

Bellamy, Joyce, and John Saville. *Dictionary of Labour Biography*. 9 vols. London: Macmillan Press Ltd., 1972–92.

Benenson, Harold. "The 'Family Wage' and Working Women's Consciousness in Britain, 1880–1914." *Politics and Society* vol. 19 (1991), 71–108.

Bock, Gisela, and Pat Thane (eds.). *Maternity and Gender Policies: Women and the Rise of the European Welfare States, 1880s–1950s*. New York: Routledge, 1991.

Boone, Gladys. *The Women's Trade Union Leagues in Great Britain and the United States of America*. New York: Columbia University Press, 1942.

Branca, Patricia. *Women in Europe Since 1750*. New York: St. Martin's Press, 1977.

Brinton, Crane. "Utopia and Democracy." In Frank E. Manuel (ed.), *Utopias and Utopian Thought*. Cambridge, MA: Houghton Mifflin Company, 1966.

Brookes, Barbara. "Women and Reproduction, 1860–1939." In Jane Lewis (ed.), *Labour and Love: Women's Experiences of Home and Family, 1850–1940*. New York: Basil Blackwell, 1987.

Claeys, Gregory. *Machinery, Money and the Millennium: From Moral Economy to Socialism, 1815–60*. Oxford: Polity Press, 1987.

Clark, Anna. *The Struggle for the Breeches: Gender and the Making of the British Working Class*. Berkeley: University of California Press, 1995.

Drake, Barbara. *Women in Trade Unions*. London: Virago Press Ltd., 1984 (1920).

Dwork, Deborah. *War Is Good for Babies and Other Young Children: A History of the Infant and Child Welfare Movement in England, 1898–1918*. London: Tavistock Publications, 1987.

Dyhouse, Carol. *Feminism and the Family in England, 1880–1939*. New York: Basil Blackwell, 1989.

Fader, Laura L., and Sonya O. Rose (eds.). *Gender and Class in Modern Europe*. Ithaca, NY: Cornell University Press, 1996.

Faderman, Lillian. *Surpassing the Love of Men: Romantic Friendships and Love between Women from the Renaissance to the Present*. New York: William Morrow and Company, Inc., 1981.

Feurer, Rosemary. "The Meaning of 'Sisterhood': The British Women's Movement and Protective Labor Legislation, 1870–1890." *Victorian Studies* vol. 31 (Winter 1988), 233–260.

Gaffin, Jean. "Women and Co-operation." In Lucy Middleton (ed.), *Women in the Labour Movement: The British Experience*. London: Croom Helm, 1977.

Gaffin, Jean, and David Thoms. *Caring and Sharing: The Centenary History of the Women's Co-operative Guild*. Manchester: Cooperative Union Ltd., 1983.

Giles, Judy. *Women, Identity and Private Life in Britain, 1900–50*. New York: St. Martin's Press, 1995.

Gittens, Diana. *Fair Sex: Family Size and Structure, 1900–39*. London: Hutchinson, 1982.

Gleadle, Kathryn. *The Early Feminists: Radical Unitarianism and the Emergence of the Women's Rights Movement*. New York: St. Martin's Press, 1995.

Gurney, Peter. *Co-operative Culture and the Politics of Consumption in England, 1870–1930*. Manchester: Manchester University Press, 1996.

Harrison, Brian. *Prudent Revolutionaries: Portraits of British Feminists between the Wars*. Oxford: Clarendon Press, 1987.

Henriques, Ursula. *Religious Toleration in England, 1787–1833*. Toronto: University of Toronto Press, 1961.

Humphries, Jane. "'. . . The Most Free Form of Objection . . .': The Sexual Division of Labor and Women's Work in Nineteenth-century England." *Journal of Economic History* vol. 47, no. 4 (December 1987), 929–949.

John, Angela V. (ed.). *Unequal Opportunities: Women's Employment in England, 1800–1918*. New York: Basil Blackwell, 1986.

Johnson, Paul. *Saving and Spending: The Working-class Economy in Britain, 1870–1939*. Oxford: Clarendon Press, 1985.

Jones, John Paul, III et al. (eds.). *Thresholds in Feminist Geography*. Lanham, MD: Rowman & Littlefield Publishers, Inc., 1997.

Joyce, Patrick. *Work, Society and Politics: The Culture of the Factory in Later Victorian England*. New Brunswick, NJ: Rutgers University Press, 1980.

Katz, Marilyn A. "Daughters of Demeter: Women in Ancient Greece." In Renate Bridenthal, Susan Mosher Stuard, and Merry E. Weisner (eds.), *Becoming Visible: Women in European History*. Boston: Houghton Mifflin Company, 1998.

Kent, Susan Kingsley. "Gender Reconstruction after the First World War." In Harold L. Smith (ed.), *British Feminism in the Twentieth Century*. Amherst, MA: University of Massachusetts Press, 1990.

———. *Sex and Suffrage in Britain, 1860–1914*. Princeton: Princeton University Press, 1987.

Kobayshi, Audrey. "The Paradox of Difference and Diversity." In John Paul Jones III et al. (eds.), *Thresholds in Feminist Geography*. Lanham, MD: Rowman & Littlefield Publishers, Inc., 1997.

Koven, Seth, and Sonya Michel. "Womanly Duties: Maternalist Politics and the Origins of Welfare States in France, Germany, Great Britain, and the United States, 1880–1920." *American Historical Review* vol. 95 (October 1990), 1076–1108.

Land, Hilary. "Eleanor Rathbone and the Economy of the Family." In Harold L. Smith (ed.), *British Feminism in the Twentieth Century*. Amherst, MA: University of Massachusetts Press, 1990.

Laws, Glenda. "Women's Life Courses, Spatial Mobility, and State Policies." In John Paul Jones III et al. (eds.), *Tresholds in Feminist Geography*. Lanham, MD: Rowman & Littlefield Publishers, Inc., 1990.

Levine, Philippa. *Feminist Lives in Victorian England: Private Roles and Public Commitment*. London: Basil Blackwell, 1990.

Lewis, Jane. "Dealing with Dependency: State Practices and Social Realities, 1870–1945." In Jane Lewis (ed.), *Women's Welfare/Women's Rights*. London: Croom Helm, 1983.

———. "Models of Equality for Women: The Case of State Support for Children in Twentieth-century Britain." In Gisela Bock, and Pat Thane (eds.), *Maternity and Gender Policies: Women and the Rise of the European Welfare State, 1880s–1950s*. (New York: Routledge, 1991).

———. *The Politics of Motherhood: Child and Maternal Welfare in England, 1900–1939*. London: Croom Helm, 1980.

———. *Women in England, 1870–1950: Sexual Divisions and Social Change*. Bloomington, IN: Indiana University Press, 1984.

———. "The Working-class Wife and Mother and State Intervention, 1870–1918." In Jane Lewis (ed.), *Labour and Love: Women's Experience of Home and Family, 1850–1940*. New York: Basil Blackwell, 1987.

Lewis, Jane (ed.). *Labour and Love. Women's Experience of Home and Family, 1850–1940*. New York: Basil Blackwell, 1987.

Lewis, Jane (ed.). *Women's Welfare/Women's Rights*. London: Croom Helm, 1983.

Lewis, Jane, and Sonya O. Rose. "'Let England Blush': Protective Labor Legislation, 1820–1914." In Ulla Wikander, Alice Kessler-Harris, and Jane Lewis (eds.), *Protecting Women: Labor Legislation in Europe, the United States, and Australia, 1880–1920*. Urbana, IL: University of Illinois Press, 1995.

Liddington Jill, and Jill Norris. *One Hand Tied Behind Us*. London: Virago Press Ltd., 1978.

Lockwood, Maren. "The Experimental Utopia in America." In Frank E. Manuel (ed.), *Utopias and Utopian Thought*. Cambridge, MA: Houghton Mifflin Company, 1966.

Loeb, Lori Anne. *Consuming Angels: Advertising and Victorian Women*. New York: Oxford University Press, 1994.

Malone, Carolyn. "Gender Discourses and the Making of Protective Labor Legislation in England, 1830–1914." *Journal of British Studies* vol. 37, no. 2 (April 1998), 166–191.

Manuel, Frank E. (ed.). *Utopias and Utopian Thought*. Cambridge, MA: Houghton Mifflin Company, 1966.

Mappen, Ellen. *Helping Women at Work: The Women's Industrial Council, 1889–1914*. London: Hutchinson, 1985.

Millar, Jane. "Women, Poverty and Social Security." In Christine Hallett (ed.), *Women and Social Policy*. New York: Prentice Hall, 1996.

Morris, Jenny. *Women Workers and the Sweated Trades*. Brookfield, VT: Gower Publishing Company, 1986.

Offen, Karen. "Contextualizing the Theory and Practice of Feminism in Nineteenth-century Europe." In Renate Bridenthal, Susan Mosher Stuard, and Merry E. Wiesner (eds.), *Becoming Visible: Women in European History*. Boston: Houghton Mifflin Company, 1998.

Pedersen, Susan. "Eleanor Rathbone, 1872–1946: The Victorian Family Under the Daughter's Eye." In Susan Pedersen, and Peter Mandler (eds.), *After the Victorians: Private Conscience and Public Duty in Modern Britain*. London: Routledge, 1994.

———. "The Failure of Feminism in the Making of the British Welfare State." *Radical History Review*, no. 43 (Winter 1989), 86–110.

———. *Family, Dependence and the Origins of the Welfare State: Britain and France, 1914–1945*. Cambridge: Cambridge University Press, 1993.

———. "Gender, Welfare, and Citizenship in Britain during the Great War." *American Historical Review* vol. 95 (October 1990), 983–1006.

Pedersen, Susan, and Peter Mandler (eds.). *After the Victorians: Private Conscience and Public Duty in Modern Britain*. London: Routledge, 1994.

Phillips, Anne. *Divided Loyalties: Dilemmas of Sex and Class*. London: Virago Press Ltd., 1987.

Pollard, Sidney. "Nineteenth Century Co-operation: From Community Building to Shopkeeping." In Asa Briggs, and John Saville (eds.), *Essays in Labour History*. London: Macmillan & Company, Ltd., 1960.

Poovey, Mary. *Uneven Developments: The Ideological Work of Gender in Mid-Victorian England*. Chicago: University of Chicago Press, 1988.

Pugh, Martin. "Domesticity and the Decline of Feminism." In Harold L. Smith (ed.), *British Feminism in the Twentieth Century*. Amherst, MA: University of Massachusetts Press, 1990.

Rendall, Jane. *The Origins of Modern Feminism: Women in Britain, France and the United States, 1780–1860*. New York: Schocken Books, 1984.

Roberts, Elizabeth. *A Woman's Place: An Oral History of Working-class Women, 1890–1940*. New York: Basil Blackwell, 1984.

———. "Women's Strategies, 1890–1940." In Jane Lewis (ed.), *Labour and Love: Women's Experience of Home and Family, 1850–1940*. New York: Basil Blackwell, 1987.

———. "Working Wives and Their Families." In Theo Barker and Michael Drake (eds.), *Population and Society in Britain, 1850–1980*. London: Batsford Academic and Educational Ltd., 1982.

Rose, Sonya O. "Gender Antagonism and Class Conflict: Exclusionary Strategies of Male Trade Unionists in Nineteenth-century Britain." *Social History* vol. 13 (1988), 191–208.

———. *Limited Livelihoods: Gender and Class in Nineteenth-century England*. Berkeley: University of California Press, 1992.

———. "Protective Labor Legislation in Nineteenth-century Britain: Gender, Class, and the Liberal State." In Laura L. Fader and Sonya O. Rose (eds.), *Gender and Class in Modern Europe*. Ithaca, NY: Cornell University Press, 1996.

Ross, Ellen. "Labour and Love: Rediscovering London's Working-class Mothers, 1870–1918." In Jane Lewis (ed.), *Labour and Love: Women's Experiences of Home and Family, 1850–1940*. New York: Basil Blackwell, 1987.

———. *Love and Toil: Motherhood in Outcast London, 1870–1918*. New York: Oxford University Press, 1993.

———. "'Not the Sort that Would Sit on the Doorstep': Respectability in Pre–World War I London Neighborhoods." *International Labor and Working Class History* no. 27 (Spring 1985), 39–59.

Rowbotham, Sheila. *Hidden from History*. London: Pluto Press, 1980.

Rupp, Leila J. "'Imagine My Surprise': Women's Relationships in Historical Perspective." *Frontiers* vol. 5, no. 3 (1981), 63–70.

————. *Worlds of Women: The Making of an International Women's Movement.* Princeton: Princeton University Press, 1997.

Savage, Mike. "Capitalist and Patriarchal Relations at Work: Preston Cotton Weaving, 1890–1940." In Linda Murgatroyd et al. (eds.), *Localities, Class and Gender.* London: Pion Limited, 1985.

Scott, Gillian. *Feminism and the Politics of Working Women: The Women's Co-operative Guild, 1880s to the Second World War.* London: UCL Press Limited, 1998.

————. "'The Working-class Women's Most Active and Democratic Movement': The Women's Co-operative Guild, 1883–1950." D.Phil. thesis, University of Sussex, 1988.

————. "'Working Out Their Own Salvation': Women's Autonomy and Divorce Law Reform in the Co-operative Movement, 1910–1920." In Stephen Yeo (ed.), *New Views of Co-operation.* New York: Routledge, 1988.

Scott, Joan W. "Deconstructing Equality-versus-Difference: Or, the Uses of Poststructuralist History for Feminism." *Feminist Studies* vol. 14, no. 1 (Spring 1988), 33–50.

————. *Only Paradoxes to Offer.* Cambridge, MA: Harvard University Press, 1996.

Seccombe, Wally. "Patriarchy Stabilized: The Construction of the Male Breadwinner Wage Norm in Nineteenth-century Britain." *Social History* vol. 11, no. 1 (January 1986), 53–76.

Smith, Harold L. "British Feminism in the 1920s." In Harold L. Smith (ed.), *British Feminism in the Twentieth Century.* Amherst, MA: University of Massachusetts Press, 1990.

Smith, Harold L. (ed.). *British Feminism in the Twentieth Century.* Amherst, MA: University of Massachusetts Press, 1990.

Soldon, Norbert C. *Women in British Trade Unions, 1874–1976.* Dublin: Gill and Macmillan Ltd., 1978.

Taylor, Barbara. *Eve and the New Jerusalem.* New York: Pantheon Books, 1983.

Thane, Pat. "Visions of Gender in the Making of the British Welfare State: The Case of Women in the British Labour Party and Social Policy, 1906–1945." In Gisela Bock, and Pat Thane (eds.), *Maternity and Gender Policies: Women and the Rise of the European Welfare States, 1880s–1950s.* New York: Routledge, 1991.

————. "The Women of the British Labour Party, 1906–1945." In Harold L. Smith (ed.), *British Feminism in the Twentieth Century.* Amherst, MA: University of Massachusetts Press, 1990.

Thomson, Alistair. "'Domestic Drudgery Will Be a Thing of the Past': Co-operative Women and the Reform of Housework." In Stephen Yeo (ed.), *New Views of Co-operation.* New York: Routledge, 1988.

Tilly, Louise A., and Joan W. Scott. *Women, Work and Family.* New York: Holt, Rinehart and Winston, 1978.

Ulam, Adam. "Socialism and Utopia." In Frank E. Manuel (ed.), *Utopias and Utopian Thought.* Cambridge, MA: Houghton Mifflin Company, 1966.

Valentine, Gill. "Making Space: Separatism and Difference." In John Paul Jones III et al. (eds.), *Tresholds in Feminist Geography.* Lanham, MD: Rowman & Littlefield Publishers, Inc., 1997.

Vicinus, Martha. *Independent Women: Work and Community for Single Women, 1850–1920.* Chicago: University of Chicago Press, 1985.

Walby, Sylvia. "Segregation in Employment in Social and Economic Theory." In Sylvia Walby (ed.), *Gender Segregation at Work.* Philadelphia: Open University Press, 1988.

Waters, Chris. *British Socialism and the Politics of Popular Culture, 1884–1914*. Manchester: Manchester University Press, 1990.

Wikander, Ulla. "Some 'Kept the Flag of Feminist Demands Waving': Debates at International Congresses on Protecting Women Workers." In Ulla Wikander, Alice Kessler-Harris, and Jane Lewis (eds.), *Protecting Women: Labor Legislation in Europe, the United States, and Australia, 1880–1920*. Urbana, IL: University of Illinois Press, 1995.

Wikander, Ulla, Alice Kessler-Harris, and Jane Lewis (eds). *Protecting Women: Labor Legislation in Europe, the United States, and Australia, 1880–1920*. Urbana, IL: University of Illinois Press, 1995.

Yeo, Stephen. "Introductory: Rival Clusters of Potential: Ways of Seeing Co-operation." In Stephen Yeo (ed.), *New Views of Co-operation*. New York: Routledge, 1988.

Yeo, Stephen (ed.). *New Views of Co-operation*. New York: Routledge, 1988.

Index

About the Author

BARBARA J. BLASZAK is an Associate Professor and the Chair of the Department of History at Le Moyne College in Syracuse, New York. She has published works about the Cooperative Movement in England and on women's roles in that movement. She is a past president of the New York State Association of European Historians and is active in the Middle Atlantic Conference on British Studies.

ISBN 0-313-30995-7

90000>

EAN

9 780313 309953

HARDCOVER BAR CODE